JUD

A Magical Journey

Jud Heathcote
with Jack Ebling

SAGAMORE PUBLISHING
Champaign, IL 61820

Production Manager, Editor: Susan M. McKinney
Dustjacket and photo insert design: Michelle R. Dressen
Proofreader: Phyllis L. Bannon

ISBN:1-57167-016-5

Printed in the United States.

To Stener, for steering me toward the coaching profession.

To Marv, for starting me on my way in the collegiate ranks.

*To Beverly, for starring as a wife, a mother
and a best friend.*

CONTENTS

ACKNOWLEDGMENTS

The best baskets always have assists. So do the best books.

This one is a product of love, guidance and teamwork over a span of more than 68 years.

The play started with my parents, Fawn and Marion Heathcote, in Harvey, North Dakota, and with my mom and grandparents in Manchester, Washington.

Credit should go to my first coach, Stener Kvinsland at South Kitsap High, and to my college coach, Jack Friel at Washington State.

Marv Harshman at Washington State was my mentor and one of the great minds in basketball history. He was a part of every win we had at Montana and Michigan State.

Many thanks to all the players who've taken coaching over 45 seasons, especially to Gregory Kelser and Earvin Johnson, who led us to the '79 championship.

From someone who knows an assistant's life, thanks to Jim Brandenburg, Don Monson, Vern Payne, Bill Berry, Edgar Wilson, Bill Norton, Mike Deane, Herb Williams, Tom Izzo, Stan Joplin and all the part-timers with all-the-time loyalty: Benny White, Bob McGriff, Fred Paulsen, Kelvin Sampson, John Holms, Frank Rourke, Silas Taylor, Jim Boylan, Jim Boylen, Tom Crean and Brian Gregory.

Thanks again to Joe Kearney, who hired me; to Doug Weaver, a great boss and a greater friend, and to Gus Ganakas, an unsung hero.

Many thanks to the Rebounders Club, especially presidents Dave Zisook, Tom Danker and Phil Irion; to two terrific secretaries, Lori Soderberg and Sylvia Thompson, and to sports information people like Nick Vista, Mike Pearson and John Farina and the SID staffs at Washington State, Montana and MSU.

Thanks to Sagamore Publishing for letting an ol' coach tell some old stories and to Robin, Zach and Alison Ebling for playing as a threesome for three months.

And thanks to the game of basketball, the greatest team game there is.

PROLOGUE

If I only had two words to describe Jud Heathcote, they would be "extremely honest." You always knew exactly where you stood with him as a player, coach, friend, etc. I did not always like where I stood, nor did some of my teammates at times. But we could all appreciate the candidness and, more importantly, the open lines of communication.

I was 18 years old just after my freshman season at Michigan State University when I learned we'd be getting a new coach from out West. We had not heard of Jud Heathcote. But wild and almost maniacal descriptions of the man and his style of coaching were quick to follow. And we were very concerned.

Upon Coach's arrival at MSU, some six months prior to the 1976-77 season, meetings were scheduled with each player to discuss the upcoming campaign. We all came away from those meetings saying, "Hey, what a great sense of humor this guy has! He can't be all that bad!"

We later learned that was the off-season Jud. When practice began on October 15, we realized some of the things we had heard were not that far from the truth.

Coach was tough, demanding and intimidating. Sometimes I wonder if he ever knew just how much team unity and cohesiveness he fostered because we had to pick one another up after his rampages. His toughness made his teams tough. The games were easier than the practices. And that's exactly the way he wanted it.

One of Coach's favorite axioms, and he had many, was that basketball was work, and the fun came from winning. Needless to say, we worked very hard. And after Coach's first season, we began to have a lot of fun.

I remember his uncanny skill of dissecting our opponents, limiting their strengths and fully exposing their weaknesses. His attention to minute details was so acute. We were, without question, one of America's most prepared basketball teams each time we stepped on the court.

Case in point: I started 88 games for Jud Heathcote and jumped center in all of them. We always tapped the ball backward to gain the first possession. In our '79 regional title game against Notre Dame, Coach noticed the Irish would not station anyone in their defensive area for the tap. The day before the game, he installed a play for me to tap the ball forward to Earvin Johnson,who would likewise tap to a streaking Mike Brkovich for an easy dunk and an early lead. The play worked to perfection and may have been the only time Michigan State ever tapped forward in Coach's 19-year tenure.

Coach's nature was to be very firm. He would not relax with success, nor would he allow his players to become complacent. If he ever detected that trend, he would rip us all. And believe it or not, we came to appreciate his unorthodox manner of motivation. We understood he saw our potential and would not allow us to sell ourselves short. We even became somewhat protective of him, as was the case in March of '79.

The Spartans were in Murfreesboro, Tennessee, for our first-round NCAA Tournament game vs. Lamar. Clarence Kea and B.B. Davis were two of Lamar's stars and had played important roles in their opening win against Detroit. Prior to the game, they were heard making flippant remarks about Coach and his hairdo.

When I looked at Earvin, we both nodded. Lamar's players would have to pay dearly for their lack of respect. Jud was our coach. And we were not tolerating any of that nonsense. We destroyed Lamar, 95-69. The competitive part of the game was over by halftime. As I said, he was OUR coach. And we were his guys.

When I reminisce about some of those times, I am reminded of how Coach would spend extra time with each player to enhance his skills. He helped me develop a fairly respectable jump shot. By doing so, defenders had to play closer to respect the threat of a shot. When they would get too tight, I could use my quickness and go strong to the basket, which was what Coach really wanted anyway.

Earvin used to get into the lane and take off-balance shots. Not wanting to disrupt his ability to get inside, Coach would encourage him to practice those leaning suspension shots. Most coaches would have suggested he stop taking them. I really enjoyed the idea we had the freedom to express ourselves and our talents on the court. Coach did not mind a fancy pass or an imaginative dunk, as long as you scored. He would say, "Give me the results."

I went on from MSU to play six seasons in the NBA for six different coaches. Each coach enjoyed teaching the game. And they were all talented. I would place Jud Heathcote at the top of that list. His knowledge of the game is unsurpassed. His method of motivation is effective. And I am not certain a more competitive person has ever coached anywhere.

But the thing that impressed me the most was the concern Coach had for me after I left. He would call to make sure all was well with the pro team I played for and always offered to help during the off-season. When I injured my knee, it was Jud who wanted to know if he could help. After my career ended and I became a broadcaster, there was Coach offering advice and sending letters of recommendation. He cared beyond my MSU playing days.

I once read a book about pro football's Green Bay Packers and their legendary head coach Vince Lombardi. The Packers were football's most dominant team of the '60s. And Lombardi was not easy to play for. He yelled, stomped, accepted nothing less than the maximum from his players and fully utilized the element of fear. Yet, when his players spoke of him, they mentioned how he made them better than they could have made themselves, the discipline he taught and how his lessons transcended the gridiron and helped with life after football.

Many of Jud Heathcote's former players speak the same of him today. He made us push ourselves to become better players. We became WINNERS. He expected us to graduate from school and would not stop chirping until we did.

One of the proudest moments for me occurred in August of '89, when our '79 NCAA championship team reunited in East Lansing. Every manager, trainer, player and coach was in attendance. Each former player and manager had successfully made the transition into the working world. And like the Packers and Lombardi, we felt we were fortunate to have spent time with Coach and benefitted from his teaching.

From 1976-95, Coach established himself as one of college basketball's best. And more importantly, he helped re-establish

Michigan State as a power on the national scene. But clearly, his greatest impact was the way he chose to use the platform that was provided by the position of head basketball coach. It is a position of tremendous influence and can sometimes be misused.

Coach Heathcote did not squander his opportunity. He led with a strong hand and later became your friend. He expected discipline. But he had the most discipline. He demanded that everyone work hard. But no one outworked him. Little did we, as players, know then how those same principles would serve us throughout our lives. Coach left his mark. He made a difference. And it was a positive one.

Best wishes in your retirement, Coach.

Gregory Kelser
MSU Spartan

P.S. Thank you!

THE DIN THAT
WOULDN'T DIE

Where does a book start? At the beginning . . . the middle . . . the end? Who cares? This one starts with the most memorable game in my 45-year coaching career.

If I'd screamed at Gregory Kelser six feet away, he couldn't have heard me. All anyone heard midway through the second half on Thursday, February 1, 1979, was the echo of 10,004 screams of joy in Jenison Field House.

Over the years, 200,000 people have said they were at that game. And that's how loud the noisiest crowd in Michigan State basketball history was when The Magic Man hobbled back to the court and rekindled a championship dream.

For 8-0 Ohio State, it was a chance to make another statement. For the 4-4 Spartans, it was a shot to stay alive in the Big Ten race and to answer our harshest critics—often ourselves.

As head coach of a team most Michigan State fans expected to win the NCAA title, or at least get to the Final Four, how we got to that desperate predicament was almost as interesting as how we fought our way out of it.

And just in time! With one more conference loss, not only would we not have won the NCAA Tournament, we wouldn't have received an invitation. There were 40 teams in the field that year, not the current 64. Purdue, which wound up sharing the conference crown with us and Iowa, didn't even make the Tournament.

The trouble started the summer before with a seemingly successful trip to Brazil. Earvin Johnson, the best guard—and in my mind, the best player—in the country, had just returned from an all-star tour of the Soviet Union. He'd played competitively all summer, and he needed to rest more than to represent the USA in the Governor's Cup in Sao Paulo.

He said, "Coach, I'm really worn out. I don't want to go to Brazil."

I said, "Hey, E, it's too late now! We have to go! I suppose we could cancel the trip. But we can't let you stay home while the rest of the team goes."

Looking back, I don't know why we couldn't have. We could have! I never even thought of that. But we could have—and maybe should have—done that.

We took that tour to Brazil in September. And those were two tough weeks. I always said I'd never take another trip that late in the summer. It's different if you go to Australia in June and have a couple of months to regroup. I say you can play basketball 365 days a year. But you can only play competitively, with pressure, a certain number of games until it wears on you mentally. It affects your preparation and your performance. That's why so many clubs, as we've seen through the years, are drained at Tournament time. They just can't play any more.

But we were always thinking "team-team-team" and wondering, "How are we going to get ready for the season?" That was why we wanted the trip, to get extra games for another young club.

The effects didn't show right away on the scoreboard, though the coaches and players knew something was wrong. We could sense our guys were tired of basketball all through the preseason. We even gave them extra days off.

That helped us roll through the Far West Classic, where we beat Indiana for the title by 17. But we had lackluster performances, too. We beat Cal State-Fullerton 92-89—just a terrible defensive game. And we were awful against Cincinnati in the first college game in the Pontiac Silverdome, pulling out a win before nearly 32,000 fans.

The intensity just wasn't there. And it wasn't one game. It was that way almost every practice.

Still, our only loss in the first 10 games was by one at North Carolina. So when we won the Far West Classic, the pollsters were fooled into ranking us No. 1 in the nation—a first in MSU basketball history.

I remember calling the team together in the Denver airport, coming back from Portland, and saying, "I've got good news and bad news. The bad news is it looks like we'll be spending the night in Denver because of the ice storm. The good news is you're now the No. 1 team in the country!"

It was a very brief salute. We rallied from a 13-point deficit in the second half and beat Minnesota by seven. But in our third Big Ten game, we were beaten on a last-second shot at Illinois by Eddie Johnson. Two days later, we lost again at Purdue on a 22-foot turnaround prayer by Arnette Hallman. That was the last time we'd be No. 1 until we earned that ranking 20 games later.

Despite three fouls on Earvin and three on Jay Vincent in the first seven minutes, we handled Indiana again—this time at home by 24. And we stayed two games behind the Buckeyes with an 11-point overtime win against Iowa, a game we probably should've lost in regulation.

If we beat the Hawkeyes on a phantom foul, we lost that way the next week at Michigan. Keith Smith made a free throw with no time remaining, after a phantom foul against Gregory. To this day, Gregory swears he never touched him.

And at 4-3, it looked like we were battling bad luck. But if you looked at the stats, you could see we were outrebounded at Illinois and Purdue almost 2-to-1. So we weren't playing very good basketball.

That's why what happened the week before Ohio State's visit was so important. You can always look for excuses. You can tell yourself you're just unlucky when you lose by one or two points. But when you go to Northwestern and you're 10 down at halftime, that's hard to do.

I went to the locker room at halftime and said, "Guys, I can rant and rave all day . . . . But you guys have to decide what you're going to do."

"Coach, we're going to be all right!" Gregory said. "We're better than they are. We were in foul trouble and had some guys out. Don't worry! We'll be OK!"

I said, "Should we go with some aggressive defense and put some pressure on them?"

"Good idea!" they all said. "Let's put some pressure on them!"

When we pressured them, they scored on a backdoor play five straight times. We didn't score on any of our possessions. And after about 3 minutes, we weren't 10 down. We were 20 down!

We tried to fight back. But Jay fouled out. Gregory fouled out. And Earvin went 7-for-22 from the field. He tried to win it himself and couldn't.

We were beaten by 18 points in Evanston—a blessing in disguise. Suddenly, the realization of what other clubs were doing to us and what we weren't doing hit us square in the face.

When you're 4-4 and lose to Northwestern the way we did, something is obviously wrong. And there were 500 different slants on what that was. But I still say the best guy to analyze it all was Mike Longaker, nearly a 4.0 student in pre-med. He had no ax to grind. Yet, he said about as much as anyone in the team meeting we had.

To this day, everyone says the guys told Jud he had to lay off. But the gist of the meeting was more than that. Maybe we said the coaches were too critical. Maybe we said the players weren't responding and playing to their potential.

But Mike said, "Hey, you guys can blame the coaches if you want . . . . But the bottom line is we'd better blame ourselves, instead of each other. We're not playing as hard as we need to or as well as we can. If I can sit there and see that, you guys ought to see it, too!"

Not everyone could. Instead of giving credit to other coaches and what they were doing to defense us, the media had a field day, tearing us apart. After all, we almost went to the Final Four the year before. And we'd only lost one key player, Bob Chapman. So they really chopped us up as underachievers. They said, "Heathcote is too emotional, too vociferous!" and this, that and the other. And they were taking potshots at the players, too, saying, "Earvin is still trying to do too much."

Every guy had an angle. And I think our guys kind of keyed on that. I've never told anyone this, but the players came to me and asked me to bar Lynn Henning, then of the *Lansing State Journal,* from our locker room. They said, "If anyone is going to write that negatively, he shouldn't be able to talk to us." When I told Lynn that, he couldn't believe it. He thought I was making it up. But that's the way the kids reacted. And they took it out on the rest of the teams we played.

From 4-4 in the league and 11-5 overall, we won 15 of our last 16 games and became one of the better national championship teams in the last 20 years. And the day Ohio State came in, I thought we'd be very lucky to get to the NIT, let alone the NCAA.

If anyone said our backs were against the wall, they had a wonderful sense for the obvious. It didn't take a genius to look at our situation and realize if we lost one more game, we were done. And how were we not going to lose in our league, as strong as it was?

I said, "Let's keep our chances alive for the NIT or something else. Mathematically, we're not eliminated. But we have to win this game."

That's one reason the Ohio State game was the most memorable night of my coaching career. Why? Because of the tension and all the circumstances.

Some things you remember all your life. If you put headphones over my ears and turned up the heavy metal as high as it would go, it wouldn't match the unbelievable din and noise when Earvin came back.

Earvin went down, clutching his ankle, with 2:23 left until the break. We were up by nine at the time and by seven at half-time. But we were sure he wouldn't play in the second half. We'd have to hold on without him.

I went in and told our trainer, Clint Thompson, and our doctors, Dave Hough and Doug McKeag, "If there's any danger to Earvin, I don't want him to play, even if he wants to play."

They said, "OK. . . . He won't be playing."

I thought it was a severe sprain, not a broken ankle. But you know how severely sprained ankles are. You can hardly move when you have one.

When Gregory didn't move enough, he drew his fourth foul and had to sit down early in the second half. The Buckeyes battled back and went ahead twice by a point before the training room door popped open and the place erupted. By the time play stopped, Jay had scored twice on putbacks to put us ahead by five.

Gregory was waiting to go back in and said, "I knew people would be glad to see me back in there. But I couldn't believe the ovation I was getting! Then, I turned and saw Earvin limping back out."

Right away, I said to Clint, "What's the scoop?"

He said, "The doctors say he can play. There won't be any lasting damage."

And Earvin said, "I can play. . . . I'm OK!"

I meditated on what to do for at least a third of a second, then sent him in with 8:42 left. But Ohio State scored six straight points and went ahead by one.

I've always kidded Earvin and said, "If we hadn't put you in, we'd have won in a breeze!"

As it was, the Buckeyes tied it up on a bizarre four-point play with :28 left. We had to win the game again in overtime. But Earvin made the difference. He had 15 of his 23 points in the last five minutes and the overtime, was 11-for-13 at the line and had seven rebounds and seven assists.

I told the media, "I thank the good Lord Earv shoots free throws with his hands rather than his ankles!"

Gregory finished with 21 points. And Jay had 19 points and 12 rebounds, outplaying Herb Williams. But the numbers that mattered most were the records: 8-1 and 5-4. We were still alive.

We didn't come out of that game and say, "Hey, we're on our way! Look out!"

We still had a lot of work to do. But we were ready to start doing it. And less than 48 hours after we beat Ohio State, we had another game—against, of all teams, Northwestern.

Before the game, I told Earvin, "You're not going to play today unless we absolutely need you."

But we struggled in that one, too. We were up by 10 with about four minutes to go. Suddenly, they cut it to six.

"Coach," Earvin said, "I'd better go in."

And I said, "Yeah, E, you'd better go in."

We won by 11, then ran past a good Kansas team by 24 the next afternoon in our first NBC appearance of the season. But the greatest run came in our next three games—all on the road.

That's when I took Ron Charles out of the starting lineup and put Mike Brkovich in. Brk had started for Terry Donnelly against Ohio State and for Earvin against Northwestern. But after the Kansas game, he was in the lineup to stay.

I said, "We have to have another ballhandler and a guy who can get out on the fast break."

It wasn't so much I thought Mike would give us a lift shooting, as great a shooter as he was, because Ron could score some points around the basket. But we couldn't get the ball to Earvin on the outlet. They always had someone there. The only other guy we could throw it to was Donnelly, our other guard.

With the change, we had two guys to throw it to. And we had a fast break again. We could outlet to Donnelly or Brkovich, then get the ball to Earvin with a full head of steam. That was probably the biggest change all season. And it had nothing to do with the meeting after the Northwestern game.

In an eight-day span, we held on to edge Iowa again, blew out Ohio State by 16 and beat Indiana by 12, our third win over Bobby Knight's team that season. That stretch was something you just don't do in our league. And I think that's when we really believed no one in the country could beat us.

Michigan definitely couldn't when we came home to play them. We were ahead by 22 at the break and led 46-16 early in the second half. Gregory also broke Terry Furlow's school scoring record with a jumper in the first half.

Next came payback wins over Purdue, with Joe Barry Carroll, and Illinois, with Gregory saying goodbye to the fans in Jenison with slam dunks for the day's first basket and his last score at home.

A 13-point victory at Minnesota gave us a share of the title. And we were surprised to learn Iowa and Purdue both lost that night. So even if we all wound up in a tie, we'd get the automatic Tournament bid because of a better record head-to-head.

Our guys said, "Finally! We've done it!"

Earvin even said, "Coach, do we have to play the last game?"

I said, "Yeah, E, we do. And let's win it!"

But there was no intensity whatsoever at Wisconsin. We just went through the motions. I know if we hadn't clinched it, we'd have won easily and gone into the tournament with 11 straight wins and finished with 16. Instead, Wes Matthews threw in a 55-footer to beat us.

Someone said, "That probably helped you."

It didn't. It was a non-game in everyone's mind. A loss in that situation can help a team a lot of times. But with this club, no. We'd done what we set out to do. And we were all ready to take the next step.

A SWEET TRIP TO
SALT LAKE CITY

The amazing thing is we were only up for two games in the '79 NCAA Tournament. And when I ask people to tell me which games those were, they never get it right. They always assume one had to be the championship game against Indiana State.

Instead, we were only up for a second-round game against Lamar, our first postseason test, and the Mideast Regional Final against Notre Dame.

Watching teams lose after first-round byes, I was so paranoid I went down to Murfreesboro, Tennessee, and scouted the Detroit-Lamar game myself. Our guys had a lot of respect for Detroit, which still had Terry Duerod and Earl Cureton and was 22-5 after back-to-back 25-4 seasons. We were preparing all week for the Titans, who wanted revenge after we'd beaten them by 29 points 15 months earlier. When Lamar won 95-87, it surprised me as much as anyone.

I came back and told our coaches, "Hey, it didn't matter who won that game. We can beat either one of those clubs by 20. But don't dare say anything like that to the players! And don't dare tell the media!"

We told our guys, "Hey, if Lamar is good enough to beat Detroit, Lamar is damn good!"

Our guys were psyched to the sky that Sunday. And as the No. 2 seed in the Mideast Region, we blew by Lamar, 95-64. Afterward, Billy Tubbs walked into his press conference and ripped up his scouting report. He said, "Here's what it says: 'Michigan State walks the ball up—no fast break.' . . . Hell, we haven't seen them yet!"

When you played Iowa and won 60-57 and beat Indiana 59-47, you hoped opponents were watching those games. Those teams all had three guys back and refused to let you run. Against Lamar, we ran right by them.

Gregory had 31 points and 14 rebounds. And that was the game that gave us Jaimie "Shoes" Huffman. He lost a shoe, couldn't get it on for what seemed like 10 minutes and finally scored his first career basket. Al McGuire had fun with that, since the game was such a blowout.

Jaimie was up off the JV team and thought he should be playing. He'd played with Earvin in high school. And he would practice really hard —almost dirty.

So the players started teasing him, "Hey, Shoes!"

"My name is Jaimie!" he said. "Don't call me Shoes!"

But pretty soon, with all that publicity, he was signing his autograph as "Shoes" Huffman.

The only negative aspect of the Lamar game was a worsening of Jay Vincent's foot injury, a problem throughout the tournament. But Ron Charles did an excellent job when we needed him the next four games.

Our second game was in Indianapolis the following Friday against LSU. Dale Brown's team had already lost one starter to injury and suspended its leading scorer, DeWayne Scales, for dealing with an agent.

So our guys said, "Hey, Coach, without their regular team, how can they possibly be any good? Don't worry, we'll play hard. But we're a lot better than they are."

And we were. We had the biggest halftime lead ever against the Tigers and outscored them 27-9 at the line. Dale was slapped with a technical. And their team doctor drew another one on the way to the locker room. We coasted home 87-71 and could've won by more.

That meant we got to play Notre Dame, the No. 1 seed, in Market Square Arena. That was the year the Fighting Irish were on TV nearly every single Sunday. Our guys really resented all the publicity they got.

I still think Notre Dame was the second-best club in the country that year. They had a team of future pros with Kelly Tripucka, Orlando Woolridge, Bill Laimbeer, Bill Hanzlik and Tracy Jackson, plus Bruce Flowers and Rich Branning.

But I didn't have to give a pregame speech that Sunday afternoon. All I did was write on the blackboard: LET'S GO KICK SOME ASS.

We had a plan to jump in front in the first few seconds and set the tone for the entire game. See, Gregory used to hold guys with his other hand when he jumped center. He got almost every tip the whole year. So we put in the tipoff play, where he tips it to Earvin, Earvin flips it back over his head to Mike Brkovich, and Brk dunks it.

A guy named Russ Marcinek, who'd worked our camp and was a high school coach in Hammond, Indiana, asked to come in and watch practice that week. Supposedly, he bet a Notre Dame guy $20 that Michigan State would score on a dunk in the first 10 seconds. It was quicker than that. Then, we put a press on, stole the ball and got another basket.

Danny Nee, the coach at Nebraska, was Digger Phelps' assistant then and said, "Digger never swore. So I knew we were in big trouble when he let loose twice in the first 10 seconds."

Gregory had 34 points and 13 rebounds. But it was a hard-fought game, with great intensity from both clubs. I still say that was the national championship game. And if I looked at a win as the second most memorable of my career, that would have to be it. It was the game that got us to the Final Four. And after working for Marv Harshman at Washington State, I knew he'd never been there. So that meant something, too.

People have said that's the happiest they've ever seen me. And they're probably right. I shook my fists over my head. It was the realization we'd made it to the Final Four, knowing how few teams had made it, and the relief from the kind of stressful season we'd had.

We left to go to Salt Lake City a day earlier than scheduled; the media attention in East Lansing was too much. Everybody was around. Plus, we were on break. And I knew the altitude is different in Salt Lake. So as the first team there by a day, we got the first wave of free-lance writers—call after call.

"Jud, I know this is a busy time for you," one guy said. "But I'd like to talk to Magic Johnson. I don't need much of his time— 15 minutes is plenty for me, either after practice or . . . what I'd really like to do is take him to lunch."

After 15 to 20 calls like that, I finally said, "We're going to honor the requests of the NCAA. Otherwise, we're off-limits to the media."

Joe Falls of *The Detroit News* still holds that against me. Even this year, he wrote, "Jud was so uptight, he couldn't even talk," and all that stuff. Joe was pissed off because he thinks he's special. He hadn't covered us all year. And he wanted a special interview with Earvin and Gregory.

I said, "No! We're off-limits. You can talk to them when everyone else does."

No one understood the number of requests we had for Earvin and Gregory. There were very few for me. . . . So be it.

I closed practice off to the media, not wanting a circus atmosphere. And no matter what I did, I couldn't get the team motivated for Penn, our next opponent. Bob Weinhauer's club had beaten Syracuse and North Carolina to get to the Final Four from the East. Still, no one believed the Quakers were a quality team.

Earvin kept saying, "Coach, they're from the IVY League!"

But to this day, I say Penn attacked our matchup zone better than any team we played all year. The thing is, every open shot they had, they missed. And we turned them all into fast breaks at the other end. I think they were just so tight, and we were so loose. Suddenly, the score at halftime was 51-17. It was the first time I could ever remember having a 34-point lead at halftime.

I told the guys, "I think we have this won, guys. Let's face facts. And let's not do anything to embarrass Penn or embarrass ourselves in the second half."

Our subs—guys like Mike Longaker, Jaimie and Gerald Gilkie —played as many minutes in the second half as they had all year.

The next day, we had a press conference. I only brought two guys, Earvin and Gregory. And I told them to be prepared. The Sycamores had beaten DePaul in the second semifinal to climb to 33-0. And it was "The Bird Man vs. The Magic Man" in every storyline.

I said, "Every guy is going to try to trap you and get you to say something negative about Larry Bird. So be smarter than they are, and say all the right things."

When we got back in the car, they started giggling and saying, "Coach, you wouldn't believe it! They kept asking, 'Is Magic as good as Bird?' But we said all the right things and didn't give them any of the answers they wanted."

Word was already out that we'd made Earvin pretend he was Bird and play the entire practice on the second unit. Before that workout, I pointed to Earvin and said, "Gentlemen, meet Larry Bird!" But at the press conference, the question was, "Magic, wasn't that a tremendous insult?" Earvin said, "We do whatever we have to do to get ready to win."

And that really helped us the day between games. Earvin did a great job at practice. Bird could so do many things to beat you. Who else could possibly have given us that look?

The question then was, "Who would be Magic?" But you could tell Brk, "You're Magic!" and he'd say, "Oh, I'm Magic! OK, Coach. Whatever you say."

The championship game Monday night was strictly business. There was no real emotion or intensity. It was, "We're better than they are. Let's get this over with and get back home."

I told the press I thought two All-Americans were better than one. But I don't think our guys even thought of that. They looked at it as our team being better than their team. I always said, "We have two superstars. They have one. And we have some great support players."

And the amazing thing is, we won the national championship almost without Jay, who was a key player. He did play 19 minutes against Indiana State, because Gregory was in foul trouble. We figured Jay could suck it up for one game. The doctors said he had a sprained foot—that's all.

I said, "No, it has to be a stress fracture."

"No, no, a sprained foot!" they said.

But stress fractures don't show up on x-rays. And Jay's didn't show up until two weeks later. Then they said, "Guess what? Jay has a stress fracture."

"No shit!" I told them.

And I still say that championship game might have been one of the all-time blowouts in Final Four history if Gregory hadn't picked up his fourth foul. We were up by nine at halftime. And less than three minutes into the second half, when he got his fourth foul, we were up by 16.

Terry Donnelly hit four straight jumpers from the corner. And we played conservatively after that. They hit a couple of outside shots to knock it down to six. But whenever you had Bird in the game, anything could happen.

We played him with a man-and-a-half the whole way, double-teaming as soon as he touched the ball. And Bird was only 7-for-21 from the field. We did a good defensive job and won by 11. Gregory's breakaway dunk on a blind, backward, full-court pass from Earvin made it 75-64. . . . Maybe we should have won by more.

Earvin had 24 points, Gregory 19 and Donnelly 15. And Earvin was named the Final Four MVP—as in most visionary passer.

After the game, I took all five starters to the press conference. The media asked question after question after question. So by the time we got back to the locker room, there was only one writer waiting for us—just the kind I'd warned the guys about.

He said, "Boy, Larry Bird really let his team down, didn't he?"

And Brk said, "Oh, no, he played hard! We just did a good job defensing him."

Then, the guy went to Donnelly and said, "Well, 'The Bird Man' kind of choked tonight, didn't he?"

"I don't know what you mean by choke," Terry said. "I thought he played pretty well."

Finally, he went to Gregory and started in again. So I grabbed him.

"Hey, who are you?" I said. "Who do you write for?" He said he was a free-lance writer from New York and gave me his name. I said, "You write what you want. But if you try to get one more negative comment from any of our players about Larry Bird, I'm going to throw your ass out of here myself!

"But while you're here, I want to tell you something. Larry Bird and Magic Johnson will be two of the greatest professional players ever. They possess two things no one ever evaluates—court vision and great hands. Now, print that!"

Naturally, it never was printed. I've always wished my quote would've been printed somewhere, so I could brag about being a basketball prophet.

After the championship game, the feeling was one of relief, not of elation. I thought it was just me. But when I told the guys to go out and celebrate, I found out it wasn't.

Earvin said, "Coach, we're going back, and we're going to bed. We're all worn out. We'll do our celebrating when we get home."

So the culmination wasn't euphoria, the way everyone thought it should be. It was "Whew, we did what we were supposed to do."

Before the season started, Joe Kearney, our athletic director, said, "Jud, the expectations for this team are unbelievable. I think you have to prepare yourself and your team not to expect too much. If you do just a little better than you did last year, that'll be good enough."

I said, "Joe, we made it to the round of eight last year. What you just told me is, if we go to the Final Four, that will be good enough. Your expectations are just like everyone else's!"

The adulation from the Mid-Michigan community was incredible. When we returned to Jenison, we had people standing there waiting for four hours. And the number of people at the parade down Michigan Avenue to the Capitol was unbelievable.

That was the first time we'd sold out our Basketball Bust. We had 1,760 people there and could've had twice that number. The whole thing was televised. Then, they had the Community of Champions Banquet with Al McGuire. So it was a love affair at a special time with a special team.

I told the guys, "You just accomplished something that's unbelievable. It doesn't seem like it now. But all the criticism we've had will disappear with this single accomplishment. And this will get bigger and bigger as the years pass."

Ten years later, we had a Reunion Game and an after-game party just for players and coaches. Each player got up and talked. And to a person, they all said the achievement had become bigger and bigger.

For Michigan State and Greater Lansing, it was plenty big enough the night of March 26 and for years to come.

COACHING SEEDS
AND EARLY DEEDS

I was born in Harvey, North Dakota, May 27, 1927. My dad, Marion Grant Heathcote, died when I was 3. And I had a baby brother who died at the same time, in the diptheria epidemic of 1930.

As much as I've tried, I can only remember two things about my dad. Shortly before my dad died, my brother, Grant, and I got kites. We were out trying to fly the kites, and they didn't fly very well. For some reason, we got the idea if we set them on fire, they'd fly a lot better. So there we were, lighting our kites on fire just as my dad came out of the house. He put out the fires, then wailed the living tar out of both of us.

The other thing I can remember was my dad was a coach and an ag teacher. We always had chickens. Whenever we were going to cook a chicken, we'd just go out and kill one. Do you know the two ways to kill a chicken? You can chop the head off. Or you can ring the head off. The neck snaps. And there's the chicken going, "Flaup, flaup, flaup, flaup, FLAUP . . . flauuuuu."

Those are the only two things I can remember about him: the business with the kites and getting the chickens ready for dinner.

My mother was a teacher. Her name was Fawn Walsh before she got married. But that was during the depression. She kept us there for a couple of years and just couldn't make it. So she sent us out to stay with her mother in Manchester, Washington.

I was 5 years old, my brother was 6, and my sister, Carlan, was 4. And we were on that train all by ourselves for a three- or four-day trip. Our grandmother and grandfather met us at the station.

My mother came out a year later and got a teaching job. We grew up very poor—and didn't know it. My mother made $90 a month for nine months—$810 a year. We lived on the beach and swam in Puget Sound.

Granddad worked on the docks as a checker. He'd take the ferry over to Seattle every day. Some days he'd work, and some days he wouldn't. He'd always catch the last ferry home.

By then, I wasn't George Melvin Heathcote to anyone. Everyone called me Jud.

The story my mother told was that my brother was 14 months older than I was and hadn't learned to enunciate. He always called me Brother and pronounced it Bubber. That was when he was 3 and I was 2.

When you're 3, geez, you're supposed to be able to talk! But with older kids around, pretty soon they started calling me Blubber. I was kind of a fat little kid. And it didn't bother me at all —"Hey, Blubber!"

But my mom wanted to find a simple name everyone could say. Out of the clear blue sky, she picked Jud, and had my brother practice saying it. She said, "You have a new name! Now, tell all your friends."

That's how I became Jud. And I've been Jud ever since. If my brother could have talked, I'd be George to this day.

We lived in Manchester the entire time we grew up. We never had a car. And my brother and I started working when we were in about the third or fourth grade. We would work for the neighbors, digging or clearing brush.

When I was in eighth grade, we got jobs as waterboys at Austin Construction. And a year later, my brother and I went to Arlington, Washington, to work. We were on our own at an early age and self-sufficient. We earned all our money for clothes and our spending money.

Grant and I used to fall trees on weekends. We were good at it, too. I'd contract a job and say, "I'm going to put that Douglas fir right there!" If I missed by three feet, I was pissed off.

One day when I was a junior in high school, I contracted for my brother and I to clear all the brush off an acre of land for $50. We got there at 6 a.m. and finished the job at about 6 p.m. We did the whole thing in one day. But when I went to get the money, the guy wasn't going to pay me.

He said, "I must've misfigured. . . . I thought that was a three-day job."

"That is a three-day job," I said. "It may be a four- or a five-day job for guys who don't know what they're doing. We worked 12 hours and got more done in 12 hours than some other guys would do in three days. Now, give me my money!"

And the guy said, "OK."

In the summers, I worked in federal programs as a recreation supervisor. Our athletic director, Maynard Lundberg, was in charge of those programs in our area. And he kind of looked out for my brother and I, knowing we had no father.

We did a lot of things with the neighborhood. My brother and I were both big for our age. We had a neighborhood football team and a neighborhood baseball team. We played tackle football six-against-six.

The first time I ever played basketball was in fifth grade. Every time I'd get the ball, the whistle would blow. I couldn't understand it. But I kept running with the ball; I thought that was what I was supposed to do.

By the time we got into organized athletics, we had five kids in our entire eighth grade at Colby Grade School. They were our basketball team. And when we played the neighboring junior-high school, we beat them, 32-2. I scored 30 points. So the next time we played them, it was agreed I wouldn't play. Instead, I could help coach. If I played, they said it wasn't fair. The second time, we won, 24-14.

The principal there was Aaron Masters. He paid a little more attention to my brother and I, because that's where my mother was teaching. In those days, I think a lot more people recognized when you didn't have a father in the home. Now, it's very common.

I think the influential people in my life at an early age were always my coaches. Stener Kvinsland was our football coach and our basketball coach at South Kitsap High. I owe that man a lot.

He was a very good football coach and knew a little about basketball. But he knew enough about coaching that he could do the job in basketball. And I became kind of the coach on the floor, even early on.

I was probably as good a football player as a basketball player. I was an end and a defensive tackle. And that's when I hurt my knee for the first time. I missed four games my senior year. I was second-team all-conference as a sophomore, unanimous all-conference as a junior and still made all-conference as a senior, but just barely.

When I got my football uniform as a sophomore, I was 6-1 ½, 193 pounds. I played at 185 for three years, once I lost a little of the baby fat. But I never grew any taller. I thought I was going to be 6-4 or 6-5 and be a great player.

Was my dad big? I don't know. In pictures, he's fair-sized; but when you see him with his teams, you don't know, because you don't know how big they are.

Art Grosso was my baseball coach. He only had one arm. But he was known far and wide as a great coach. We held the state record for years with 41 straight wins. I was the only guy who played every inning of all 41 games.

The streak started in my sophomore year. We could only play 10 games a year in the regular season. With the war, you couldn't get gas to go many places. As a junior, we won all 21 games we played. And when I was a senior, we won our first 10 games before losing to Bremerton.

In basketball, our freshman team went 15-0. A lot of people thought a guy named Eddie Brown and I should be playing on the varsity. But that team was all seniors. The coach said, "Let's keep the older guys together. We don't need to bring in the freshmen."

I started on the varsity and was the leading scorer as a sophomore, junior and senior. I was first-team all-state as a senior, the first all-state player in the history of the school. And our team finished seventh in the state.

I was also mythical all-state in baseball. I was a third baseman, then a catcher. Our senior year, we played in an invitational tournament in Walla Walla for the state championship. Gonzaga High finally beat us in 15 innings. And a guy named Scarpelli made the catch of his life on a ball I hit that would've won the game.

Every time I see him, he says, "Remember that catch I made off you?"

They retired my number—No. 11, so I went there for our 10-year reunion and saw my jersey in the trophy case, kind of tattered. But when we had our 20th reunion at the new high school, there was nothing in the trophy case. I got a basketball program and saw someone else was wearing my number. They must have unretired it. As they say, "Fame is fleeting."

What I'm trying to say is, I always said I wanted to be a teacher and a coach. Everyone said it was because of the influence my coaches had on me. To a degree, I think that's true. But I really think it was from the memory of my dad. I knew he was a coach. I knew he was a teacher. And that's probably why I did what I did.

I couldn't even talk about my dad without crying for years and years. Why? I don't know. I think it was because I was so conscious that everybody else had a dad and I didn't.

I'd like to think that helped me relate to kids when I became a coach. Yet, all the kids I coached who didn't have dads were black. So it was a little different, in terms of experiences. But I'd like to think I've been able to sit down with a Daimon Beathea or an Ed Wright and empathize some with their situations.

My mom never saw me play. But she always stayed up to talk about the game when I got home. We lived seven miles from school. A few times, I had to walk those seven miles home. More often, I'd get a ride from someone on the swing shift at the Bremerton Navy Yard at midnight.

We hitchhiked everywhere we went. I never rode the school bus. I hitchhiked to and from school. If you had your letterman's sweater on, guys would stop and pick you up. They'd say, "Hey, Jud! How's the team doing?" You could hitchhike across the country in those days. It was a different time and a different lifestyle.

But my mom never liked our coach. When my brother was a senior, he was our backup center, and I was the starter. The only time he played was when we were way ahead or when I was in foul trouble. Grant didn't think that much of it, because he wasn't very good in basketball. He was a very good baseball player and a catcher on two of our championship teams.

In football, he was the reserve quarterback. When I was a sophomore, we were way ahead, and Grant was in there. He got sacked really hard. And it was fourth down and about 20 yards to go.

A kid came running over and said, "Coach! You'd better get Grant out of there! He just called a buck on fourth down!"

Sure enough, Grant had a concussion. After a couple of days, he seemed absolutely normal. But he couldn't do simple math problems. He was salutatorian of his class and had always been very good with math.

One day, I said, "Hey, help me with this math problem."

Grant said, "Jud, I can't!"

But I was pretty good in math, too. After my sophomore year, three of us had 4.0 grade-point averages. Then, I took chemistry and just hated it. So I got a B in chemistry. I also got a B in physics. And they talked me into taking typing my senior year. I was such a clod that I wound up getting my only C and graduating fifth in a class of 152 with a 3.68.

I only keep in touch with about a half-dozen of those guys today. I remember when we went to the Great Alaska Shootout in '89, Jack Peterson, our second baseman, and George Smith were there. Jack is still the faculty rep at Alaska-Anchorage. And George is retired.

I spent some time with both of them, and my wife, Beverly, said, "Don't tell anyone those guys were your teammates! They look so much older than you do!"

"No, they don't!" I said. "They're probably saying the same thing about me."

There were about 300 kids in the junior class, including my sister, Carlan, Grant's and my greatest fan. She was active in everything. She was a baton twirler, a cheerleader, a class officer and had leads in the school plays. To this day, I believe Carlan would've been a great athlete if there'd been the emphasis there is today on girls' and women's athletics.

We were a close family growing up, with the three of us just a year apart in age. Grant was the smartest. I was the best athlete. And Carlan was the most aggressive.

There was a boom economy with the war and the Bremerton Navy Yard right there; you know the story of Rosie the Riveter.

During our senior year, it was obvious we were going to go in the service. We were either going to get drafted or enlist. Three of us took the Navy V-5 test to be fighter pilots. I was the only one who passed. And after graduation, I was assigned to Butte, Montana, and Montana School of Mines in 1945 as a V-5 cadet.

When we got there, they had all this football equipment. There were about 80 guys in the unit. So they decided they'd split us into two teams and play a football game. They only had one coach. So the chief officer coached one team, and I wound up coaching the other team. There I was, 18 years old, coaching against a 30-year-old. We won the game, 7-6.

I'd always wanted to be a fullback. So, as coach, that's where I played. And I carried the ball almost every single time. On the winning touchdown drive, I made 3 yards, 3 yards, 2 yards, 3 yards—first down. And we did that over and over again.

We also had a baseball team in Butte. I was the all-league shortstop and, incredibly, led the team in stolen bases. If I'd been fast, I'd have really been something. I was always slow afoot, with great hands.

In '46, we got transferred down to Colorado College. There were three games left in the football season. So 10 of us decided to go out, and they kept three of us. I didn't get to play in the first game or the last game. But in the next-to-last game, I went in at fullback. I carried the ball once—for 22 yards! If I'd had any speed at all, I'd have had a touchdown. That hole had to be a mile wide.

At least, I can always say, as a college football player, I had a 22-yard rushing average.

Then we went out for basketball. I was the starting center and leading scorer. One write-up in the paper said, "Led by high-scoring center Jud Heathcote, the team went 12-6."

You can sense that I was always a leader of some kind. They had three of what they called house adjutants. They told me I was supposed to march 80 guys over to breakfast. We'd have about 20 guys there. Everyone else would still be sleeping.

But I'd say, "All present and accounted for, Sir!"

We were just like regular students, except for wearing uniforms. And like regular students, the guys would rather sleep than eat. So when they found out they had all these eggs and all this ham left over, they weren't very happy.

The chief said, "Damn it, Jud! If they're not there, you've got to turn them in!"

"OK," I said, and never did turn them in.

When the war ended, we had the choice of signing on for three more years or being discharged in another six months.

The lieutenant said, "Jud, you're well known around here. You're on the basketball team. You're the house adjutant. You probably have more influence in our unit than anyone else. I'm counting on you to make sure the majority of these sailors sign on for three years."

I couldn't wait to get out of there and said, "Sir, I really appreciate the confidence you have in me. But I will not be signing over. I have a life to live that doesn't include the service, in all honesty."

For the next few minutes, he reamed my ass up one side and down the other. He called me a traitor to my country and said I had to reconsider.

"Sir, there will be no reconsideration," I said. "I've already made up my mind."

"Well, from this day forward, you and I will have no communication and no relationship!" he said.

It took another month for our release to come. When we left, we were taking a train to Great Lakes Naval Station for boot camp. And here came the lieutenant again.

"Heathcote!" he said.

"Yes, Sir!"

"Here are the orders for the unit," he said. "You're in charge. . . . Good luck."

After everything that happened, there I was, still in charge of the group going back.

Before we were discharged, I wound up at a Naval air station in Maryland, where —of all things—they put me in an office typing. But we worked a scam there, too. If you said you owned a car, you could get discharged in Maryland and get the money for driving home, wherever that was.

We had fake orders a guy had typed up that got us aboard one of those big Navy air transports. So we got our mileage, plus the trip home—big money, maybe a couple of hundred bucks. After that, it was decision time. Where to go? What to do?

Juan Reid, the coach at Colorado College, wanted me to come back there. But who wanted to go to Colorado College?

I had a scholarship offer to the University of Washington and one to Washington State. I'd already told Washington I was coming there to play for Hec Edmundson. But I broke up with my girl, put all my stuff in the car, drove to Pullman and told the coach, Jack Friel, I'd changed my mind. They didn't have any scholarship limit. And he said, "Good! C'mon!"

We had a Northern Division and a Southern Division in the old Pacific Coast Conference, then played off for the NCAA Tournament bid. The other four teams in the North were Idaho, Oregon, Oregon State and Washington. And we played each of those teams four times—16 league games. We'd go to Oregon and Oregon State and play Friday, Saturday, Monday and Tuesday.

The other division had Stanford, USC, UCLA and Cal.

We had 5,000 students at Washington State. The scholarship was room, board, tuition and books, which was next to nothing, plus $75 a month. But there, you had to work for it. I did odd jobs until my junior year, then ran the intramural program for Jack Friel.

We had 125 guys out for basketball my first year there, with everyone back from the war. And just because you were on scholarship, it didn't mean you were going to make the team. Seven guys who'd played the year before got cut. We only had two guys from the year before who made the team.

I was a starting guard. My center days were over. I had a set shot Jack really loved. But I only learned that to beat guys at h-o-r-s-e.

Vince Hanson, who was a Helms Foundation first-team All-American in '45, was still on the team. He was 6-8 and scored 592 points the year he was selected. They redshirted Vince in the fall of '46. The reason Jack always gave to the media was Vince's shoe size was only 9 ½ and they wanted his feet to grow. It was supposed to be to Vince's advantage and to ours to let him sit out a year so he'd have better stability. Of course, the media bought it.

Your feet don't grow when you're 21 years old. The truth was Vince could only play in the low post. Because of the other players' versatility, Friel had decided to run a no-post offense.

I was slated to start until I got a blister on the bottom of my toe. The next thing I knew, I had blood poisoning and missed two games. Bob Gambold, who later was a long-time assistant football coach at Illinois, took over. And I never got back in the starting lineup. I only started three games at Washington State. After that, I played a key role as a sixth or seventh man.

I was in a fraternity that year. And the first two days I was in the hospital, it was like Grand Central Station. Every guy in the house dropped by. And every guy on the team dropped by. The last seven days I was there, not one person came to see me.

In my playing career, I was a star in high school, a star on the small-college level, but just a role player or a substitute at the major-college level. So I can relate to guys sitting on the bench, always wanting to play. I never had any hard feelings about it. I always thought I was better than the guys playing. But I accepted it. What was important was what the coach thought. That has always been my philosophy. I've always been a good team guy. And I've always felt the team came first.

If I'd gone to Washington, I think I'd still have been a coach. But I probably would've played a lot more. I was one of the first guys to have the semblance of a jump shot. That was because I had to. When I played in the pivot, at 6-1, I had to turn and try to jump over guys.

But Jack wouldn't let anyone shoot a jump shot. He said he'd run statistics on Eddie Sheldrake at UCLA and other guys, and they only hit 16 percent of their jumpers. In those days, if you shot 33 percent, you were considered a great shooter.

By that point, I'd probably torn a cartilage in football, but didn't know it. In those years, all you did with an injury was put ice on it. I hurt my knee a lot of times over the next 20 years. Once, I was laid up six weeks. But in those days, you never had a knee operation unless you just couldn't function.

I finally had surgery when I was 38 years old. I was playing competitive handball and thinking, "Hey, they just got a new division, the masters, for 40-and-over! If my knee was better . . . " I could never play in tournaments because my knee would stiffen up.

If I was just playing one match with somebody, I was probably in the top 30 in the country. I beat a guy who was ranked No. 8 and beat a couple of guys badly who were in the top 16. But if I entered a tournament and had to play Friday night, Saturday afternoon and Saturday night, I couldn't do it.

When I'd play a really tough match, I'd wake up in the middle of the night, and my knee would be aching. I couldn't sleep, so I'd take a couple of aspirin. And I was still playing half-court basketball, too.

We'd had a lot of football and basketball players go up to Spokane for knee surgery. They'd operate on them, put them on crutches and start some rehabilitation right away. In four days, they'd be walking. So I thought that was all right.

When I decided to go up there, my wife said, "How are you going to get home?" I said, "I'm going to drive. I'll take the car and just drive back. I'll probably be in the hospital two or three days at the most."

I was in the hospital for 11 days and on crutches for a month. And they made a mistake by not getting the OK to take out the kneecap. They couldn't do that without prior permission.

The doctor said, "Except for the ones we have to reconstruct, this is the worst knee we've ever seen."

My knee never came back. And one summer, I got very ill. I took every test there was. But there was something they couldn't figure out. The doctor thought it was all psychological.

He said, "Jud, you had that knee operation, didn't you? . . . It never came back. And you're very competitive. . . . That's really bothering you, isn't it? . . . It's probably bothering you to the extent that it's affecting how you feel, right?"

I thought, "Boy, is this guy full of shit," and said, "Doc, don't try to psychoanalyze me! I know what my knee was. I know what it is. I'm disappointed. But that has nothing to do with how I feel—absolutely nothing."

You know what I think it was? When I played golf, and I still do this to this day, I never washed my golf ball. I had a habit of putting it in my mouth. I think some fertilizer got in my system.

Maybe when people said, "Jud's full of it," they were right.

WEST VALLEY AND
MARVELOUS MARV

My first year of real coaching was at Washington State. I was only eligible for three years, after transferring. So after I got a bachelor's degree in mathematics and physical education, I stayed and got my education degree in '50. My last year, I was kind of a graduate assistant coach.

Friel kept me working with intramurals. And he gave me all the basketball redshirts. We didn't have a freshman team. So I arranged a 10-game schedule, usually against the football team. They had a guy named Don Paul, who played a long time with the Browns, and was very good.

We had a 6-8 guy from South Kitsap, Dave Roberts. We had Pat Streamer. And we added Scott Foxley. So we had some pretty good players on my first team.

The next year, there were only two Division A high school coaching jobs available—one at Hoquiam, Washington, and one at West Valley High in Spokane. Bob Elliott, our starting guard, got the Hoquiam job. And I got the West Valley job. I started as a head coach at the high school level at 23 and stayed for 14 years.

I taught social studies for three years until I could get into the math department. Then, I taught math for 11 years. I was also the freshman football coach and freshman baseball coach. I finally got rid of freshman football and became the trainer for the football team—specializing in knee injuries.

As trainer, I had a kid named Dick Ome, who hurt his knee. He was a tough, hard-nosed kid who said, "I'm OK! . . . I can go back in."

I manipulated the knee a little and asked him, "Does that hurt?"

"Yeah," he said with a grimace. "Not that much, though!"

Tom Ventris, the football coach, said, "Hey, is Dick ready? We need him in there!"

I said, "Give him a little more time."

Finally, Dick was walking around, but not very well. I didn't know anything about athletic training. But I told Tom, "Dick's not going in."

"He's not?" Tom said. "He says he's OK!"

"And I say he's not!" I told him.

"What's wrong with him?" Tom said.

I said, "I don't know. . . . But he's not going back in."

They took him to the hospital and found he had a broken kneecap. The doctor said if Dick had gone back in, he might have been crippled for life.

Gene Rieger was our assistant football coach. He'd won the Mr. Hustle Award as a guard at Washington State and was just a real go-go guy. But he had a guy with a lot of running back talent on the JVs, except for being kind of a chicken.

One day, the kid got tackled—not very hard—and just laid there. Finally, I figured I'd better go out.

Right away, the kid said, "I hurt! . . . I hurt! . . ."

Rieger came over and chewed him out, saying, "The trouble with you is you've got no guts! You don't have a gut in your body!"

I said, "Hey, we'd better get him to a doctor."

It turned out he had a ruptured spleen. How it ruptured, I'll never know. But if we didn't get him to the doctor, the kid would've died. For years, I'd say, "Hey, Gene! You don't have any guts! No guts at all!"

"Damn you!" he'd say. "Quit reminding me!"

During the summers, I played semipro baseball for four years. The first summer, I played on eight different teams. Then, I was an all-state semipro player in Montana. We went over and played for Libby. I was a catcher. And we'd get from $20 to $50 a game. I played in Alaska for three summers, then went back to school to work on my master's degree.

Finally, I lost interest in baseball and started playing competitive handball. So I traded the baseball job for the tennis job, because I wanted more time to play. I was the tennis coach for eight years and really enjoyed that. I'd make my basketball players come out for tennis if they weren't out for another sport.

West Valley was the smallest school in our league. It had only won one game and two games in basketball the previous two years. And my first year, we struggled and only won four games. But at least we were competitive.

That's when our principal said, "We're thinking of dropping out of the league next year. What do you think?"

I said, "Hey, we'll win the league next year!"

That's what we did. In fact, we won the league three of the next four years. We had everyone back, so I could put a few things in. I've always put in a lot of plays.

Someone said, "It's hard to play for Jud. You have to worry about all the plays, as well as playing."

We had a guy named Dave Eikerman, who was 6-8 and got straight D's in the classroom. Everyone thought he was dumb, but he wasn't. He was just lazy. So when we put in a play, Dave would pick it right up.

We also had a guy named Mike Anderson, a minister's son and a kid a lot like Matt Steigenga at MSU —good-looking, about 6-3 and a straight-A student. But when we put a play in, he ran it wrong.

I said, "Mike, no! You go in here and cut around here."

So we ran it again. And he still ran it wrong.

I said, "Mike! Mike! Remember? . . . I showed you to go around here!"

He said, "Oh, yeah."

We ran it over. And it was wrong again. Now, I'm really upset.

"Mike!" I hollered. "Christ, Mike! Can't you figure out where you go on these damn plays?"

He said, "Coach, if you wouldn't use profanity, I think I could pick up the plays a lot better."

Maybe profanity doesn't help. But I'll remember that until the day I die. Mike ran it wrong three times. And he blamed it on the profanity. He was a real smart kid with what I call a low basketball I.Q.

After our fifth year, we struggled for awhile. We had about 750 students and played schools in the city league like Lewis and Clark, Rogers, North Central and Shadle Park, all with enrollments of 2,000 or more. We also played Gonzaga, a Catholic school—and you know how Catholic schools are. That's where John Stockton went.

We won the league title five times in 14 years. But when we went to the state tournament, the highest we ever finished was seventh. It seemed we always got beat in the first or second round.

My first year there, I coached the freshmen and the varsity. We couldn't find a freshman coach. And we had a 6-0 freshman named Roger Walser, who was so uncoordinated it was almost pathetic. I made him stay after practice every day and work on some drills.

The guy I replaced, an older guy named Ward Maurer, was the athletic director and said, "Jud, if I gave you any advice, it would be not to spend any extra time with Walser. That's just a waste of time."

I said, "Ward, I think you're right. But he's the only tall kid in the class."

Roger grew to 6-4 and was a starter in his junior and senior years. He was first-team all-state in his senior year and got a scholarship to Idaho.

I had a kid named Ed Luedtke, who went to Oregon on a full scholarship. John Maras started for three years at Washington State for Marv Harshman. Dave Eikerman started for four years at Whitworth College. Harry Watson started for three years at Gonzaga. And Larry Winn, who was one of my favorite players, had a scholarship and was sixth man at Rice.

He just started a business called Hoopaholic with another guy. I'm not into art. But he owns Winn Galleries and is a multi-millionaire from selling paintings.

He's also the one who tells the story about trying to impress me in a pickup game in open gym when he was about 14. He said he was jumping up and down and checking me on an inbounds pass, when I supposedly threw the ball in his face and said, "Maybe now you'll give me room, Winn!"

I tell Larry, "I happen to know that story isn't true, because you never came that close to anybody in all the time you played basketball."

But it was at West Valley that I first met Marv Harshman. He was the coach at Pacific Lutheran and ran a high-low post offense. I ran a similar offense; it was very structured. Marv made his more guard-oriented, while mine was more inside-oriented. When we got together, we combined the two and had a better system.

When I was at West Valley, I'd go see Marv's teams play Gonzaga or Eastern Washington. And my last four or five years there, I talked to Marv quite a bit.

I'd decided, after 10 years, I was tired of the bells, the repetition and the regimentation of the classroom. It was time for me to leave.

I put in for the Columbia Basin Junior College job. My good friend, Len Pyne, was the baseball coach there. And he told me I was the leading candidate. When I didn't hear a thing for three weeks, I'd decided I didn't want to live down there and didn't want to coach junior-college kids. Of course, that's when they offered me the job. I turned it down, thinking other jobs would come up. I was really on Dial-a-Clue.

I finished second for the Eastern Washington job. Ernie McKie, another high school coach, got the job, mostly because he was a graduate there.

They told me, "Jud, you're right in there. In fact, we're going to offer to it to Ernie. If he doesn't take it, we're going to offer you the job." Now, I hoped he wouldn't take it. But he did.

Then they built Spokane Community College right in town. I figured that was a natural for me. But I applied and didn't even get an interview. When the chancellor's son got the job, I figured maybe there was some nepotism there.

In the meantime, I'd been going to school on Saturdays and during the summers, working on my Ph.D. I figured maybe I'd go into administration. I knew I was going to make a change of some kind. I'd decided I wasn't going to coach in high school the rest of my life.

That was when they approved the idea that you could put in for a year's sabbatical. You had to have been there seven years. I'd been there twice that long. So I went down to Washington

State to finish my doctorate. There was no guarantee I'd ever get my coaching job back.

When I told Marv I was coming down and would like to help, he said, "Great! Great!" and we decided I'd be his volunteer assistant.

Marv was the only coach in the Pac-8 who didn't have a full-time assistant, just a graduate assistant who'd help with the freshman team. Bobo Brayton, the baseball coach would help. But when January rolled around, he was busy with the baseball team.

Suddenly, they decided they were going to hire a full-time assistant. And since I was already down there in Pullman, I got hired. After all the near-misses, I was at exactly the right place at the right time and the first full-time assistant Marv ever had.

I coached the freshmen for five years. Freshmen weren't eligible to play varsity basketball. And my first freshman team went 22-0, finishing with two wins on the West Coast against Highline Community College and Olympic Community College in, of all places, Bremerton.

That was the first time my mother had ever seen me coach. And she commented that I really seemed to get worked up during the game. I said, since we were getting "homered" by the officials, I was a little more animated than usual. Of course, she didn't understand what that meant.

My second freshman team went 21-1, winning 38 in a row over a two-year span before losing. I was away with the varsity at UCLA and USC when we finally lost. I remember calling for the score from the L.A. Airport and actually crying when I heard the news.

The next two seasons, we were 22-1 and 19-1, giving us a four-year record of 84-3. My fifth team was 15-6. And after five years, with a 99-9 record, it was time to bow out. Since I was working with the varsity, doing most of the scouting and handling a lot of the recruiting, it was obvious we needed more help.

I was instrumental in getting Denny Houston, the coach at Clark Junior College, hired as a grad assistant. Later, Denny served as Marv's long-time assistant at Washington before becoming the head coach at Western Washington and Weber State.

I've been knocked a lot as a recruiter. But I was a great recruiter at Washington State. I was a great recruiter at Montana.

And I was a better recruiter at Michigan State than I was ever credited for being.

I believed in Washington State, because I went there. And I believed in Marv. So I did a pretty good of good job of selling the program and Marv those seven years.

Guys like Mike Deane, Tom Izzo and Brian Gregory worked 15 or 16 hours a day on my staffs at Michigan State. But my wife always said, "No one could have put in the time you did."

I'd go in at 7 a.m., sometimes go home for lunch but usually pack one, come home for dinner, then always go back. I'd work until 10 or 11 p.m. I handled the defense and thought I helped on the offense. And I tried to play a little handball on the side.

I've always said that Marv was an offensive genius. To this day, he remembers every offense he has ever run and the guys who ran it. He was just unbelievable in terms of his offensive approach to the game. And he never got any credit for it.

I've been around a lot of great coaches. And most of them couldn't have carried his jock. Marv was my mentor and my inspiration. He's the guy I'm most indebted to for all the years I've coached.

He was one of the great coaching minds the game has known –maybe not one of the greatest coaches, but one of the great minds. He was always changing something.

"Wouldn't it work better, Jud, if you moved this guy there?" he'd say whenever I'd show him a play. It was always better his way.

When Howie Dallmar was coach at Stanford, he wouldn't even scout us. He said, "Hell, why should we? You run a different offense every time we play!"

It wasn't really a different offense. But we'd always put in a couple of different plays for each team. We tried to take advantage of what the other club didn't do or hadn't seen.

Marv knew a lot about defense, too. But Brayton and I made us better defensive clubs. We'd really get on guys. Marv would talk about defense but never really demand it.

To have a good defense, you have to understand it, you have to believe in it, you have to teach it, you have to sell it and you have to demand it be played. Marv understood it. He believed in it. He could teach it. He could sell it. But he wasn't great at demanding it'd be played.

At one clinic, we were sitting around when Hank Anderson, the coach at Gonzaga, said, "Jud, you're a better defensive coach than I am. You're no smarter than I am. But you're a sonofabitch. And I'm not."

That was a compliment. But we started out 9-17, then had five straight winning seasons. We were second in the Pac-8 in three of those five years. But that was when only one club from a conference went to the Tournament. UCLA was so dominant we only beat them once in 14 tries.

The story Marv has told 50,000 times was we were playing West Virginia in the Far West Classic and were on the officials pretty hard. They'd already warned us not to get up again or we'd get a technical. But there was a play right in front of us, so I jumped up.

"Geez! Don't do that!" Marv said, snapping his arm out like a safety restraint.

I went backwards right over my chair, got back up and sat down like nothing had happened.

Very calmly, I said, "My attorney will be talking to you Monday morning," and kept on coaching the game.

Marv and I even won a handball tournament or two. He'd hide over there on the right and let me cover the rest of the court. But he always had pretty good hands and a good dump shot. Best of all, he liked to play.

You know, Marv was one of about four athletes in NCAA history to make first-team All-America in football and basketball in the same year. When I mention that to people, I always say, "Before you get carried away with that fact, remember, there weren't too many Americans then." Marv was one of the earliest settlers. He was also one of the best guys you could ever work for in the game of basketball.

We've had four distinct periods in my coaching career and our married life. We spent 14 years at West Valley. And I really enjoyed 10 of those years. We had seven years at Washington State, five at Montana and 19 at Michigan State.

The only time I was an assistant coach was at Washington State. So if we picked the most fulfilling years, they wouldn't have been those seven. But if we looked at the happiest years, they might have been the years from '64-'71.

It was the first time I was coaching college basketball. I loved coaching with Marv. I loved working with Bobo. And Pullman, Washington, was a good place to be.

At Pullman, you didn't go places. You went to someone's house. You were almost forced to make a lot of friends. Wherever else we've been, you went out. And you didn't get quite as close that way.

The other important thing was that our kids were growing up there. Even though I wasn't around all the time, it was a very good time for us as a family.

I remember when a next-door neighbor told Bev, "Oh, I feel so sorry for you! Your husband is gone so much."

"Don't feel sorry for me," she said. "We may not have quantity time. But when he's here, we have quality time."

I liked that.

BREAKING UP IS
HARD TO DO

As much as I loved working for Marv, I liked the idea of being a head coach again somewhere, some day.

I put in for the Portland State job, interviewed and even went down there with my wife. But I finished second to Marion Pericin.

I put in for the Idaho job and interviewed there, too. I've always felt that I interviewed well and knew how to express myself. But one question there did me in.

A guy asked me, "You went to Washington State and coached there for seven years. Wouldn't it be hard to change your allegiance from being a Cougar to a Vandal?"

I said, "It might be hard at first. But it certainly wouldn't be hard for very long."

They didn't like that. I shouldn't have said "hard at first." I should've said I could do that overnight. There were 15 people on the voting board. Wayne Anderson got the job, 9-6. And they said there were two or three who would have voted the other way if I'd answered that one question differently.

And I applied at Colorado because I knew Irv Brown, the baseball coach and one of the best basketball officials in NCAA history, but got nothing.

I wasn't actively searching for jobs. But I was always interested in being a head coach. It didn't look like Marv was ever going to retire. There was a 10-year difference in our ages, which wasn't enough.

Suddenly, I got the Montana job—over the phone. Jack Swarthout was the athletic director. I knew Jack when he was the football coach at Hoquiam High School. He went down to Texas as an assistant to Darrell Royal, then he got the Montana job. But I'd known him for years.

One of the assistant football coaches there was Jack Elway, who later became known as John's father. He was a fraternity brother of mine at Washington State and a good friend, even though I was a senior when he was a sophomore. We'd kept in reasonable contact, as you do with coaches.

Before I was hired, they offered the job to Dean Nicholson, the long-time coach at Central Washington in Ellensburg. But they were always having financial problems at Montana. And they'd frozen all the salaries. The salary for the basketball coach was $13,500. Dean Nicholson had been making $15,000.

Thinking he could negotiate a little, he said, "I'll have to have the same salary I'm making now."

In talking to Dean since, he told me, "Geez, I thought they'd go up $1,500! That's not a lot of money!"

They wouldn't go up one dime. So I got a call from Jack Elway, asking if I had any interest. When I said, "Yeah," he put me on the phone with Jack Swarthout.

"Jud, we'd like you to be our new basketball coach," he said, with the shortest interview in NCAA history. "I'm offering you the job. But I need an answer right now."

I said, "I'll take the job."

I was down at the Portland State Tournament, just in shock. I didn't go to the games. I went to the bar and had a couple of drinks. I called home, told my wife and said, "Hey, don't tell the kids!"

When I got home, I said, "We're going to have a family conference. We don't have many of these. But we have some things we have to talk about. Your dad has decided to take the University of Montana job. We're moving to Missoula, Montana."

At first, the kids thought I was joking. Then, my daughter, Carla, asked me why I didn't want to coach with Marv any more. I explained it was a chance to become a head coach.

Then, my son, Jerry, who was 10 years old, said, "Geez, Dad, the Big Sky!" He started crying and ran to his room.

Marv had always said, if it was just him, we'd get upset by a smaller school from time to time. But he said as long as I was around to get on the guys, we'd never lose to a Big Sky team.

I'd always harped to the guys, "That's the Big Sky! We're the Pac-8! You don't lose to a league like that!" And our kids had picked that up.

But when I went over for the announcement, they had to go through a formal process. So I met with the A.D., the sports information director and the president. And I wasn't quite comfortable about something.

"Let's go have a couple of beers," Jack Elway said.

When we got there, he knew something was wrong and said, "You're not going to take the job, are you?"

"How'd you know that?" I said.

He said, "Because I can read you."

"No, I don't think I am," I said. "In talking to Jack Swarthout, I saw no commitment to basketball whatsoever."

Elway said, "Look, I know Jack like the back of my hand. He has great interest in basketball. But he doesn't want to do anything. He'll let you run the program yourself. And he'll give you as much as he can to run it."

The recruiting budget was $6,000. But it was understood you could go as high as $10,000 if you had to. When I got there in mid-March, they were already at $11,000. And they hadn't had one guy visit. The guy I replaced had spent a lot of money with no tangible results.

So the recruiting budget was completely spent. All they could do was give me a school car and $2,500. I was used to operating on a low recruiting budget. But I didn't see how I could recruit anyone with that.

"If you take the job," Elway said, "I guarantee you Jack Swarthout will find a way to get you more money. Jack really does have an interest. When we came here, this was not a good football job. We made it a good football job. And you can make this a good basketball job."

Jack Elway convinced me of that. And I've thought about that every time Big Sky jobs have opened up over the years.

When I'd get calls from guys, asking if this job or that job was a good job, I always said, "No. If it was, it wouldn't be open. But you can make it a good job!"

If I hadn't gone out with Jack Elway, I probably wouldn't have taken the job. I was still happy where I was. And I didn't need a move to a coaching graveyard, a place where I'd be three years and get fired.

Even after I took the job, there was still enough drama to make things interesting. With all the things that happened, it was a strange set of developments.

The president at Washington State was Glenn Terrell. Joe Kearney was the athletic director at Washington then, and he liked Marv. So Marv went over and interviewed in Seattle. Meanwhile, there was a party in Pullman for Stan Bates, the athletic director, who was moving to the WAC as commissioner. And I made a point of saying something about Marv to the president.

"If you don't do something, you're going to lose your basketball coach," I said. "Is that what you want?"

"No!" he said. "We need to keep Marv. What do we need to do? Is it money?"

"Mr. Terrell, money means nothing to Marv," I said. "Certainly, a guy would like to have a raise. But I think what Marv needs is to be told he has security here."

Also, the athletic director's job was open. The physical education staff drafted a unanimous letter in support of Marv becoming A.D. He never applied officially. And he never heard one word. They never asked him to apply or contacted him and said he was doing a helluva job, but that they didn't want a combination guy.

Plus, the three best friends Marv had were gone. Stan Bates, our A.D., had just retired. I'd already taken the Montana job. And Dick Vandervoort, our trainer, had taken a job with the Rockets because he wanted to live in San Diego. Of course, as soon as he took the job, they moved to Houston.

So I told the president, "If you give Marv a raise and maybe make him associate athletic director, that might do it. But the important thing is, somebody has to let him know they want him here."

We had no long-term contracts in those days. We were all on year-to-year contracts, except the football coach. But when Marv told the president he was going to Seattle for a second interview, Terrell told him to get back in touch before he made a decision. That made Marv feel better.

Joe Kearney wanted to hire Marv and wanted a decision that night. Marv knew Terrell was at a meeting at the Union and tried to reach him there. He said, "This is Marv Harshman trying to reach Glenn Terrell. Would you please give him the message?"

The message came back: "President Terrell is very busy right now. He can't come to the phone."

So Marv said, "Would you please tell him it's very important and I'm following instructions to call him before I make a decision."

Finally, Terrell came to the phone. But he was very curt.

"What is it?" he said.

"They've offered me the job at the University of Washington," Marv said. "And they said they want a decision."

"I suggest you take it," Terrell said.

Marv was just crushed. He was a small-town guy. He didn't want to go. But he had to take it.

Right away, there was a tremendous backlash, with alumni saying, "How could you let Marv Harshman get away? He has been here 13 years and done a great job."

With the natural rivalry between the schools, it would have been like Michigan hiring Nick Saban away from Michigan State when Gary Moeller was fired —or hiring me when Bill Frieder left for Arizona State.

So Glenn Terrell had to alibi and said, "I couldn't believe it. But they bought him. He just went for the money."

I was already working at Montana. But I wasn't taking that shit. I made a lot of phone calls and let the real story out. Marv did get more money, but not much more. If he was making $21,000, he got about $25,000. And he coached at Washington for 14 years with pretty good success.

Marv won the Pac-10 title in '84 and '85, his last two years, and finished with 642 career wins—22 less than the great John Wooden. He was inducted into the Basketball Hall of Fame in '84.

But that move left Washington State without a head coach. During that time, I heard from a lot of alumni who wanted to hire Jud back. I know there were a lot who wanted a fresh start, too. But Ray Nagel, the new athletic director, called and wanted me to meet him in Spokane.

He told me he wanted me to be a finalist for the job. He wanted to find two or three other finalists. Then, he said he'd interview everybody and . . .

"Hold it, Ray!" I said. "If you're not prepared to offer me the job right now, forget it. I'm not sure I'd take it anyway, because I'm so upset at the way Marv was treated. But I am not a candidate for this job. I can't wait for a decision. I've got two or three recruits hanging on at Montana. I can't afford to lose them."

So I met with Ray for about two hours and told him all the things I thought the program needed. Some time later, Ray said they were having a press conference on Wednesday to announce the new basketball coach. They'd had Eddie Sutton of Creighton in the weekend before and offered him the job.

Bobo Brayton, my old buddy, said, "Hey, I know Eddie Sutton! He's not going to take that job!"

"Of course, he'll take this job!" Ray said.

When Eddie called and turned it down, Ray just panicked. He called Bob Greenwood, who'd been an assistant coach at Iowa when Ray was there as football coach. Greenwood had been in Denver, not even coaching. But Ray offered him the Washington State job over the phone.

Greenwood hired Dale Brown as his assistant. And Dale couldn't believe what he'd gotten himself into.

He said, "We'd have a meeting in the morning, and Bob would say, 'Dale, let's talk a little basketball! What do you like to do on offense?'"

Of course, Dale was really flattered. And when he got up and drew some things, Greenwood said that was good. The next day he asked Dale how he'd attack a 3-1-1 UCLA press.

Dale was up there, drawing and drawing, and said later, "It took me about a week to figure out he was pumping me. He had to have something to go by. And he knew very little about basketball."

They were 11-15 that season. Then, they let Greenberg go and brought in George Raveling. George said when he was being driven around campus, he saw huge "WE WANT JUD!" signs hanging from the dormitory windows. He said he thought there was probably some kid named Jud who was running for class president.

They'd made the decision they wanted a black coach, which wasn't me. They were getting a lot of pressure for affirmative action. But I wasn't even contacted that year.

By that point, I had enough problems of my own getting things going the way I wanted in Missoula.

I was 43 years old, which was old for a first head coaching job in college. Everything I did in my career came late, except my start. I was old to take a college assistant's job at 36. I was old when I went to Montana. And I was old when I coached my first game in the Big Ten at 49.

And as I've often been reminded, I was old when I quit.

But that was 24 seasons later —long after becoming a Grizzly and a grizzled Spartan.

GRIZZLY
HEATHCOTE

You can only coach so long with the kind of enthusiasm and energy you need. That's why guys run out of gas in college after 25 or 30 years. But I never hit that wall. I hadn't been at it as long as others my age.

When I got to Montana, I'd get in the car and drive to Portland to talk to someone that night. That was 500 miles. I'd drive to Vancouver, Washington, or Seattle to follow up on contacts I still had from Washington State—kids from the backup list. And somehow, with a ridiculous budget, we put together a good recruiting year.

We got a 6-7 kid out of Portland, Tim Stambaugh, who'd been hoping to go to Oregon or Oregon State. We got Larry Smedley, a 6-6 kid from Vancouver, Washington, who'd been on Washington's list for a long time. And the best kid we got was Ken McKenzie from British Columbia, a 6-9 guy who didn't meet most schools' entrance requirements. His classes wouldn't transfer from Canadian schools to U.S. schools.

We would have loved to have him at Washington State. But out-of-state students had to have a 3.0. And Ken was below that.

At Montana, if you were a graduate of a high school in the state of Montana, you were admissible in Missoula. We were also able to admit out-of-state students under a 3.0, so Ken qualified for admission. He became the leading rebounder in Grizzly history and was the all-league center his junior and senior years.

Our guards were Tom Peck from Libby, Montana, and Robin Selvig from Outlook, Montana.

But Montana was kind of a different place. I remember going to a restaurant and meeting a booster who said, "Ah, you're the new basketball coach! How many niggers are you going to start this year?"

I said, "Well, now that you mention it, we're going to start five!"

We only had three blacks on the team.

I was really naive on the black-white thing. I had a little guard from junior college, Mike Murray, who was on a Ford Foundation scholarship. We didn't even have to count him against our limit. And he got more money than the other kids did, based on need. Somehow, he was short of money one spring and needed to make about $200—not a lot of money, but more then than it is now.

I went to a booster, Don Huggins, and said, "Get me a part-time job for Mike Murray. We've got the pulp mill here. Can't he get on the night shift for a couple of weeks?"

Don couldn't get him on out there and said, "How about if I just raise the $200 and give it to him?"

"No, we're not going to start that stuff!" I said. "I thought you said you could get him on out there?"

"I thought so, too," Don said. "But from what some of the other guys told me, it probably wouldn't be safe for him."

I couldn't believe it. But there were only two black families in Missoula and about 20 black kids in the school. Then they got a federally funded program that brought in 1.0 students off the streets of St. Louis. Those were the wrong guys to have there. They had no interest in school and made things worse.

Things were pretty bad in some ways already. I'd contracted with Raymond Disposal Service. But another guy knocked on my door and wanted my garbage business. I said, "No, I'm already with Raymond Disposal."

"I know that," he said. "But have you ever met that guy? Did you know he's black?"

I said, "That's all the more reason he'll have my business. Now, get the hell out of here!"

That was the kind of attitude you found there. It was really a redneck area. I'm sure it has changed somewhat over the years. But we had three black players that year, including one of my favorites.

Willie Bascus was 22 years old with a 50-year-old body. It would take him half of practice to get warmed up. Later, I helped him get an assistant's job at Washington with Lynn Nance. He was going with a white woman named Isabel. And they fought the racial thing. Everyone said it wouldn't work, but they got married, had two great kids and are very happy to this day. Willie stayed on for two years when he was finished playing and helped us coach. He was still on scholarship.

My first game with the Grizzlies, we went down and played Oregon. We played Washington State on the way to Wyoming. Then, we went to Tacoma for a four-team tournament and had to play Long Beach State when Jerry Tarkanian was there.

They had a luncheon before the tournament started. And someone asked what the enrollment was at Montana. It was about 8,000. But at Long Beach State, it was 26,000.

A guy said to Tarkanian, "Well, it's no wonder you have a better team and a better program!"

"Wait a minute!" Tark said. "The enrollment at your school has nothing to do with the caliber of your basketball program. It's the number of scholarships and the budget you have. Do you think we have the same resources USC has with 8,000 students? Do you think Jud has the same resources Notre Dame has with 8,000 students?"

We didn't. We played five games in a row before we got a home date. So I asked Jack Swarthout who the hell arranged that schedule.

"We have to do it that way, because the football team goes to the Camelia Bowl almost every year," he said. "We need the facility to practice. And we can't put the floor down until football is over."

That wasn't the only inconvenience. A guy named Sharkey would come in and have his class jog around the outside of the court while we were practicing.

Right away, I told him, "Hey! You can't do that!"

"Why not?" he said. "It shouldn't bother you."

After we put up with it for a week, I told my assistant, Jim Brandenburg, "C'mon, just do what I do."

We both went into his classroom and started jogging around. I said, "Keep teaching! Don't let us bother you!"

That was the end of that. And in '72, they renovated Adams Field House, added 3,500 seats and put in a Tartan floor. Football could use the facility. And we could still schedule games.

Our second year, we played Morningside College and Stout State in the first two games. The alumni always felt we should be playing Kentucky and UCLA. And when I spoke to a Rotary group, they wanted to know where Morningside was located.

"You know, I really don't know," I said, only caring that Morningside would come to Missoula for $1,000, with no return game.

"Well, who scheduled these games?" the guy said.

I said, "I did!" explaining that we were trying to build a program and wanted some wins before the league season started.

I guess I was the original Bill Frieder. But that's how the turnaround started. We had to get some confidence.

We also had to generate some excitement. The first season we were at Montana, there was lukewarm interest in basketball. Then, we got guys to organize The Zoo, our student cheering section.

We were 14-12 the first year and 13-13 the second. But we went 19-8 and tied for the Big Sky title the third year, then won it outright and went to the NCAA Tournament in '75, finishing 21-8.

The fifth year, we were rebuilding with four starters gone and only Micheal Ray Richardson back. But by the end of the year, we were as good as anyone. If we'd had a conference tournament one year earlier than we did, we might have been in the NCAA again.

It was kind of funny the way we built the program. The first year, it was key recruiting time, and where was Brandy? Out at the Missoula Country Club, playing golf. When someone asked me why he wasn't recruiting, I said, "Hey, we've got one car. We don't have enough money in our recruiting budget so both of us can be on the road, unless we're together. And there's no need for us to both be where I'm going."

They thought I was unaware. But I knew what Brandy was doing. That's how strapped we were in terms of a budget. We had to watch the dimes so close it was unbelievable.

The odd thing was, the key to turning it around was that first recruiting class. That guaranteed that we were going to have a pretty good team the next three years. And we did. It got better each year. Plus, we got lucky. Eric Hays transferred from Washington State.

When I was in Pullman, we were always trying to get kids to walk on. I did the same thing at Michigan State the first five years, when we had a JV program. But when freshmen weren't eligible to play with the varsity, you might have four or five guys on scholarship and another 30 who'd walk on and think they could help you.

Eric Hays was from Junction City, Oregon. His dad had played at Oregon. But Oregon showed no interest in Eric; it was kind of a slap in the face. So he wrote us a letter at Washington State. I wrote back and told him if he could make the first five, we'd consider him for a scholarship the next year. We only had 22 of them then. The University of Washington had 28!

Eric started out on the third team and would always come into the coaches' office. My desk was in front. Marv's was in back. And he'd always want to know what he had to do to move up. You'd tell him he had to do this, this and this. The next week he'd be back, saying, "Coach, how do you evaluate my progress? How am I doing?"

We'd almost hide when we'd see him coming. But the guy was so intense. We didn't think he'd amount to much. He was left-handed and really slow. And at 6-3, he was a non-position player. Suddenly, he worked his way up to the second team. Then, he became a starter. He finished as the second-leading scorer on the freshman team.

Before Marv went to Washington and I moved to Montana, we recommended that Eric Hays get a scholarship the following year. Instead, I got a call from Eric, saying he wanted to transfer.

"I got cut after three practices," he said. "They told me I was too slow for a guard and too small for a forward."

I said, "Eric, they probably told you the truth. You are too slow for a guard and too small for a forward. You probably should go to Lewis and Clark in Portland or some other smaller school."

"Coach, I'm a Division I player!" he said. "I've always felt you knew basketball. If I transfer, will you give me a chance?"

"Eric, you know I'll give you a chance," I said. "But I still think you'd be better going some other place."

He transferred in anyway. And when he visited, he stayed in my basement. That shows you how dumb I was. That was an

NCAA violation. He stayed at Brandy's for nearly two weeks. That's how oblivious we were.

Eric didn't become eligible until the following year, when winter quarter began. It was after practice had started. And he really got down and didn't play that well. But he became a starter the next two seasons and was all-conference both years. When times got tough, that's when Eric was at his best. In the first NCAA Tournament appearance in school history, he got 25 against Utah State and 32 against UCLA.

In those days, teams were placed in the NCAA Tournament strictly by region. The year before, I scouted Arizona and figured we'd win. But you can always beat the clubs you don't play. We were upset by Idaho State in the league championship playoff and didn't make it into the tournament.

In '75, when I knew we were in and might play Utah State in the first round, I drove down and saw them play Utah—500 miles. Utah State had two good forwards and not much else. Of course, we were the underdog. And playing that game in Pullman, I knew the surroundings well enough.

We beat them, 69-63. It wasn't an easy win. But it wasn't a nailbiter, either. Then, we went to Portland for our second-round game against UCLA.

Everyone assumed we couldn't match up with the Bruins inside and would probably have to zone. But I knew the UCLA offense like the back of my hand. And we looked at their overplay on defense and figured we could use the back door. We scored five buckets that way.

I told our guys we had nothing to lose, but we should take some pride in who we were and what we were. We weren't afraid of UCLA. Our kids had a lot of confidence.

We took a bus, rather than flew, so we could bring a lot of people to Portland. It was a 10-hour trip. And so we didn't have to stop and eat, we brought along some box lunches.

Were we the hicks from Montana or what?

Right away, the guys said, "Hey, don't you wonder where the UCLA bus is? . . . They probably have better box lunches than we do! . . . That must be the UCLA bus up there. Guys, hide your box lunches!"

If UCLA had seen us, they'd have really been afraid. We took our cheerleaders and all our administrative people with us.

As it turned out, it could've been a wild ride home.

We were probably a 15-point underdog. But we had the ball with 30 seconds to go, trailing by one. We'd come back from eight down in the last three minutes.

Suddenly, Eric Hays went up for a shot—I can still see it as clearly as the bald spot on my head—with Larry Smedley all by himself under the basket. When Larry turned to get inside rebounding position, Eric dropped the ball off to him. The ball went out-of-bounds. After that, we had to foul. They made the foul shots. And we lost, 67-64.

If Eric had taken the shot, it might have gone in. If Smedley had seen the ball and caught it, he would've made a basket.

After the game, John Wooden gave us a lot of credit, saying, "Don't talk about how we didn't play. Talk about how Montana played. We played pretty well and struggled to beat them."

That's the way John was. He was never one of those arrogant, we're-better-than-you type of guys. But it wasn't a moral victory, despite what everyone said.

It was my 12th straight loss to UCLA and 14th in 15 games. Once when I was at Washington State, we were up by nine with six minutes to go and saw it slip away on a freak tip-in at the end of the game.

There was a freaky play in this game, too, though I'm not sure it would've affected the outcome. Charlie Fouty was one of the officials. And when Eric Hays drew an offensive foul early in the second half, he hit the floor. Unfortunately, he got up just as Charlie demonstrated the foul with a wild elbow.

When Charlie connected square to the jaw, Eric was out cold for a minute or two. It took that long for him to regain consciousness.

Charlie said, "Geez, Coach, I'm sorry! It was an accident!"

I knew it was. But I said, "No, it wasn't! You did it on purpose!" Charlie and I have laughed about that a number of times over the years.

But I don't think that changed the game. And when we analyzed it later, we said it was a well-officiated game. There was no big-time, little-time treatment.

We had a third-place game left against Nevada Las Vegas and didn't play well. We were just dead and lost, 75-67.

UCLA beat Arizona State to go back to the Final Four, then beat Louisville the following Saturday. Before the championship game, John Wooden announced his retirement. And the Bruins went out and beat Kentucky in San Diego to win their 10th title in 12 seasons, a record that will never be touched.

Curt Gowdy was broadcasting our game against UCLA. And he said Eric was one of the best postgame interviews he'd ever had.

With a TV game, if they have extra time, they usually try to get the winning coach and a couple of his players. But instead of the All-Americans, Marques Johnson and David Meyers, from the winning team, they ran out and got Eric Hays from the losing team.

Eric was an Academic All-American and was very articulate. He gave credit to his coaches, the Big Sky, John Wooden and UCLA, saying all the right things. Curt said it looked like he'd almost played himself into exhaustion and wondered how Eric could play so hard for so long.

"I play for my brother," Eric said. "He had cancer and had his leg amputated just below the knee when he was 11 years old. As soon as he had his prosthesis, he was out there shooting baskets and limping around. When I watched him do that on a wooden leg, I decided I would play as hard as I could to represent the family. . . . And my brother is now the leading scorer on his high school team as a junior."

His brother wound up with a scholarship to Southern Oregon. We looked at him at Montana, too. He was 6-7 and could really shoot. But that story is one I've told a lot of players, about reaching their potential.

Eric wound up getting drafted by Milwaukee. Larry Costello loved him, because he was so smart. And he probably would have made their team if they hadn't traded Kareem Abdul-Jabbar for three players who all had no-cut contracts. Suddenly, there was no room for a rookie.

But back in Missoula, there was another rookie everyone loved—even if we hadn't known what we were getting.

We had a kid named David Berry, a 5-11 guard from Denver, visit. We offered him a scholarship, but he went to Adams State, a Division II school. He needed to stay closer to home. His mom wasn't well. And it was a family decision.

Then, I got a phone call from a friend of his.

"Coach Heathcote, this is Micheal Ray Richardson," he said.

I said, "Yeah," with no idea who that was.

"My friend just made a visit up there and said it was a nice school," he said. "I'd like to visit and look around."

"Just a minute, Micheal Ray," I said, then put the phone down. "Hey, Jim! Do you know a Micheal Ray Richardson?"

He said, "Yeah. He plays on the state championship team at Denver Manual. He's a 6-3 forward, but a pretty good athlete."

So I picked up the phone and said, "Micheal Ray, we're looking for guards."

"Coach, I can play guard!" he said. "I was a forward, but I can play guard!"

We were trying to get into Denver anyway, so we brought him in for a visit. Our kids always used to get together and play. And after I watched Micheal for five minutes, I said, "That kid has great hands! He'll probably be a sub forward. But we're going to give him a scholarship and try to make a guard out of him."

When Micheal Ray came to Montana, he couldn't dunk a basketball. He could really jump. But he didn't have the timing or something.

"Micheal Ray!" I said, kidding him. "I've got to be the only coach in America who recruited a 6-3 black guy who can't dunk! I know 5-9 black guys who can dunk!"

"I can dunk! I can dunk! Look at this!" he'd say, then bang it off the rim.

He grew about an inch before his sophomore year, got a little stronger and could backhand dunk or do anything you wanted. We ran a high-low post offense, with Micheal Ray at weakside guard. He was a defensive specialist his first year and All-Everything as a sophomore. The last game he played for me, he had 40 points against Montana State.

And he went on to become the all-time leading scorer in school history—not bad for a "Micheal who?"

Both Jim Brandenburg and I have always claimed the credit for recruiting Micheal Ray. In reality, he recruited us.

FROM MISSOULA
TO MID-MICHIGAN

When Joe Kearney was hired as Michigan State's athletic director in April '76, he wanted to hire Marv as his basketball coach—again.

Marv said no and gave Joe a list of people he should consider. My name was on that list. And it wasn't the first time our paths had crossed.

Joe and I weren't what you'd call long-time friends of any kind. We were long-time coaching acquaintances. That was it.

When I was at West Valley, he was the coach at Sunnyside High near Yakima. We coached against each other a couple of times. And when I was taking grad classes at the University of Washington, Joe was an intern there. We'd go down to the gym and play one-on-one.

But I hadn't seen him for a long time until he became athletic director at Washington, while I was an assistant at Washington State. Later, Joe got fired at Washington for no good reason—mostly due to a change in administrations—long after he'd hired Marv.

Now, he was looking to hire another coach with the Harshman stamp of approval. And despite what everyone thought, Joe never did call me until he actually offered me the job.

Instead, I got a call at Montana, saying, "This is Gwen Norrell at Michigan State University. I'm calling to see if you have an interest in the basketball head coaching position."

I thought for a minute, figured I didn't have anything to lose and said, "Well, . . . yes, I do."

I thought I was probably talking to a secretary of Joe's. But I found out later it was the school's faculty representative.

Then, I got a call that said, "We are interviewing the candidates this weekend in Chicago. You're scheduled for an interview at 1 p.m. Saturday."

It was Gwen again. But I still thought it was a secretary.

I said, "That's a key recruiting weekend for us. We're having two of our top recruits in. I can't interview at that time."

She said, "That's the last time we have interviews scheduled."

And I said, "I'm sorry, then, but I guess I'm not a candidate for the job. Thank you very much." I hung up and figured that was that. I had no burning desire to leave Montana anyway.

A little while later, I got a third call, saying, "We've decided to extend the interviews by one day. Could you interview at 3 p.m. Sunday?"

I said, "Yes, I can," knowing I could have the recruits in, see them and leave for Chicago Sunday morning.

I was the last guy they interviewed. They'd talked to Don DeVoe of Virginia Tech, Lee Rose of North Carolina-Charlotte, Bill Hess of Ohio University and Darrel Hedric of Miami (Ohio). They'd also given Dick Versace, Gus's assistant, a courtesy interview. But the selection committee didn't interview Versace. Joe did.

In Chicago, I met with the president, Clifton Wharton, and several others. Gwen Norrell was there. Clarence Underwood, the assistant A.D., was there. And Jake Hoffer from the faculty was there. There must have been eight or nine people in the room, including a couple of students.

They asked about the black walkout of '75 and wanted to know what I would've done in that situation. I said, "To me, that's almost beyond my scope of comprehension as a coach. If I didn't have more control over my team than that, I'd resign immediately. I couldn't imagine that happening to a team of mine. Maybe I'm naive. But with the control I've always had with my program and my players, that couldn't happen."

That was the answer they wanted. I think I got the job because I was a strict disciplinarian. And maybe that game against UCLA had convinced a few people I could coach. . . . I don't know.

But I had no idea I had the job when I left. I figured I'd had a good interview. Then, I flew back home in all kinds of storms. I was supposed to get home that night at 11 and got there at 2 a.m. My wife was just on pins and needles, not knowing if we had to move or what was happening. Moving is always traumatic when you have three kids.

And when I came in the door, Bev said, "You had a call a couple of hours ago from Joe Kearney. He said to call him regardless of the time you get in. He knows there were some problems with the weather."

"I'm not calling Joe Kearney," I said, just exhausted. "If they're going to offer me the job, they'll offer it to me tomorrow as well as tonight."

So I went to bed and conked right out. Bev tossed and turned and didn't sleep a wink. I got a call the next morning from Joe, offering me the job. Bev and I had made up our minds because of the situation—where I was coaching and where I'd like to be coaching— if they offered, we'd take the job. We knew that before I went to Chicago.

But when I took the job, I wanted to keep it quiet so I could tell the president, the athletic director and my team at Montana. Instead, while I was driving home from school, I heard it on the radio.

I'd already gone to the president and gotten a guarantee that Jim Brandenburg would get the job if I left. So I felt good about that. But when I got home, Micheal Ray was at my house.

"I just heard on the radio you're leaving," he said. "That isn't true, is it?"

"Yeah, it is true," I said.

He said, "Coach, you can't leave us! You can't leave me!"

"Micheal Ray, sometimes we have to make decisions that are best for us professionally," I said. "I'm not enthused about leaving. But it's best for me and my family."

He said, "Coach, you can't leave! You've been like a father to me."

I said, "Micheal, I haven't been like a father to you. I've

been on your butt every day in basketball. And I've been on your butt to get to class."

"You don't understand," he said. "I don't have a father."

Then, he started crying. And I started crying.

He said, "I'm coming with you!"

"No, Micheal, you're not," I said. "You're very successful. Right now, I belong there. And you belong here."

The next day he came in and said, "Coach! Everything's cool. You belong there. I belong here. That's what's best. . . . But if you want me, I'll come with you!"

I wish now I'd have brought him. He had two years left. And it would've been tough to sit out a year. But if Brandy hadn't gotten the job, it would've been another story.

I didn't come to East Lansing for a week. I stayed in Missoula for three days. Then, I flew down to California. Everyone thought I was down there recruiting. It was more than that.

Suddenly, they said Jim was only going to be a candidate for the Montana job, not my successor. And that wasn't what we'd agreed would happen.

The new athletic director, Harley Lewis, always kind of resented basketball's success. We only had two cars for the department. And when he always said he needed our car. I'd tell him to go get football's car.

But when Harley was hired, he was named acting athletic director. Then, Jim and I supported him for the full-time job. So we both went over to his house, and I reminded him of that. We tried to back him in a corner and weren't getting anywhere.

Finally, I said, "Harley, if Jim doesn't get the job, I'm taking him with me. . . . And I'm also taking Micheal Ray."

"You couldn't take Michael Ray!" he said. "You wouldn't."

I said, "Go ask him!"

When he did that, Micheal Ray said, "Yeah, I'm going with Coach!"

That would've looked terrible for Harley. Micheal Ray was the crowd favorite. Plus, I got 16 businessmen to say they'd withdraw their support for the program if Jim didn't get the job.

They did open the job up. Jim was one of the two candidates. But we'd guaranteed Harley's support for Jim. And he was the one they hired.

When I finally got to Michigan State, it was the first time I'd been on the campus. And right away, Joe Kearney took me into Jenison Field House and turned on the lights.

I looked out and said, "Joe! . . . We had a better place than this at Montana!"

He said, "Well, I'd certainly hope so!"

I knew that Jenison was old. But it was worse than I'd ever thought it could be. Gus Ganakas told me they used to bring recruits in and never even take them to Jenison. Can you believe that? They'd just assume the kids knew they had to play somewhere.

That was almost as bad as when Jim McGregor was at Whitworth College. He'd take all the recruits to the Spokane Coliseum and tell them that was where they played all their games. The Coliseum seated about 8,000. And he'd tell them the gym on campus was their practice facility. The truth was, they'd play one game at the Coliseum and all the rest on campus.

Otherwise, I had enough knowledge of the Big Ten to know what it was all about. I'd seen maps. I knew where it was. And I'd seen brochures. I knew how big the campus was. I knew how big the University was. I knew how big East Lansing was. I didn't go in like a total idiot.

Still, that's how some people saw me. I was this rube from Montana. And apparently, they thought it was up to them to try to set me straight.

I didn't keep Dick Versace on the staff. He came on a little too strong in our interview. Plus, I already knew I wanted to hire Don Monson. I'd tried to hire Mons when I went to Montana. This time, it all worked out. But I did keep Vernon Payne, Gus's other assistant.

One day, Vern came in and said, "I've got three guys who've been influential in helping the program. They want to take you to lunch and meet you."

I said, "Good!" and drove downtown to meet three minority businessmen—Joel Ferguson, Greg Eaton and Rickey Ayala.

It wasn't a lunch. It was an absolute interrogation. And it wasn't a friendly interrogation. They said, "Why do you think you can coach black players? And what makes you think you can recruit black players?" Everything was black, black, black.

Finally, I said, "To hell with you guys! I didn't come down here for this. We're going to have a program here whether you support the program or not. If you want to support the program, that's fine. If you don't, that's fine, too. I don't give a shit!"

Rickey Ayala, the first black player in Michigan State history, said, "I don't like your attitude. I don't like you. And I'm not going to support the program."

Joel Ferguson, who'd later be the Chairman of the Board of Trustees, said, "I've always supported the program. I live in Lansing. And Jud, I want you to know I'm going to continue to support the program."

And Greg Eaton said nothing—not one word.

But Greg called the next day and said, "Jud, I'm going to support the program. I didn't want to say anything yesterday. It isn't that I had to think it over. I would have told you privately if the opportunity had been there. But Rickey Ayala is a good friend of mine. I didn't want to antagonize him."

He said, "I operate a little differently than Joel. Joel will be up front supporting the program. I'll be in the background. If you need anything at any time, I'm there."

And he has been. He has helped guys with summer jobs. That's all we've ever asked of our alumni.

Once, when I went up to Bay City for a meeting, a bunch of guys said, "We'd like to make some extra money available to you."

I said, "If you want to help the program, give to the Ralph Young Scholarship Fund through the University."

They didn't like that. I wasn't a popular guy suddenly. But I've always believed in running a clean program. If you can't win without cheating, I don't want to be involved. I also believe a coach has to defend the things he believes in, even if it's not what people want to hear.

When I was down there with Joel, Greg and Rickey Ayala, they said, "How would your Montana team do against the team we have right now?"

I said, "The team I had coming back would beat this team by 20 points." Oh, did that piss them off!

Then, they said, "How many black players do you have on that team?" I said, "I have one black player. His name is Micheal Ray Richardson. And there's another black player we recruited. So next season, they'll have two."

"You mean two starters?" they said.

I said, "No. . . . Two, period. You know, not every black kid in the world can play basketball."

That's true. And the team I left in Montana went 17-9 with Brandy, only to forfeit some games with an ineligible player, then was 20-8 the next year.

At Michigan State, it was a little different. Right away, I went to Vern and got the list of the top 10 guys they were recruiting. I called all 10. And with one exception, they'd all signed somewhere else or lost interest. I also saw that they never had that strong an interest in being a Spartan anyway.

But we went down to see the No. 1 guy, Stuart House, a big center and one of the best players in Detroit. It turned out his dad worked at a hospital run by Rickey Ayala.

We got out of the car, and Vern said, "Did you lock your door?"

I said, "No."

"Jesus Christ!" he said. "Don't ever come down to Detroit and not lock your car!"

So we went in and talked to Stuart House's dad. He promised me Stuart wouldn't sign until we had a chance to visit with him.

As we walked out, Vern said, "Great job! Now, at least, we've got a chance. We're back in the ballgame with Stuart."

"Vern," I said. "We have no chance. When his dad said Stuart wouldn't sign until he talked to us, do you think he was looking me in the eye? He was looking at the damn floor! That tells me he was trying to get rid of us. I guarantee you it's over."

He said, "Well, I'm going to go find him and talk to him!"

I said, "Good! You do that!"

Vern looked for Stuart House all night. George Raveling had him stashed away somewhere. And he signed with Washington State at 8 a.m. the next morning.

Then, we went up and saw Jim Swaney, a kid from Traverse City St. Francis. His mom and dad and brother and sister were there, too. When we walked out, Vern said, "We've got that kid! That's the best home presentation I've ever been part of. Jud, you did an unbelievable job of selling the program and . . . "

"Vern," I said, "We're not going to get Jim Swaney. We could sign his mom. We could sign his dad. We could sign his brother. We could probably sign his brother's wife. But we're not going to get Jim Swaney. There's something wrong. You noticed all the enthusiasm from the family. Jim didn't show any enthusiasm at all."

Jim had already visited Michigan State. And we found out later that Terry Furlow had told him, "If you come down here, we're going to beat the shit out of you every single day in practice!"

Jim Swaney went to Toledo.

The other thing was, we had so many rules and regulations when I came in. I was told you couldn't give a national letter-of-intent unless you had a conference scholarship with it.

But we were going up to White Cloud to recruit a kid named Ernie Riegel—like Swaney, a Class C all-stater. I knew the only chance I had was to throw the scholarship down and say, "Here's your chance to play in the Big Ten!"

Clarence Underwood, who was in charge of scholarships, said, "This person has not made application for admission, so you can't have a scholarship. We have to ascertain whether the players are eligible for admission before we offer them a scholarship. And there's a time frame involved. It's tough on you. But that's the rule."

I told Vern, "Damn! That's a tough Big Ten rule when you're coming in late and . . ."

"Coach, hold it!" he said. "That's not a Big Ten rule. That's a school rule."

I couldn't believe it and went and told Clarence, "I'm going up to White Cloud. I want that scholarship on my desk by noon tomorrow before I leave. And if you can't get it, let me know, because I'm going through the president to get it!

"Clarence, we're in a bind in recruiting. Don't put hurdles in front of me. If you have to make a phone call, do it. But this kid is the salutatorian of his class. And for us to sit here because of some bureaucracy is ridiculous!"

Clarence was really pissed. But I had the scholarship on my desk at noon the next day. The kid wound up going to Davidson. The black walkout in '75 really hurt us. A lot of guys were afraid.

While I was still at Montana, I tried to recruit a kid named Dean Decker from Long Beach City College and said, "There's the kind of point guard we need."

But they won the California JC title and, in the worst luck we could possibly have, he was named the MVP. In three games, he scored a total of 12 points. That shows you how much he did for that team. And after that, we knew he wasn't going to Montana.

When I got the job in April, the first thing I did was go back down to California. Finally, we got Dean Decker to visit Michigan State. And he went upstairs in Jenison and started playing with Furlow, Pete Davis and Gregory Kelser.

Later, he said, "It's a good thing Terry Furlow is leaving, because he could never play for Coach Heathcote."

There's a guy who didn't even know me. The funny thing is, he was right.

We used to have the gym open Tuesday and Thursday nights that first year. With three teams, the winners were supposed to stay out there. But when Furlow's team lost, he stayed on the floor.

He said, "I always stay out. I never come off."

"Not here you don't!" I said. "Every time you lose, you sit out. That's the way we play here."

"That's not the way we play here!" he said. "That's not the way I play here!"

"Fine! Then, don't play!" I said.

I understand Terry was different off the floor. But we didn't see eye-to-eye when he was playing.

Dean Decker never played for us, either. His visit came when we had a horrible ice storm. I didn't even know it, but he sat in the Lansing airport for six hours and in the Detroit airport for 12 hours. It took him 28 hours to get home.

Needless to say, we lost him.

But we signed two legitimate recruits, Terry Donnelly and Ron Charles. The others were just to fill in.

We signed Donnelly from St. Louis without ever seeing him play. We hadn't been recruiting him at Montana. All our scholarships at guard were filled. But he was being recruited by Washington State. And I figured, if he was good enough for them, he was good enough for us.

We talked to his coach and knew the kid was averaging 22 points a game. Hey, at that point, we had to take somebody!

And I knew about Ron after seeing him play for the Virgin Islands in the Pan American Games in '75, when I was Marv's assistant on the U.S. team. Ron was only 16 years old. So when he came to Michigan State and played, he was 17.

I'd tried to recruit Ron at Montana. And if I'd stayed there, he might have been a Grizzly. I knew he had a lot of potential. But when I switched jobs, I had him visit Michigan State instead of Montana.

We also signed Jim Coutre, a junior-college center from Illinois who started and played quite a bit before we got Jay the following year.

And we brought in two other JC players, Les DeYoung and Nate Phillips—not great players, but players we had on our Montana recruiting list. We had to have bodies.

Eric Hays, who came from Montana to be a grad assistant, told me, "Coach, don't get too impatient! What good is a junior-college player? Remember, it takes two years to learn to run your offense anyway."

In two years, we were Big Ten champions. In three, we were the best team in college basketball.

THEY WERE DANCING
IN LANSING

As soon as I took the Michigan State job, Fred Stabley Jr., a writer for the *State Journal* and the one who named a 15-year-old "Magic", said, "Surely, you've heard about Earvin Johnson."

I said, "Yeah! Yeah!"

But I really hadn't.

We didn't get all the recruiting services at Montana. So I went back to the office and looked him up. I saw he was listed as a 6-8 forward from Lansing. I figured he must be a pretty good prospect.

But I was gone most of that summer. I didn't see Earvin play, not even in pickup games, until his senior year at Lansing Everett. As soon as I did, I knew what all the commotion was about. It didn't take a genius to figure out Earvin was a great player. And right away, I saw him as a guard. I don't think anybody else really saw that.

The first time I went to Everett, I received a lukewarm welcome. I was the new hick from Montana. And they all thought Gus Ganakas should never have been fired.

Earvin loved Gus. And he loved Vern Payne. They'd done a very good job of recruiting him. And he'd always loved Michigan State.

That's why I didn't have to hard-sell Earvin Johnson. All he had to see were three things: I could coach, I knew how to take advantage of his special abilities, and I wasn't the one who fired Gus.

I always say Earvin's heart was at Michigan State the whole time, and his mind was at Michigan.

He talked about North Carolina. Bobby Knight went to see him at Everett. And he did visit Notre Dame. But he narrowed it down to three schools—Michigan State, Michigan and Maryland. And I don't think Maryland was ever really in it.

Maryland had an assistant, Will Jones, in here all the time. The idea was if the pressure got too great for him to pick between Michigan State and Michigan, Maryland would be an out. They knew it was a longshot. But Earvin told them not to give up.

We weren't about to give up, either, despite some discouraging signs from time to time.

At one Everett game, there was a raffle drawing for a basketball. And of all people, I won the ball! They kind of assumed I'd give it back. After all, what was I going to do with another basketball? Instead, I figured this gave me an excuse to go to the locker room.

I wasn't allowed to talk to the players. But they told everyone they'd have to sign the ball for Coach Heathcote before they left. Earvin said, "That's the only autograph he's ever going to get from me!"

As time went on, that started to change. We encouraged Earvin and Jay, another great player from Lansing Eastern, to come to all our games. And so they could stay away from all the people wanting autographs, we gave them one of the radio booths. They were usually up there with a half-dozen guys.

Of course, you can't do that any more. In fact, Earvin had an easier time getting a box in Jenison as a high school senior than he did last year in Breslin Center as part-owner of the Los Angeles Lakers. But that's another story.

Pretty soon, other people started to get involved. We didn't encourage the community to actively recruit him. But kindergarten kids and first-graders would write him and beg him to stay in the area.

Then, he went to West Germany for the Albert Schweitzer Games, where he played with Larry Bird. When he came back, they had thousands of people at Capital City Airport with signs, including a petition from 5,000 kids, asking him to stay home and play at Michigan State.

All that time, Michigan was there. Johnny Orr's program had just played for the national championship in 1976 and been ranked No. 1 the next year. And Bill Frieder, Orr's chief recruiter, was hanging around all the time.

But when I visited with his parents, Earvin Sr. and Christine, I knew they wanted him to come here. The question was, "What did Earvin want?" We wouldn't know that right away. And while we waited, everything else heated up.

I got a call from Clifton Wharton's office, saying he wanted to talk about the Earvin Johnson situation. He wanted Joe Kearney and me to come right over.

The president's mood was tied to a meeting we had the fall before, just about the time he became upset with his new football coach, Darryl Rogers.

At Michigan State our first year, we were allowed 10 special admits as an athletic department. Football was supposed to get eight of them. And basketball got the other two. But if we didn't use them, the other sports could bid for them.

You have to remember, Michigan had no limit. Ohio State had no limit. Illinois had no limit. And we were trying to get that policy changed. When we met on it, a few deans and a trustee or two were there with the president and the coaches.

With that smile he always had, the president said, "I want you all to know how much I support athletics. We can have excellence in academics and excellence in athletics. The two go hand-in-hand. But we have very grave concerns about our image. We have to maintain that."

The guy could really talk. Actually, I was kind of impressed. But when he asked if anyone had any questions, Darryl got up.

He said, "You know, I haven't heard one word here that's going to help me be competitive in the Big Ten as a football coach. Everything that has been said here sounds good—and absolutely doesn't work. I'll tell you, ladies and gentlemen, if you think I can compete with Michigan, Ohio State and Illinois when they have no limits on special admits and we can only have 10, you are absolutely stupid!"

The president just glared at him. But what happened? Eventually, we got some relief. The pressures of those comparisons were too great to ignore.

I told Darryl, "I kind of thought the same thing. But you've got more guts than a burglar!"

"Jud," he said, remembering his program was already carrying the burden of a three-year inherited probation. "I've got to compete! I can't compete with 10 special admits!

"What do we do if I use all 10, and you've got a chance to get Earvin Johnson? Do we hold on the 10? Do we make an exception for Earvin? And if we make an exception for Earvin, if we have the greatest baseball player in the world, do we make an exception there?"

But this all happened a year earlier. So we went to the president's office for what I figured would be a friendly little talk. Instead, the president said, "Gentlemen, I do not like the position you have put me in!" He just glared. And Joe didn't say a single word.

I was waiting for him to carry the ball, but finally said, "Mr. President, I think you'd better explain yourself, because I have no idea what you're talking about."

He said, "Oh, yes, you do!"

And I said, "Oh, no, I don't!"

The president said, "I'm referring to the Johnson recruiting and the position you've put me in, where I'm supposed to go to their house. I have made it very plain that I will talk to them if they come to Cowles House. Now, I'm caught in the middle. I've got people telling me that I should go to their house. And you have put me in that position!"

Again, I waited for Joe to say something, then said, "Mr. President, we haven't put you in that position. Maybe other people have put you in that position. Maybe you've put yourself in that position. But we have nothing to do with it.

"Let me clear this up for you. You do not have to meet with the Johnson family at Cowles House. You do not have to meet with them at their house. That is completely irrelevant. It has nothing to do with Earvin's recruiting. The impression you make on Earvin's parents means nothing. They already want him to come to Michigan State. The only thing that would do is enhance your position in terms of what other people expect you to do.

"If I could give you any advice, it would be to let it go, let it pass, and tell the people who are putting pressure on you that it has no bearing on Earvin's recruiting. But whatever you do, don't blame us, because we have not put you in that position!"

That pissed the president off even more. And as we left, his administrative assistant said, "Jud, uh, you were very emphatic with the president."

"What should I have done?" I said. "Should I have let him sit there with a false impression?"

He said, "Well, you could have been a little more . . ."

"No, I couldn't!" I said. "If I'd done that, he wouldn't have believed me. If I'd come in very, very mamby-pamby, he never would have been convinced."

When we got on the elevator, I started laughing and said, "The president is really pissed, isn't he?"

I thought the whole thing was somewhat humorous that recruiting pressures had reached the president's office. But Joe was just petrified, wondering if the president would hold it against him and the athletic department. A lot of people in the Lansing area were probably petrified as Decision Day neared.

I was supposed to sit down with Earvin one more time. And he was supposed to make a decision that week, with a press conference planned for Friday, April 22. I had a meeting scheduled with him that Monday. But he didn't show up. Now, I was pissed.

I figured we were about to lose him. I hadn't been able to talk to him since he'd been back from overseas. So I got a hold of Charles Tucker, his long-time friend and adviser from the Lansing School District, and said, "What the hell is going on?"

Tuck said, "Just a little misunderstanding."

I said, "Tuck, I want to talk to him. I want to talk to his folks. I want to talk to you. Then, wherever he goes, let's wish him well. But I haven't talked to him since he left for Germany."

So we set the thing up for Tuesday night. Michigan had convinced him that if he came to Michigan State, since he'd be our tallest player, he'd have to play center. And that was after we'd already signed Jay.

But I said, "From the first time I saw you, Earvin, I knew you'd be a guard. If you come to Michigan State, you'll be running the fast break. And you'll be handling the ball. You might be checking a bigger guy on defense, that's all.

"Earvin, you can take our program somewhere it hasn't been. You can be special. If you go to Michigan, you're just another one of their great players. But we're going to give you an opportunity to do more things here than they could."

He said, "What about me playing center?" never realizing he'd play center with the Lakers when he won his first NBA championship three years later.

And I said, "Hey, when I came here, you thought I was a hick from Montana. I've been here a year. And you have more respect for my coaching than you did. Look, I'm not stupid. I know basketball. And you will NEVER be a center at Michigan State!"

We still didn't know where we were. But Vern went to Everett Wednesday morning and talked to him later that day. By this time, Vern had just taken the Wayne State job. But he was very instrumental in establishing my honesty, saying, "If Coach tells you something, that's the way it is. He's not going to make things up."

After a long talk, Vern called and said, "Earvin is ready to sign!"

He signed with Michigan State at school the next day. And we managed to keep it quiet until the press conference Friday.

That morning, with everyone waiting to hear and TV crews all over the place, Earvin leaned into the microphone and said, "Are there any questions?"

When the laughter stopped, he leaned forward again and said, "Next fall, I'll be attending Michigan State University."

All that time, Tuck had a great influence on Earvin. And Tuck saw his friendship and influence would be easier to maintain here than at Michigan. So I think Tuck always wanted him to go to Michigan State. But Tuck also wanted him to make that decision himself, instead of telling him where to go.

When they'd talk about it, Earvin would say, "What do you think?"

And Tuck would say, "Both programs are good. . . . But there's nothing wrong with this program."

By saying both programs were good, he helped us. He didn't say, "This program sucks. And Michigan has a great program."

Another thing that helped was Earvin had worked for Joel when he was growing up. But was Joel essential in Earvin's recruiting? I don't think so. I really don't. I think Earvin had respect for Joel. He had respect for Greg Eaton. And the fact that there were successful black businessmen in town helped him feel good about Lansing.

When you talk about a superstar's recruiting, little things can become big things. So when you say, "Was he instrumental?" No. "Was he a factor?" Yes.

That friendship and the respect is there to this day. Earvin said, "I used to sit in Joel's office, put my feet up on the desk and imagine I'd be a great businessman some day."

For us, it wasn't a matter of giving him anything but respect and earning his trust. They said when he went to Notre Dame, there was an envelope with $500 in it. . . . I don't know.

There's a story that when Michigan learned it was losing him, Tuck got a call from someone saying there was $20,000 waiting if Earvin came to Ann Arbor. The second call was $40,000. But I have no knowledge of that.

I can honestly say if he ever got anything at Michigan State, from anyone, I have no knowledge of it. I heard a rumor one time that some businessmen paid for his apartment. I know nothing about that.

All I know is he is the greatest player I'll ever coach and as exciting a player as there has ever been in college basketball. What would have happened if Earvin had gone to Michigan? . . . I really don't know. And I'm glad I didn't find out.

I know we weren't enamored with the Midwest the first couple of years we were there. The kids had a hard time adjusting to the change. But if we'd moved to Siberia, Beverly would have made the best of it.

In that way, Earvin's decision helped not only our program but our family's move to the Midwest and to a soon-to-be-joyous Mid-Michigan.

ONE MAGICAL
TRANSFORMATION

My first season at Michigan State was an exercise in survival.

Gus's last team had gone 14-13. And that was with Terry Furlow averaging 29.4 points per game. Furlow was a first-round pick of the Philadelphia 76ers in '76. So we had to find some scoring, along with our other needs: rebounding, defense, leadership, etc.

We had the makings of two pretty good players in Gregory Kelser, a sophomore, and Bob Chapman, a junior guard.

Chapman had already had two operations on his knee. But when we started practice, the knee swelled up again. Dr. Lanny Johnson, who's recognized today as a pioneer in arthroscopic surgery, drained the knee. And when Bob got back, I asked him how everything went.

He said, "Uh, Coach, uh, I'd like you to talk with the doctor."

I wondered what the hell was going on and called Lanny Johnson in Lansing. I said, "You looked at Bob Chapman. What do you think?"

He said, "Here's what I told Bob we could do: You play most of your games on Thursdays and Saturdays, right?"

"A lot of them," I said.

"Good," he said. "Bob can play in the Thursday games. But the knee will give some him some problems. No practice Friday. He can play Saturday. He should ice it down Sunday, then come to our office Monday. We'll drain the knee. With no activity Tuesday and some light shooting Wednesday, he should be ready to play again Thursday."

I said, "Thank you very much, doctor," and went down to see Bob.

He said, "Did you talk to the doctor? What do you think?"

"You have two choices, Bob," I said. "Either turn in your uniform or get a new doctor. There is absolutely no way you can play basketball for me without going through practices."

The knee gave him some problems. But Bob practiced and practiced hard all year. Bob was a very hard worker.

I told him, "Don't think I'm not sympathetic. I hurt my knee in high school football. I'm limping right now. I have pain. I have swelling. My knee is not functional. But I do the things I have to do. Don't think I don't know what you're going through."

We were all going through a huge transition. My style of coaching has always been negative. And that was nothing like what they were used to with Gus.

At the second practice, I told the guys a free throw is a jump shot without the jump. I said they didn't have to spend a lot of extra time on free throws, provided they shot them the same as their jumpers. And I said a good example was Eric Hays, our grad assistant.

I told Eric to shoot a couple of jumpers, just like he had against UCLA, then said, "Now, shoot some free throws until you miss."

He made 128 in a row.

The most I'd ever made was 65. And a lot of times, I'd go out and try to break that record. But I never could.

The thing was, we needed free throws and a whole lot more to be successful that year. We needed players we didn't have.

We opened with a loss at Central Michigan, came home and lost to Western Michigan, then got ripped by North Carolina in Jenison. We crushed Eastern Michigan by two, then faced Detroit and Dick Vitale.

We lost 99-94 and sat there saying to each other, "Did you ever think you'd see a game where we'd score 90 points and lose?"

Just then, Joe Falls of *The News* walked in and said, "Hey, great game!"

That was the wrong thing to say to Don Monson.

He said, "Great game? . . . GREAT GAME? . . . Have you ever coached? You dumb sonofabitch!" and stomped out.

Later, he came back in and said, "Who was that dumb bastard?"

I said, "That was Joe Falls."

Don said, "Joe Falls? . . . You mean the writer from Detroit? . . . Oooh, maybe I came on a little too strong!"

But there were signs what we were doing was right. We beat North Carolina State. We won at Indiana. And we were in most of the games, losing eight times by five points or less.

We lost in triple-overtime at Wisconsin, when Terry Donnelly played all 55 minutes. And it should never have lasted that long.

Gregory was fouled in that game and hit the floor. I knew he wasn't hurt. But he just stayed there. When Clint Thompson ran out to check on him, Gregory had to come out of the lineup. So I had a choice to put in Dan Riewald or Tanya Webb. Dan was a good shooter, but was shaking. And I didn't figure Tanya could throw it in the ocean. Finally, I sent Dan in. He missed it off to the side and barely hit anything.

Michigan was ranked No. 1 that year. And when we played down there, we had a chance for an upset. But Tanya missed a one-and-one that would have won it for us. Instead, we went into overtime and lost, 69-65.

The funniest game was the last one at Illinois. It was tied with about 15 seconds left. And to this day, I swear Edgar Wilson thought we were ahead.

We had to get the last shot. Suddenly, we all hollered, "SHOOT! SHOOT!"' And he nonchalantly shot one that went in. Everyone was mobbing him. But I still don't think he knew what was going on.

We finished 12-15. And we really weren't that good. We got two of those wins later on forfeits from Minnesota.

We ran a lot of Montana plays at first. Then, I realized, at this level, a guy couldn't play effectively in the high post. Even Earvin, as good as he was, couldn't do it, we found out later.

But along with Earvin and Jay the second year, we brought in Mike Brkovich from Canada, Sten Feldreich from Sweden, Rick Kaye from Detroit Catholic Central and Len Williams from Chicago.

That was also the year I came out of the Big Ten meetings, after I saw the schedule, and said, "Whoever came up with this is either the village idiot or the town drunk!"

Now, Wayne Duke, the commissioner, was pissed off. He said we had to live with it and he'd appreciate it if no one would criticize the schedule any more.

There I was, one of the newest coaches in the league, and I said, "If we can adopt a better schedule two years from now, why can't we move it up a year? I don't know about the rest of you guys, but I'm going to rip the conference for the stupidity of this schedule. And I'm going to rip it every chance I get!"

Every other coach said, "So am I!" and we wound up adopting that new schedule a year sooner.

The scheduling change was nice, but not as nice as the upgrade in talent in '77-78 and '78-79 —a time that'll always be known as "The Magic Years."

Our first year, we went to the dorms and did anything we could to generate interest. Once Earvin signed, you couldn't buy a ticket in Jenison. We had to tell everyone not to expect miracles right away.

When Earvin was a freshman, Chapman was a senior and Kelser a junior. But before that, I remember they were playing in Jenison when Gregory made a couple of great passes. It was almost contagious.

He said, "I know I'm going to get some great passes from Earvin this season. I'd better be able to give a couple back."

Our players had all played with Earvin. They knew he was going to be something special. And they were excited about winning more games.

Maybe Bob Chapman saw a diminished role for himself. But I think everyone knew the program was about to move up. So there was never any hostility, animosity or adversarial relationship.

All along, we thought we'd have a good team in '77-78. We were competitive the year before, when the league was down. So I figured we didn't have to be a lot better to beat a lot of clubs in our league.

I never figured we'd do what we did, going 15-3 in the league and 25-5 overall. But we were 7-0 and 15-1 in the league before anyone noticed.

Our only early loss was at Syracuse. And when we opened the Big Ten season by overcoming a nine-point deficit and beating Minnesota, we gained a lot of confidence.

We really snuck up on a lot of people. There were no TV games to speak of in those days. And we were as hard to prepare for as we were to play.

For years, I used to do a lot of our scouting myself. I maintain you don't send the fourth guy on the totem pole to scout and try to explain what Earvin Johnson does. But a lot of teams did that and struggled with us the first time or two they played us. The next year, they'd faced Earvin twice and seen him on TV. They knew what he could do. The defenses were so much better, even the second time around in '78.

Still, Earvin and Gregory did things that were a little bit ahead of their time. And we were using the matchup zone a lot, always adjusting to the ball and the man. People were still trying to attack it as a straight zone.

People had used matchup zones before. It wasn't something we just devised. We just did it better than anyone else. And we won the Big Ten by three games, a huge margin in a conference like ours.

We lost three times: at Indiana after the freeze-out when we were stuck at Ohio State, to Michigan at home on a long shot at the buzzer by Mark Lozier and at Purdue when we got absolutely killed, 99-80.

But we beat Iowa in Iowa City. And I remember Lute Olson saying we'd intimidated the officials. Monson said, "Lute's always bellyaching! Why can't he just give us some credit and admit that we beat him? . . . We did intimidate the officials. But so what?"

We'd won eight of our last nine when we entered the NCAA Tournament. It was Michigan State's first postseason bid since '59 —and almost its first Final Four appearance since '57.

We opened against Providence at Market Square Arena in Indianapolis. The Friars had a pretty good team. Dave Gavitt was the coach there then. But we ran right through them, 77-63.

Then, we went to Dayton and just played awful against Western Kentucky. Everyone thought we were so much better. And we won 90-69, scoring a lot of points at the end.

Finally, we got to play Kentucky in the Mideast Final, with the winner going on to St. Louis. But Kentucky was rated No. 1. And there was tremendous pressure on Joe B. Hall and his players to bring home a championship.

They had Rick Robey, Mike Phillips and James Lee inside, Kyle Macy and Truman Claytor at guard and, of course, Jack Givens, who'd go on to be the MVP of the Final Four.

To this day, I say if we'd made more adjustments and Earvin hadn't gotten his fourth foul with 10 minutes left, we'd have won that game. We were up by five at halftime and scored off the tip to start the second half. But we couldn't quite hang on. It wasn't our time yet.

Earvin only had six points in that game and eventually fouled out. When the Wildcats went to a zone trap, we didn't handle it well. And they kept running a high pick-and-roll with Robey and Macy—with an illegal roll.

I was going crazy on the sideline. But every time Donnelly fought through the pick, they called a foul on him. Macy was 10-for-11 at the line. And the game slipped away, 52-49.

Of all the games in my coaching career, that's No. 2 on the list I'd like to have back. It may have meant another national championship. Kentucky went on to beat Arkansas and Duke and won the title.

Afterward, there was tremendous disappointment. Yet, there was satisfaction, too, that we'd gone as far as we did and more than doubled our win total.

When you looked back at that game, you wanted to kick yourself in the butt. You knew you didn't do a very good job of adjusting to what they did.

But as a coach, you knew you didn't play the game, either. So do we blame the coaches? Do we blame Earvin? Or do we give Kentucky credit for becoming NCAA champion? People always talked about what would've happened if we'd played Kentucky again. Maybe we'd have lost again. Who knows?

I knew we had the makings of an even better team the next season. The only player of note we lost was Chapman. And that was a strange goodbye. Bob, to this day, blames me for not being drafted that year.

He was picked fifth the year before by Kansas City, based on the fact it was his fourth year and his class would graduate. He checked it out. And they offered him nothing—no bonus, no no-cut contract, just a make-good. So he decided to stay.

After the '78 season was over, guys were calling, wanting to know if Magic was coming out as a freshman and wanting to talk about Micheal Ray Richardson. Bob's name never came up. So I brought it up nearly every time.

I said, "What about Bob Chapman?"

"Oh, yeah," they said. "He's a big, strong guard. He should probably go in the third or fourth round."

I said, "Is he on your list? Are you looking at him?"

"Uh . . . no, Coach, we're not looking for that type of player," they always said.

Bob already had an agent who told him he was going in the first or second round. And I was starting to get concerned. I said, "Bob, everyone I talk to says you're going to go in the third or fourth round. But I haven't had one guy yet say you're on their list. And I've talked to 10 guys! I'm selling you as a player every time I pick up the phone. But I'm telling you, don't get your hopes up."

"Don't worry, I'm going in the first or second round," he said, pissed off at me because I was telling him the truth.

I figured he'd go in the fourth or fifth round. But in 10 rounds, he didn't get drafted.

Maybe it was the knee question. And maybe the pros forgot he was a pretty good player before Earvin arrived. All we know is he was a starter on a Big Ten championship team and player who helped Michigan State arrive.

MICHEAL RAY AND SPECIAL K

After one of Earvin's great games his freshman year, I was talking with the media—always one of my favorite ways to kill time when my dentist is busy.

"Have you ever had a player who could do the things Magic Johnson can?" one writer said.

"Yes, I have," I answered. "Remember, I coached Micheal Ray Richardson two years at Montana."

Everyone looked at me like I was crazy. If I was, it had nothing to do with Micheal Ray.

The last game he played for me, he tied what's still the school's single-game scoring record. He took very few shots that night. But I always teased him about hogging the ball. If he'd played with Earvin and Gregory—and Jay and Donnelly and Brk and Ron Charles—Micheal Ray would've been even more spectacular than he was. And so would we.

Gregory was already at Michigan State when I arrived. He'd been a very good high school player at Detroit Henry Ford, but hardly the kind of recruit you looked at and said, "There's an All-American!"

By the time he left East Lansing, he was an All-American on and off the court and, later, as good an ambassador for your program as you'd ever want.

Gregory played one year under Gus and started all but four games as a freshman. I claim he could run and jump, but couldn't play basketball. Still, he had a very good freshman year for a guy with no moves and no shot. What Gregory should have done at that point was just play around the basket and capitalize on all his physical gifts.

For most of his college career, Gregory didn't have an outside shot. But he always looked at himself as a shooter. He always wanted the green light to shoot the 17-footer.

I told him, "One out of three is great in baseball. It'll lose for you in basketball. And one out of four, you should never take a shot!"

But we worked and worked on a hook shot inside. I'd keep Gregory after practice and work on inside moves every day. That was when I still used to teach the hook.

He could always rebound. And he could always run. But there was enough potential there that we knew he should be doing more than he was. What helped Gregory tremendously was he was a great worker. He worked and worked and made himself into a very good basketball player.

That work ethic showed in everything he did. And that's why Special K was more than another catchy nickname. It was a description of a truly special student-athlete. How special? Special enough that at 6-7, he stood above the rest.

As coaches, we were always trying to get jobs for guys. When I came, we had about six Oldsmobile jobs. They were inside. They were shift work, from 4 p.m. to midnight. And they paid big money. But we couldn't get anyone to take those jobs. In fact, one year, my son, Jerry, and Clarence's son, David Underwood, took two of those jobs.

Finally, I said, "Hey, I'm not going to try to hold Oldsmobile up! If no one wants to work there, they can work somewhere else for less."

I guess those were jobs our guys considered too much work or maybe too dangerous. Even then, every guy we had, with a couple of exceptions, thought of himself as a future pro.

Gregory said, "No. I just want a half-time job, either in the morning or the afternoon. The rest of the time, I'm going to work on my game."

Everyone says they're going to work on their game. It's a cliche every summer. But Gregory did it. And to me, that was pretty intelligent. It was working toward the future.

One year, he worked for the telephone company and did such a good job they asked him to work more hours. I think he did work as many as six hours a day. But he was very insistent he wanted to work on his game every day, too.

Gregory got better every year. At least, that was true until he got in the pros.

He averaged 21.7 points my first year, before Earvin arrived, and was at 17.7 and 18.8 his last two years. When he left, he was Michigan State's all-time leading scorer with 2,014 points and is still No. 1 with 1,092 rebounds, including 28 in his first conference game.

Only three players in Big Ten history have finished with more than 2,000 points and 1,000 rebounds: Gregory, Joe Barry Carroll of Purdue and Herb Williams of Ohio State.

Joe Barry Carroll was a 7-footer. Williams was 6-11. But Gregory was the only non-center in the group.

He was named the team's MVP by the media as a sophomore and by his teammates as a junior. His senior year, he and Earvin shared the media award—and the captain's role.

Gregory had a great game against Notre Dame in the '79 Tournament. And we ran a couple of lob plays that everyone remembers.

After the game, Earvin said, "It was eye contact. I'd look at him, and he'd look at me." That was all media hype. They were set plays. But when they'd lob the ball on the break, that was timing.

We worked on the alley-oop a lot in practice and really encouraged it. And I think Earvin and Gregory kind of made it an art form. They worked on it so much, they were really excited when they could pull it off in a game.

Earvin and Gregory were really close when they played at Michigan State. There was kind of a love for each other. They roomed together on the road. And their relationship went way beyond the game of basketball.

They're still close in some ways. With the distance that separates them in their professional careers, they're not as close as they once were. But they're still great friends.

But as good a player as Gregory was for four years, he was —and is—every bit as good a person.

In Gregory's last home game, our old friend Charlie Fouty was officiating. And on the opening tip, Charlie's glasses were knocked off. As everyone ran past him, Gregory ran back, picked up the glasses and handed them to Charlie. After all, how could Charlie call a foul on Illinois if he couldn't see it?

But my favorite story about Gregory is I was on him continually, saying, "Hey, you have to come back and finish your degree!"

He was two quarters short. In those days, everyone was on the five-year plan for graduation. Now, they're back on the four-year schedule, because they all go to summer school. But we thought, since you got a scholarship for five years in the Big Ten, why not take advantage of it?

The problem with that was everyone started going to the NBA, to Europe or somewhere else. If you didn't finish in four years, a lot of times, you never finished.

So I told him, "Hey, it's really good to go for home visits and say, 'We had Gregory Kelser, a bonafide All-American and also a first-team Academic All-American.' They say, 'What did he graduate in?' And we have to say, 'Oh, he didn't graduate! . . . He was just an Academic All-American.'"

But after he was picked fourth overall by the Pistons in '79, the team had two more down years. They were finished so early he was able to get back up here for spring quarter.

One day in May, when we were in the upper gym at Jenison, Greg walked in and said, "Coach, I just took my final test in my final class. . . . I'm all done. . . . I'll have my degree."

I said, "Greg, that just has to be an anvil off your back!"

"No," he said. "It's YOU off my back!"

It was another important achievement for him. And it personified what Gregory represented. It's never easy for a player to come back after he has been in the pros.

Gregory wasn't short any hours or short any talent on the basketball floor. He could run and jump like Micheal Ray. And our paths—Gregory's, mine and Micheal Ray's—all crossed one day in '79.

In Gregory's rookie year, the Pistons played an exhibition game in the Lansing Civic Center against the Knicks, who'd drafted Micheal Ray fourth overall the year before.

Micheal Ray was really struggling that fall, so I took him out to breakfast. Supposedly, he wasn't happy with his role.

Micheal said, "Coach, I can't come off the bench."

"Oh, bullshit!" I said. "You can come off the bench! Have you always been a starter your whole life? What about when you were a sophomore at Manual High School?"

He said, "Well, I don't know if I'm a guard or a forward. Sometimes I go in at forward. Sometimes I go in at guard."

I said, "What the hell difference does it make? Remember your sophomore year? Your freshman year, we played you at guard all the time. But your sophomore year, one game we played you at guard, and the next game we played you at forward. We did that because you could play both positions. And you can play both positions now."

Finally, I said, "God, Micheal, it has been two years! I was so glad to see you. And for 15 minutes, all I've done is chew you out."

He said, "Coach, that's just what I needed!'

Micheal Ray went back and played brilliantly the rest of the season, leading the league in steals and assists. One game, he had 10 assists in the third quarter alone.

At 6-5, 195, he became a four-time all-star and a two-time member of the NBA All-Defensive Team. He led the league in steals three times and had a Playoffs-record 21 steals in one five-game series against the 76ers.

Then, he got involved with cocaine.

Everyone assumed he must have had that problem back in college. But he didn't when I was at Montana. And he didn't while he finished up there.

Playing in New York, he went to a party when cocaine was a recreational drug. He tried it. Then, he tried it some more. And pretty soon, he was addicted.

That was a long time after he'd been in the pros. And he fought back once to be the NBA Comeback Player of the Year. In '84-85, he led the league in steals, was sixth in assists, was first in guard minutes and third in guard rebounds and led the New Jersey Nets with 20.1 points per game.

But once it got him again . . .

He tried to get back in with Albany in the CBA. I'd get a phone number—disconnected. I called the Nets, his last NBA team. They didn't seem to know how to reach him.

Finally, I got him and said, "Micheal! You've always been a competitor. You can beat this!"

"Yeah, I can beat this!" he said.

But he had a relapse and got a lifetime suspension—two years, according to the NBA. He went to Italy and did really well there. And when an NBA club wanted to pick him up, he said he'd rather stay over there.

Drugs were harder to get in Italy.

It cost Micheal Ray millions of dollars. And it cost him a marriage. Cocaine just destroyed him.

Drugs were never an issue with Gregory Kelser. But his health was always a problem for him as a pro. I've always said if Gregory could've put on 20 pounds, he'd have had a great NBA career. He'd still be in the league today, if his body hadn't disintegrated on him. He played with reckless abandon. And his body wouldn't let him do that.

Some guys, like Jamaal Wilkes, Bobby Dandridge and Reggie Miller can get by with that type of body. Maybe they learn to protect themselves. But Gregory was jumping into guys and didn't know how to stay free from injury.

He played six-and-a-half years in the league. And he was healthy for about two years total. But the three years Gregory played for me, he was healthy.

And the last two seasons, so was our record.

Jay Vincent shoots over Notre Dame's Bill Laimbeer in the 1979 NCAA Mideast Final—the real national championship game.

Earvin dunks and draws a foul on Indiana State's Bob Heaton in the triumph that meant NCAA supremacy. (Lansing State Journal)

Gregory Kelser wears a priceless necklace after the Spartans dropped Indiana State to 33-1 in Salt Lake City. (Lansing State Journal)

Big Ten Commissioner Wayne Duke presents the winning coach with Michigan State's 1979 national championship trophy. (Michigan State University)

The 1979 Spartans: (back) Terry Donnelly, Greg Lloyd, Gerald Busby (left team), Don Brkovich, Rick Kaye, Gregory Kelser, Ron Charles, Earvin Johnson, Jay Vincent, Rob Gonzalez, Gerald Gilkie, Mike Brkovich, Jaimie Huffman, Mike Longaker; (front) manager Randy Bishop, equipment man Ed Belloli, coaches Dave Harshman, Jud and Bill Berry, trainer Clint Thompson, and manager Darwin Payton. (Michigan State University)

Who knew how many wins and how many jokes were yet to come? (Washington State University)

Jud and mentor Marv Harshman with their team, the Washington State Cougars. (Washington State University)

In his first college head coaching assignment, Jud puts new fight in the Montana Grizzlies. (University of Montana)

Eric Hays, one of Jud's hardest workers, nearly carried Montana past UCLA in the NCAA tournament. (University of Montana)

Micheal Ray Richardson, a spectacular talent, was a star at Montana and in the NBA. (University of Montana)

Jud and Bob Chapman confer in 1976 in a half-empty Jenison Field House.

Lansing Eastern's Jay Vincent shoots over Everett's Earvin Johnson and Paul Dawson in a series of classic prep matchups.

Lansing Everett's Earvin Johnson flies by another future Spartan, Birmingham Brother Rice's Kevin Smith, in the 1977 Class A Final.

Spartan guard Bob Chapman drives around Michigan's Steve Grote in Jenison Field House. (Lansing State Journal)

Earvin Johnson and Jay Vincent celebrate after their first Big Ten win, an 87-83 comeback against Minnesota.

Gregory Kelser maneuvers for room and puts a shot up against Kentucky's Rick Robey in the 1978 NCAA Mideast Final.

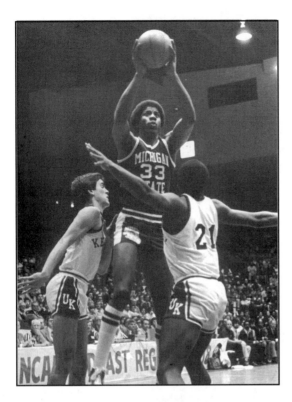

Earvin Johnson splits Kentucky defenders Kyle Macy and Jack Givens in a near miss against the national champs.

Everyone laughs except the speaker at the Michigan State Basketball Bust. (Michigan State University)

Gregory Kelser flashes across the lane and signals for a pass against Purdue's Joe Barry Carroll. (Lansing State Journal)

Who gets the ball? Only the Magic Man knows. (Lansing State Journal)

Terry Donnelly puts the ball off the glass over Minnesota's Mychal Thompson.

Ron Charles, the most accurate shooter in Michigan State history, scores against Western Kentucky in the 1978 NCAA Tournament.

Mike Brkovich moves inside and shoots over Minnesota's Trent Tucker.

Earvin Johnson and Gregory Kelser with their gray and red Mercedes Benzes after signing their first NBA contracts. (Michigan State University)

THE GREATEST GUARD
TO PLAY THE GAME

People said Earvin Johnson was a once-in-a-lifetime basketball player. But from a coaching standpoint, I can tell you that's wrong.

A lot of coaches have worked a lifetime and never had anyone anything like him.

It's no surprise when I say he's the greatest player I ever coached. But it's always a shock when I say Earvin was also the hardest worker I've had. Most of all, he was the greatest winner.

If you look at Earvin's career from Lansing Everett to the Dream Team, he has always had the Magic touch.

At Everett, he led a team with no other outstanding players to the '77 Class A title in Michigan.

The following year, a 12-15 Michigan State team was transformed into a 25-5 Big Ten champion and an NCAA Mideast runner-up. In '79, he led the Spartans to a share of the conference crown and to five postseason wins by a total of 104 points, a Tournament record.

As an NBA rookie, he was the catalyst in turning a club that was 47-35 the year before into a world champion, scoring 42 points in the sixth and deciding game at Philadelphia as a fill-in for an injured Kareem Abdul-Jabbar—or as Peter Vecsey wrote, "in Lew of Alcindor."

And over a 12-year NBA career, when you ask him about his greatest triumphs, he doesn't talk about his MVP awards—three for the regular season and three for the playoffs.

He talks about five world championship rings, not to be confused with the five Olympic rings he wore in '92 for the USA.

He was the greatest passer in basketball history and arguably the greatest player. The reason I say that is Earvin did what only a few have ever been able to do: make everyone else on his team play better than they actually were.

I always said he was Cyclops in reverse. He had a big eye in the back of his head and always knew where the other nine guys were, including the five behind him.

When Earvin first came to Michigan State, he roomed with Jay Vincent, who was finally on the same team. But both being from Lansing, they weren't in that room a whole lot.

The second year, Earvin got an apartment. He lived with Andy Wells, the son of our track coach, Jim Bibbs. And he was a regular guy—as regular as anyone could be with their picture on the cover of *Sports Illustrated*, shooting a layup in a tuxedo and top hat.

In those days, they'd bring the stat sheets in right after the game. And Earvin wouldn't even look at them. He'd say, "I'll look at it in the morning. We won the game. That's all that counts."

In Michigan State basketball history, there have been eight triple-doubles. Earvin had all eight at ages 18 and 19.

He also has one of the highest basketball I.Q.s you could ever imagine. We'd run a play once, and he'd know what all five guys were supposed to do. Earvin would say, "Jay! No! . . . Remember, you're supposed to go here."

He had a way of telling other players what to do and having them accept it. And if he had the ball on the break and didn't hit you, he'd always give you a wink or a nod and say he'd get you the next time. It made you run just a little bit harder.

He listened to what the coaches had to say. But he wasn't that open to suggestion from everyone. It was funny, but when Jay or even Gregory would try to tell him something, he wasn't listening! He knew he knew more than they did about basketball.

When Mike Longaker, who wasn't nearly the player those guys were, said, "Earvin, that guy is playing you to your right a whole step-and-a-half! You've got to go to your left more," that was different. He'd say, "Thanks, Mike."

Any time Mike would talk, Earvin would listen. He had great respect for Mike's intelligence, maybe not recognizing the difference between intelligence and basketball I.Q.

I'd never coached a guy who was always up like Earvin. He'd get upset now and then. But when he was down, it was so temporary. And if he was mad at the end of a practice, it was completely gone the next day.

I think that's why the two of us had such a good player-coach relationship. We both knew how to put those things behind us and go on from there. No question, Earvin and I have strong personalities. But I think we made a great combination, because we both wanted the same thing.

When he signed with the Lakers and people asked him what it was like to play for Jud, he said, "If you think he's a crazy man, you don't understand him. He wants to win. I want to win. We were always on the same page."

After his injury against Ohio State, he wasn't supposed to play two days later against Northwestern. But we needed him to close out a victory. He played four minutes, scored four points and never thought, "Now, I'm going to have another game to cut into my stats." And we had a nationally televised game against Kansas the next day, so he wasn't thinking about resting and saving himself for that one, either.

At Michigan State, we always had a rule that players couldn't call a timeout on their own. All timeouts had to come from the bench.

But the third time we beat Indiana his sophomore season, we had a five-point lead in Assembly Hall with about six minutes to play. We were stalling it out—something you could do in those days before the shot clock —and playing what we called "Five man, main man," where Earvin had the ball, passed it and got it right back.

There was a timeout with about four minutes left, and Earvin said, "Coach, . . . can I call a timeout if I need one?"

I said, "Yeah, E. If you think you need one, go ahead."

He was just exhausted. He never called the timeout that day. But he wanted to be able to call it if he had to. Earvin was just a coach on the floor.

And amazingly for a superstar, he never dogged it in practice. I was talking to the team about that last year, and Silas Taylor, a coach with us for a year and a guy who was always around, was there.

I said, "Silas, in the two years with Earvin, how many practices did you watch?"

He said, "Just about every one."

I said, "How many bad practices did he have?"

He thought a minute, then said, "None."

"Guys," I said. "That has to tell you something."

Earvin never had a bad practice. Some were better than others. But he was never in a funk. And that was just unbelievable.

After we won the national championship, Earvin was really a hot ticket. So I'd go to clinics and say, "I told E this. And I told E that."

A guy said, "Wait a minute! Everyone calls him Magic. We know his name is Earvin. But you call him E. . . . Why?"

The truth was, I didn't want to call a freshman Magic when he came in. And I thought Earvin was hard to say. So I called him E. That wasn't a very good answer for a group of coaches. So I came up with this one:

"I call him E because E stands for excitement and enthusiasm," I said. "There has never been a guy in basketball who has played with more enthusiasm or brought more excitement to the game than Earvin Johnson.

"And there's a message there. If you put more enthusiasm into your life, I guarantee you'll get more excitement out of it."

I used that whenever I gave a speech. But that's what he did. He was exciting to watch. And he was enjoyable to coach. You can take all those E's and make a list of them. In Los Angeles, the players either called him E or Buck. He was almost never Earvin or Magic.

I have a theory that all guys who come out early aren't exactly the most coachable. And Earvin wasn't the most coachable guy in the NBA. He did his thing—and that was plenty. But Earvin was kind of an exception, because of the way he'd take over a game.

He took a lot of guff about getting Paul Westhead fired. Everyone wanted Westhead gone. Kareem was pissed at him. And so were some others. But when Earvin spoke up, the guys were all mummies. He got all the blame.

What he never got credit for doing was working harder than anyone else in the off-season and constantly improving his game. Each year it was something different.

He'd come back to Jenison, a place he always loved, and I'd say, "E, I'll help you whenever you want. Is this the summer you want to work on a jump shot?"

He'd say, "No, I still don't need it."

And he was right. He shot everything on the move, aside from that long push shot he had.

I still remember when he hit that hook shot in the '85 Finals against the Celtics and said he learned that shot from Kareem. I had to laugh. When I was working on that shot with Gregory, Earvin would come down and say, "Hey, Coach, I'll work on that, too!" And he had a pretty good one, even then.

Earvin used to play one-on-one with Tuck in the morning, then play with the guys in the afternoon and evening every single day. Before he'd go to camp, he was always running. No one knew how hard he worked, every single year—even after 10 years in the league.

I always tried to stay in touch. But I never bothered him during the season. I'd call Darwin Payton, our manager in '79 and a guy who worked for Earvin, and see how things were going.

I'd say, "Tell E to hang in there!"

And he always did. He'd come by in the summer and talk. We talked a lot about basketball. But we talked more about other things.

There were no words to express the way I felt on November 7, 1991. When people came over, I couldn't even go to the door. When Earvin got up and said he was HIV-positive, didn't have AIDS and was retiring, I just shouted at the television.

"WHY? . . . WHY?" I hollered.

I figured, "He must have AIDS." Then I found out he didn't.

He really wanted to come back the next season. And not only should he have come back, he should never have retired. But he hated all the controversy. Suddenly, it was no fun any more. Everywhere he went, he was bombarded with negativism and people saying, "Magic shouldn't be playing!"

Eventually, it would've all blown over. Maybe it would never have been totally forgotten. But it would have been a part of the past. There might have been reference to it, but only in passing.

Earvin has a great love for basketball. But when he tried to coach, he couldn't stand the attitudes. Guys were more interested in their cellular phones, checking the stock market and talking to their agents than they were in playing the games. I think Earvin puts such an huge importance on winning, above all else, that he resents that mindset.

I remember talking to Reggie Fox, who went to Wyoming and played on a couple of Earvin's traveling all-star teams in international play.

I said, "You guys been beaten yet?"

"Nope!" he said.

So I said, "How's Earvin to play for?"

"Some of the practices are really long," he said. "But it's hard to complain because he's there the whole time, doing everything we're doing. One game, we were behind by about 10 points at halftime. And Earvin came in, just in a rage. He told us he was going to send us all home and bring other guys in if we didn't want to play any harder than we played. Then, we went out and made a great second-half comeback, Earvin scored 37 points and we won."

I said, "Well, wasn't he happy then?"

"No," he said. "He came in after the game, chewed us out again just as much and said, 'I'm the playmaker! I'm not the scorer! Don't put me in this position again!'"

Most guys would have been happier than 10 men to score 37 points, but not Earvin. He has never liked to lose. And he has never had much practice at it.

You can talk about all kinds of personal accomplishments. But with Earvin, the bottom line was always WINNING. That's why I'm so proud to say, for two years, I coached the greatest guard to ever play the game.

HELP FROM TERRY,
BRK AND BOBO

Basketball, not baseball or football, is the greatest team game there is.

End of debate.

No matter how good any one player is, it takes at least five to win a game and more than that to win a championship. As Exhibit A, I offer Michael Jordan's first six years as a solo artist with the Chicago Bulls.

He won an NCAA title as a freshman at North Carolina, and not just because he hit a jumper against Georgetown. As great as Jordan was, and is, the Tarheels won because they also had players like James Worthy and Sam Perkins and a coach like Dean Smith.

In Earvin's case, he won championships with increasing degrees of support—more at Michigan State than at Everett, more with the Lakers than the Spartans and more with the Dream Team in Barcelona than he ever had in L.A.

He never had a Kareem Abdul-Jabbar in East Lansing, though Jay Vincent could score with anyone when his pride was on the line.

And he never had a Worthy in Jenison Field House, though Gregory Kelser did the same spectacular things a few years earlier.

But with Jay, Gregory and a thin-but-enthusiastic support-ing cast, Earvin had enough help so 13 players, two managers, two doctors, one trainer, one equipment man, four assistant coaches and one gimpy, grumpy head coach can carry one label the rest of their lives:

1979 NCAA BASKETBALL CHAMPIONS.

Some played a major role. Some hardly played at all.

But only five players in Michigan State history—Matt Steigenga, Shawn Respert, Steve Smith, Scott Skiles and Gregory —started more games than a 6-2 guard from St. Louis Parkway North, Terry Donnelly.

Terry was always so steady. It didn't matter that in '79, with everyone else available to score, he only averaged 6.0 points per game, his career low. What mattered was he did the other things we needed, like covering a lot of ground in the matchup zone and handling the ball when Earvin couldn't.

Everyone remembers his five jumpers in the win over Indi-ana State. But Terry could've scored a lot more points if he wanted to—or if he had to. He always took the approach that he'd only shoot if he was wide, wide open.

He'd say, "I'm not a scorer," and was almost too willing to accept that.

I don't want to say he cherished or relished that secondary role. But he welcomed it. And a lot of times when he had good shots, he'd hesitate and pass them up. He figured it was best to get the ball inside to Gregory or get it to Earvin and let him figure out what to do with it.

There was never any urgency for Terry to get a shot. He might pass up a shot three times, then end up taking it the fourth time.

But I told him during the tournament, "You're going to have to shoot more than you have been. They're going to double-team Gregory. They're going to put pressure on Earvin. And they're not going to leave Brkovich alone, because he has a reputation as a shooter. So, at times, it's going to be up to you."

When it was, one of our first Spartan recruits was up to the challenge.

The other key addition from '76 was Ron Charles —Bobo, to all his teammates. We signed him from St. Croix in the Virgin Islands, after he nearly chose St. John's.

At 6-7, Ron could do a lot of things. But he never seemed to be working very hard. Whereas Jay practiced harder as a sophomore than as a freshman, with Ron it was always the same. Don Monson gave him another nickname—No Sweat.

He'd say, "Hey, the athletic department is going to save money on you, Ron! You never have to shower after practice, because you never sweat."

"I do, too!" Ron would say.

He was laid-back for four years at Michigan State, even when he was pulled from the starting lineup the second week in February. He was very disappointed about it. But he wasn't the kind of player who'd openly complain.

We tried to explain to him, "Hey, you're a better player than Mike Brkovich. But for the good of the team, Mike now becomes a guard and you're in a position where you can fill in at guard or forward."

We tried to sell him on the idea he'd play just as many minutes. Well, he didn't play as many minutes. And that was disappointing, but not devastating to him.

He idolized Gregory and Earvin. So if they said, "This is best for the team," he accepted that a lot easier than if I'd said it was best for the team.

Ron's best game came in '80, when we won by one at Michigan. He was 12-for-12 from the field, which is still a Spartan record. And so is his lifetime field goal percentage, .639.

When Ron started coming off the bench, we were a much better team. But before that, we needed Brkovich to send us into overtime in a game we had to have against Iowa.

The Golden Arm, a 6-4 sophomore from Windsor Lowe, had to make two free throws with no time left in regulation. There'd been some strange calls in that game. And when Brk shot at the buzzer and missed, I'm not sure he ever got hit.

But Lute Olson called a couple of timeouts. And Brk was just a basket case. Right away, I started talking about what we were going to do in the overtime period.

Later, the media asked Brk, "What were you thinking during the timeout?"

He said, "I was just thinking about what we had to do in the overtime."

Then, a guy said, "What were you thinking about before the second shot?"

And Brk said, "What second shot?"

He'd blocked it out completely. Then, we killed them by 11 in overtime.

I remember when I got Brk and Jay on an all-star team one summer. It was pretty funny. Brk came back and told me, "Coach, you wouldn't believe how those guys talk about their coaches! They just hate their coaches!"

I said, "Yeah, then you chimed in and ran me down!"

"Oh, no! No!" he said.

"Oh, yeah!' I said. "I know you did! You told them how much you hated me, too, didn't you?"

He thought I was serious and said, "Coach, Coach, Coach! I'd never do that!"

But that's Brk for you.

I talk a lot about shooting at camps. Shooting is confidence and practice. And I tell people the best shooter I ever coached was Mike Brkovich. He averaged 7.0 points a game for his career. So how can that be?

After practice, Brk would say, "Coach, can you spend 5 minutes working on my shot? It doesn't feel right."

Forty minutes later, we'd still be shooting. Mike would be out past what's now the 3-point line, making seven or eight out of 10. And every one he'd miss, he'd say, "Coach, what'd I do wrong?"

I said, "Mike, you're not supposed to make every shot!"

"But that one didn't feel right," he'd say.

Mike was always so conscious of the shots he'd miss. But when Earvin was here, he'd say, "Brk, when you get the ball, shoot it!" He never thought about missing with Earvin around. But after that, he'd miss a couple, then pass up shots he had to take. He'd say, "Coach, my shot is off tonight. Let someone else shoot it."

But I still say if Earvin had stayed another two years, Brk might have been an All-American. He'd have gotten a lot more shots. Instead, he went back to the city league in Windsor and averaged 36 a game in a comfortable environment.

The thing that made the '79 team special, or even great, was we really had some terrible subs. So where was the challenge in practice?

The year before, Earvin got to the point he just hated to play against Dan Riewald. And the next year, everybody hated to play against Jaimie Huffman. All they did was chop guys. They couldn't check them, so they'd chop them. Dan would play hard, because he figured that was the only way he could help the club. But a guy would beat him, and he'd chop him. Jaimie was the same way.

See, Earvin never liked contact in practice. And Gregory never did, either. They couldn't have cared less in the game. They knew it was part of winning.

But our practices were probably unique. In all my years of coaching, I probably had 10 really hard practice players. Earvin and Gregory, if they weren't Nos. 1 and 2, were definitely in the top three or four. They practiced hard every single day.

If we didn't have the deepest bench in '79—and we had 13 games where only six guys scored—at least we never had any team problems. Our guys got along so well.

We had one guy leave in the middle of the season, a freshman guard named Gerald Busby. Bus didn't want to go. But he ran up a big phone bill, was homesick and was struggling in class. We kept it quiet. But we said, "Bus, it's time to go. Hit the road!"

And Earvin and Gregory weren't the only ones to leave after the championship year. Don Brkovich, Mike's brother, transferred to New Mexico. Rob Gonzalez, who played quite a bit as a freshman reserve, left, too.

I've always said, "Freshmen don't just want to start. They want to star." And there was no better example than Rob. He came into the office one day and said, "Coach, I can't believe I'm not starting."

I said, "Well, let's see, Rob. . . . You're a forward. Our two starting forwards are Earvin Johnson and Gregory Kelser. Do you think you should be starting ahead of Earvin?"

"Oh, gosh no," he said. "Earvin is really good, Coach."

I said, "Then, you think you should be starting ahead of Gregory?"

"Yeah, yeah," he said. "I'm playing better than Greg in practice almost every night."

Now, if Gregory was a dog in practice, I could understand that. But as I said before, Gregory played hard and well every practice.

So I said, "Rob, maybe you ought to talk to some of the other players. I think you have a distorted view of how you're playing. None of the coaches think you're playing that well. If you get any playing time at all, it'll be as a backup."

But here's what happened with Rob. He went to Howard Garfinkel's camp. Now, here was a 6-7 white guy who'd take the charge and dive for balls on the concrete. So, the final five schools recruiting Rob were North Carolina, Kentucky, Michigan, Indiana and ourselves. As they came and watched him during the year, they started dropping off—but not in his mind. He still had an overinflated view.

What we were trying to do was get a kid from a Catholic school in the suburbs who could help us. We were thinking he was probably good enough to be a sixth or seventh man.

But he still wasn't happy after his sophomore year. So I had a meeting with his parents that spring. I'd already talked to Rob.

I said, "I think it's best Rob transfer."

"Why?" they said.

"Well, it's obvious he's never going to be happy here unless he's starting," I said. "He can be an excellent sixth or seventh man. But he can't accept that. You can't accept that. Then, all he is is a malcontent. And I can't accept that! So I think we've reached the point of no return. . . . I'll help him find another school. There are other schools that must have an interest."

That's what we did. He transferred to Colorado. But to this day, Rob looks on me as his coach. He calls me. He has been down in Mexico playing. And when I saw him at the Pan Am Games, he came right over and talked.

I haven't had a kid yet who has transferred and hasn't wished he'd stayed. To some players, the grass always looks greener somewhere else. More often than not, that green turns to brown.

"...BEST FOR MY FAMILY"

We were sitting at the Community of Champions Banquet they had for us at Long's of Lansing, when Al McGuire said, "Hey, I hate to tell you this, Magic, but Gregory Kelser is the best player on your team!"

I was sitting across from Earvin. And when our eyes met, we winked at each other. That was all that needed to be said. As good as Gregory was, we knew—and the other guys knew, too—the best player on the team was No. 33.

So did the pro scouts. Larry Bird, a fifth-year player, had been drafted by Boston the season before. And it was clear Earvin could be the No. 1 pick as a sophomore—if he decided to leave.

People have said he was close to leaving after his freshman year, when the Kansas City Kings had the first pick. But I don't think he was close at all.

Earvin never would've left after the Kentucky game. As proud and competitive as he was, he couldn't have gone out with a 2-for-10 performance. And I'm not sure he could've left with any kind of loss.

I think he wanted to listen to what the offers were and get a measurement of where he was. And I think he kind of liked the speculation he might leave. He liked the mystique that he had to make this big decision.

Tuck said Earvin had a letter of application written and sealed in '78. And I believe that. You have to be ready in case you do leave.

But I think Earvin was smart enough to know he wasn't quite ready. He loved the college scene. He hadn't accomplished what he'd hoped to accomplish. As a freshman, he was only third-team All-American. And his team hadn't won a national championship.

I don't think playing for Kansas City appealed to him at all. And I don't think he was ever really enthused about the idea of leaving school and leaving the scene.

I might be totally wrong. That first year, we hardly discussed it at all. He didn't come to me for advice or opinions. And he didn't ask me to check out any monetary situations. The next year, we had some discussions. Earvin didn't really want to leave Michigan State that year, either. The thing people don't understand is that money was never important to Earvin. He said, "We always had plenty of money at my house."

Well, they didn't. His dad always worked two jobs. And his mother worked at the middle school. Earvin always worked in the summer. And he used to drive an old '74 beat-up Buick. But they always had plenty of food. In his mind, money wasn't a factor.

I still remember when I recruited Tim Andree, a big center from Birmingham Brother Rice. I drove up and parked next to this long green-and-white Lincoln Continental and said, "Hey, Tim! Guess who's car that is?"

"Earvin's! . . . That's Earvin's!" he said.

I said, "No. That's Darryl Rogers' car. . . . There's Earvin's car over there, the one with the big dent in the front."

"That's Earvin's?" he said, so disappointed that a guy like Earvin wouldn't have a nice, new car. So it wasn't money that made Earvin decide to leave. I still think if Los Angeles didn't have the first pick, he would've stayed.

The way the Lakers got that pick still boggles the mind. In '76, they traded Gail Goodrich to the New Orleans Jazz and got a first-round pick in '79. No one knew the Jazz would be the worst team in the league three years later.

And no one knew L.A. would win a coin flip with the Chicago Bulls for the first pick. If the commissioner, Larry O'Brien, had flipped heads, instead of tails, Chicago would've won. And so would we for at least one more year. If you ask Earvin now, he'll tell you he wouldn't have gone to Chicago. He would've come back to East Lansing.

But the Lakers? That was a different story. His heart still said, "Stay." And his mind said, "It's time to go!"

I've always said, when Earvin and I talked, I told him it would be best if he stayed—best for my family. He'd sit there and say, "Coach, I just really love being around school! We're going to have a good team next year. And wouldn't it be great if we could win two in a row?"

Bill Gleason, a writer from Chicago, wrote a scathing article that Earvin would be stupid for leaving, because he wasn't good enough. He wrote, "I've seen the Magic show, and I'm not impressed." Joe Falls and some others also questioned Earvin's ability.

But I told Earvin, "E, I don't care what you read. There are probably only two guys who know how good you are—you and me."

He said, "Yeah."

I said, "You'll start for any pro team that drafts you."

"I think so," he said.

"So when we talk, we're not going to talk about basketball at all," I said. "We're gong to talk about the other things. The basketball is there. You know what you can do. And I know what you can do."

We talked about lifestyles. We talked about the things he hadn't accomplished. For one thing, he hadn't been Player of the Year. They gave that honor to Bird. Those things meant something to Earvin. And all that time, he was wavering.

The Lakers seemed to be wavering, too. According to Earvin, the owner, Jack Kent Cooke, was leaning toward Sidney Moncrief from Arkansas or David Greenwood from UCLA. But he had a deal in the works to sell the team to Jerry Buss. And Buss said, "No Magic, no deal!"

Finally, Earvin went out to Los Angeles. And the word on the street was before he went he was 70-percent stay and 30-percent go. When he came back, he was 90-percent go and 10-percent stay. The word was he got stars in his eyes, got carried away with Tinseltown and met some Hollywood stars and Kareem Abdul-Jabbar.

In truth, none of that had any effect. What did have a tremendous effect was when Bill Sharman, Jerry West and Cooke sat him down and said, "Earvin, what's the most important thing to you when you play basketball?"

That was the easiest question he'd ever been asked.

"Winning," he said.

"Earvin, we have a unique situation," they said. "We're one of the best clubs in the league. And we have the first pick in the draft because of our trade with New Orleans. This will never happen again in the history of pro basketball.

"You have an opportunity to come to us and be a winner for your entire career. Or you can wait a year and go to Kansas City or Cleveland or whatever team has the first pick. You'll be a great player. But you can be a great player like Oscar Robertson, who never won a championship until he was traded to Milwaukee. He has one championship ring, from the twilight of his career, to show for being one of the three or four greatest players ever.

"Earvin, is that what you want?"

The importance of being on a winner was what made the difference.

They had the farewell press conference on a Friday, May 11. Before he went out, he said, "Coach, I've got to talk to you first." I said, "No. We're not going to talk, E. . . . I'll find out like everyone else."

I knew he wanted to tell me he'd made his decision. And I still felt, come announcement time, his heart would overrule his mind. I still felt he was going to say he'd stay. Or maybe I was holding out hope for that.

"I'll be at the press conference, E," I said. "That's how I prefer it."

He even told people afterward, "I wrestled with this until after 3 a.m."

I think he'd already made his decision. But he wrestled with it. He wanted to make sure it was the right thing to do. There are still people who say that wasn't the case. If you asked Earvin now, maybe he'd say, "Oh, I knew I was going all the time!"

Hey, he wasn't that sure about going.

Did he make the right decision? That seems like a ridiculous question with all the success he had—five NBA titles, three MVPs and the money he has made.

I've always said, "When the price is right, the time is right."

Why do you go to college? To prepare yourself for your lifetime's work. If you're good enough to do that when some basketball and football players can, I have no problem with that. And I never have.

We programmed Micheal Ray Richardson to leave Montana after his junior year. He wasn't a student. He couldn't have cared less about a degree. With the coaching change and the forfeits, he wound up staying four years. But I said afterward he made the right decision for himself.

Earvin made the right decision, too—the one he had to make for his future.

It was a unique situation in the community. Everyone was disappointed. Yet, no one was angry with the decision. People felt Earvin had given us two special years. They felt it would have been great if he could have stayed. But they knew why he had to go.

It was a little like a funeral when he left. There was an outpouring of grief, mixed with appreciation. There was no anger, no bitterness and no real conjecture it was the wrong decision. It was accepted. It was predicted. And it was still disappointing.

Ever since, we've had our cycles—up, down and in-between. But it was never quite where it was in '79.

After Earvin left, I used to joke, "We have five of the seven players back who won the national championship and two Big Ten titles. . . . Our biggest problem is they're the wrong five."

But believe it or not, we had a pretty good team the next two years. The problem was the league was the strongest it has ever been—with the possible exception of '89, when Michigan and Illinois met in the Final Four.

In '80, Purdue and Iowa, our third- and fourth-place teams, were in the Final Four. And the conference was tough from top to bottom, even Northwestern and Wisconsin.

We were competitive. We just weren't quite good enough. If we could have been in a different league for a couple of years, we'd have had a very good record. Instead, I think we were about a player short. We never quite had enough at forward.

We were 6-12 in the conference and 12-15 overall. We lost to Wichita State in the last seconds, lost to Weber State and dropped some others we could have won. So we were a competitive team, just not one that could win.

If Earvin had stayed, I think he would made the difference for another Big Ten title. After that, how far we could have gone, no one knows. We might have won another national title.

He made the announcement he was leaving the second week in May. And that meant it was going to be a disappointing recruiting year. We were able to get in a lot of homes. But we finished second on guys from New York to California. You're better off finishing 10th than second. If you're second, you've wasted a lot of time. And that recruiting year really hurt us down the road.

We had a couple of transfers already on campus, Kevin Smith and Steve Bates. Kevin became a good guard in our program. And Steve had one great moment.

We used to have the Spartan Mini-Clinic for high school coaches. And when I talked about pivot moves, I had Steve Bates demonstrate the step through, the hook shot, the roll hook, the power move, the stick shot and the drive to the basket. I'll bet, out of 100 shots, he probably made 95.

"Boy, that kid is really going to help!" one coach said. "He's really going to be good this year!"

I said, "That kid won't play much. Hey, he can make all the moves with no defenders. But you don't see how slow and methodical he is. You're watching the end result. And the end result, the basket, is there. But as far as doing things quickly, he can't."

Kevin Smith was always very, very good with the basketball and not very good without it. He was never a very good defensive player. But I always thought Kevin would be better than he was, though at times he was awfully good. He was with us three years, after transferring from the University of Detroit. And he was probably as good the first game he played with us as he was at the very end.

It wasn't that Kevin resisted coaching. But he didn't like weight work or off-season work. Another guy like that was Eric Turner at Michigan. And when you refuse to get stronger physically, suddenly, you tend to plateau.

Yet, in his junior and senior years, Kevin made first-team All-Big Ten. If you can do that on a lower-echelon team, you've got to be damn good. Kevin was good. He just never took us as far as I thought he would or could.

When I went down to recruit Kevin, his dad immediately challenged me and said, "Why don't Mike Robinson and Lindsay Hairston have their degrees?"

I said, "I don't know. . . . Why don't they?"

He said, "Well, they went to Michigan State. And the school never got them degrees."

"Whoa, wait a minute, Bob!" I said. "The school doesn't give out degrees. The kids earn degrees! We give them all the help we can with support services. But if you think your son is going to walk in and we're going to give him a degree, he'd better go somewhere else!"

That wasn't a good thing to say.

Then, I said, "Bob, you're in education! How can you even ask that question?"

But that's how a lot of coaches thought in Detroit. If a guy showed up, you were supposed to give him a degree.

I said, "I'll guarantee our guys will have a chance to get degrees, because I'm going to make them go to class and monitor what they do. But don't think there isn't responsibility for the student. And don't hold me responsible for guys I didn't recruit and didn't coach!"

It's interesting to note, after Mike Robinson's playing days were over, he returned to school. He got a bachelor's degree and a master's degree, too. I don't believe Lindsay ever returned to school.

But when Kevin was in school, the three seasons after Earvin left, we could never get quite enough basketball to beat the really, really good teams. And in those years, we weren't one of them.

HARD TO SELL WHEN YOU'RE NOT BUYING

We had two or three big names who might have come here if Earvin hadn't left. We had Sidney Green set to come from New York. James Worthy made a visit from North Carolina. And we were recruiting Ralph Sampson from Virginia.

I remember we had a home visit with Ralph. He had two sisters about 6-2. And when I went in, he just sat there. We went over everything. Then, he got up . . . and got up . . . and got up. He only weighed about 210. And even then, he was 7-foot-4.

Ralph was a giant. But he wasn't as tall as Manute Bol. We were playing at Cleveland State when he was there for his visit. He had on these tight pants that only came halfway down his leg. It looked like he'd suddenly grown out of his pants.

But after the national championship, we were probably doing more national recruiting than was wise. We had a lot of near-misses in recruiting. And near-misses don't score many points for you.

The strangest example of that was in '80 with Vern Fleming from New York. He wasn't Earvin. But he was the kind of player we thought could do a lot of the same things. We were always looking for a big guard after that. And Fleming was nearly 6-6.

I put Edgar Wilson, a second-year assistant, in New York for 21 straight days. That's when we were recruiting the city. We saw

Vern and his twin bother, Vic, from Mater Christi. And we had a kid from his hometown, Tracy Robinson, on our JV team. So Vern came in and had a great visit. Everyone thought he was coming. But I sent Edgar to New York and said, "Keep a handle on this guy! There's going be some skulduggery if we're not careful."

His high school coach wanted him to go to North Carolina. So Vern said he wouldn't sign until he took a trip there. And he couldn't make the trip until early May, about three weeks after the signing date, because he had to play in some all-star games.

It was down to Louisville, North Carolina and Michigan State, and Edgar said, "Hey, Coach! Don't worry about it! We've got him!"

I said, "I just talked to him. He told me how great Michigan State is. But he never told me he's coming. He told you. He told Tracy. He told his girlfriend. But he never told me!"

"Well," Edgar said. "He's probably a little apprehensive. Maybe it's because he has to take that trip to North Carolina." I didn't ride in on the turnip truck. I'd been through this before.

So I had lunch with Rob Johnson, a street agent who was eventually written up in *Sports Illustrated*. And I pretended I didn't know what was going on. The guy figured I was dumb anyhow.

He said, "You know, Mrs. Fleming is really worried about how she's going to going to get along when the two boys are gone."

I said, "Oh, she should get along fine. It'll probably be a little different for her. She'll probably miss the boys, but . . . "

"No, I don't mean the relationships," he said. "I mean how she's going to get along when they're gone—how she's going to get by."

I said, "Geez, they're both really involved in athletics. Is either one of them working? . . . If not, with the cost of caring for both those boys, she's going to have less expense when they're gone than she does now, don't you think?"

"She's REALLY worried about how she's going to get by," he said, not giving up.

I said, "She'll get by fine!"

That ended that. He knew I knew what he was talking about. And he knew I wasn't buying it.

But after saying he couldn't sign until May, Vern Fleming signed at 8 a.m the first day you could sign in April—with Georgia.

He said he didn't want to go to Michigan State and be compared to Magic Johnson, didn't want to go Louisville and be compared to Darrell Griffith and didn't want to go to North Carolina and be compared to Phil Ford. He wanted to go somewhere he could just be Vern Fleming.

Talk about recruiting surprises!

But, hey, I could tell you about a half-dozen players in Detroit we lost at signing time. I got criticized my entire career at Michigan State for not recruiting Detroit. And you couldn't recruit a lot of players in Detroit in those days unless you went through a middle man. They usually had their hands out, so I steered clear of those situations.

We were trying to get Demetreus Gore from Chadsey, who was Mr. Basketball that year. Supposedly, it was down to Pittsburgh, Detroit, Missouri and us.

Tom Izzo had just come to Michigan State in '83. He'd talk to Demetreus on the phone and say, "Hey, guys, we're still in it!" Mike Deane, our top assistant, and I said, "Tom! Get a life! Wake up! Demetreus Gore isn't coming here." And he didn't. He wound up at Pittsburgh, which went on probation shortly thereafter.

Here's what usually happens in recruiting. When you lose a player, the assistant coaches panic. They know they have to get players or they'll get fired. And the easiest way for assistants to justify things to the head coach is to say, "Hey, they flat-ass bought him!"

When one or two guys say that about a program, it's a copout. But when it comes back from 10 or 20 assistants at different programs, then, where there's smoke, there's fire. Does the coach always know? He usually has an idea and chooses not to know.

But there are still quite a few coaches who are strong enough not to bend the rules—and wouldn't let anyone else do it. The Bobby Knights and the Gene Keadys aren't going to put up with that.

Guys have tried to write theses on the decision-making process. And most kids don't even understand the factors that go into their decisions. If you listed 20 things, you could talk about geography, you could talk about publicity, you could talk about anything you want. The most important factors are a school's style of play, the opportunity to play and whether he likes the players he's going to play with and the coaches he's going to play for.

Yet, a kid might come because a school is close, because he has a girlfriend there, because he had a great time on his visit—all kinds of factors.

We probably worked harder on Jeff Grayer from Flint Northwestern than any other kid and went to game after game. He wound up going to Iowa State.

B.J. Armstrong from Birmingham Brother Rice was a different situation. Iowa told B.J. he'd be their starting point guard as a freshman. He almost transferred after his freshman year. We tried to sell B.J. on sitting for a year. We had Sam Vincent and Scott Skiles. We knew he wouldn't start. And he knew that, too.

The opportunity to play is just about the biggest factor these days. No one wants to sit, watch and learn. They want to play, start and star.

I could tell you a lot of horror stories about the recruiting process. But this book isn't about accusations with no proof. We heard all the rumors about big booster cash buys and know that one player in the NBA signed two weeks late, with the scholarship post-dated.

Where do players get luxury cars, posh apartments and expensive wardrobes? And why were we leading on so many great players, only to lose them at the last minute to schools that all the coaches knew were buying players?

I have a number of coaching cliches. And one is, "It pays to cheat." Schools cheat for years and years. If they're caught, the coach gets a slap on the wrist, and the school goes on probation for a couple of years. Then, it's back to "business as usual."

I've always proposed that we should be punishing players and coaches, rather than schools. If a player knew he would never play again if was caught taking anything illegal, there'd be much less cheating. Players would think twice before they jeopardized their pro careers. And if a coach knew he'd lose his job and could never coach again, he'd hesitate to be involved in illegal inducements.

Under our present system, NCAA investigations take forever. And more often than not, when schools are found guilty, the players punished have nothing to do with the original allegations.

Another recruiting theory I have is, "Cheaters know how to cheat and not get caught." Enough said.

But we've also lost some players because of weird recruiting situations, as all programs have. Two recent examples were Voshon Lenard and Chris Webber.

Voshon wanted to come to Michigan State. And his family wanted him to come to Michigan State. However, we only had two scholarships available. We wanted to sign Voshon and Chris, the best player in the country and our No. 1 prospect.

Out of the clear blue, Chris informed us he thought he'd like to play college basketball with Jalen Rose, Voshon's teammate at Detroit Southwestern. Jalen had shown no interest in our program and was almost signed, sealed and delivered to UNLV.

Suddenly, with probation hanging over the UNLV program, Jalen started checking his other options. He indicated he'd like to play with Chris. So we had both players make an official visit to campus.

In the meantime, we canceled our home visit with Voshon. We didn't have a third scholarship to offer and didn't want to go into the Lenard home and pretend we did.

Voshon was disappointed and hurt. And months later, when we tried to make a late bid after Chris and Jalen signed with Michigan, he wanted no part of us. I don't blame him for that. But to this day, I really believe Voshon wanted to play his college basketball at Michigan State, not Minnesota.

The Chris Webber story was an absolute nightmare. From his freshman year on, Tom Izzo and I spent more time on his recruitment than on any prospect before or since. We had an excellent rapport with his family and his coach at Detroit Country Day, Kurt Keener.

When Chris visited in the fall, he told us he was going to sign early and was coming to Michigan State. He also indicated that in a thank you note he sent me after his visit. Then, the bizarre happened.

Chris made his official visit to Minnesota the weekend Michigan State played football in the Metrodome. And Clarence Underwood, our compliance officer, saw him sitting in the press box. Since NCAA rules say prospects can't have "special seating," it was a violation. I guess "Sherlock" Underwood thought he was seeing another Brinks robbery, so he had pictures taken of Chris in the press box.

The following Monday, Clarence called me and told me what had happened. I told him to throw the pictures in the waste basket. It was no big deal. I told him I'd mention it to Clem Haskins when the recruiting was over and informed Clarence it was probably an honest mistake, since the "press box rule" had been changed two years earlier.

I also told him it was a stupid rule. Why should basketball players be expected to sit in the rain and snow on their official visits, when most of them aren't that crazy about football anyway?

I thought the matter was closed. But the next day, I got a call from a TV station about "some pictures." I played dumb and passed it off. But the same station called the NCAA. The NCAA called Clarence and requested the photos. So Clarence sent them.

Goodbye, Chris Webber!

The NCAA came to visit Chris, his father, Mayce, and Kurt Keener. As Kurt explained it, it wasn't a visit. It was a three-hour interrogation. They accused Chris of accepting illegal inducements. And the three of them had to defend themselves. Mayce was irate. Kurt was upset. And Chris was confused.

We convinced Kurt and Chris that we didn't turn Minnesota in over a picayunish recruiting violation. But to this day, I think Mayce believes we did. Because of the interrogation, Mayce convinced Chris not to sign early.

Then, strange things began to happen. Michigan had a coaching vacancy, since Mike Boyd had taken the Cleveland State job. And Michigan decided not to fill that position for a full season. Suddenly, Jalen and Perry Watson, his coach at Southwestern, were at all Chris's games, even during the quiet period when we weren't allowed to recruit off campus.

Ed Martin, Perry's good friend, was always available to provide transportation for Chris and his friends. The more Perry became involved, and the more Ed Martin became involved, the slimmer our chances became. At the end, I felt we had no chance whatsoever.

A month after Chris and Jalen signed with Michigan, Perry Watson was hired as an assistant on the Michigan staff. According to the press release, "After interviewing several top candidates, we have chosen Perry Watson." Who's shitting who?

Even *Sports Illustrated* wrote that what Michigan did was legal but unethical. I agree. But if it hadn't been for the pictures, it never would've come to that.

I often wonder how much better a coach people might've thought I was if Chris Webber had come to Michigan State instead of Michigan.

But that's the way it goes in recruiting. Sometimes you win. Sometimes you lose. And sometimes you have no chance.

Sometimes the reasons for that are obvious. And sometimes they're not.

BROTHER, COULD
THEY SCORE

Indiana had the Van Arsdale brothers. But we had the Vincents.

They combined for 3,765 points and had their name announced in Jenison more often than any other over an eight-year span.

Jay Vincent always felt he didn't get the recognition he deserved. And that's probably true. In high school, he always played in the shadow of Earvin. Then, he came to Michigan State as the No. 2 recruit, not No. 1.

When we were recruiting Jay, Don Monson and I said, "This proves you're declaring yourself your own man. You're not leaning on Earvin. We don't know if we're going to get Earvin. But you're a key! By signing early, that makes a statement all by itself."

Jay bought that idea and signed in March of '77. But after he signed, he still wanted to go to Texas and see two or three other places. He said, "Gosh, I haven't been around that much. I still want to make these trips. So don't tell . . ."

"Jay!" I said. "It's over! You can't!"

And Monson said, "You just signed with us. We're going to take it down and give it to your mom. You can't go anywhere."

He said, "I can't?"

Jay was disappointed he signed so soon. He wanted to make some recruiting trips, just to make the trips and be recruited, because everyone else made trips.

But Jay was our first really big recruit. You wonder if Earvin would have come here if Jay hadn't signed. . . . Maybe. Maybe not. What we needed to turn Earvin's head were little things. Maybe that was one of those things.

Whether Earvin had come or not, we wanted Jay. We knew he could play. We saw he had tremendous hands. And he could really shoot. At times, Jay was an absolute offensive machine. He had so many moves, inside and out, he was almost impossible to stop—especially his last two years, when he led the Big Ten in scoring.

Big Daddy was one of those players who seemed to play so effortlessly. I don't think most people really appreciated all the things he could do. You'd watch him in a game, pick up the stat sheet afterwards, see he had 25 points and 10 rebounds and say, "Wow! . . . When did he do all that?"

A lot of times, he did it when we needed it most. He always seemed to have big games against Ohio State. He didn't like the fact Herb Williams got so much publicity.

Before the '79 game in Jenison, I taped a note to his locker that said, "We know you're the best center in the Big Ten. Go out and show your critics." Jay did just that. And with 1,914 points, he's the fifth-leading scorer in Michigan State history—63 points and one spot ahead of his younger brother, Sam.

Sometimes, as the third option, which Jay was his first two years, you're getting the third-most emphasis from the defense. When they were putting a man-and-a-half on Gregory and a man-and-a-half on Earvin, the other guys got a little more freedom.

But if Jay thought other guys were rated higher than he was, that motivated him to play a little better. Jay was not an intense, hard player. Sometimes, he needed a little extra. And he'd go out to prove he was just as good as the other guy. I think Jay always thought I picked on him. I was always on him to play a little harder. I knew how good he could be.

Sometimes, I'd say to Earvin, "E, I'm not going to get on Jay and Ron at all today. But you've got to get them to play harder." He'd get all over them, saying, "C'mon, Jay!"

Earvin was a master at being able to get all over guys and not have them resent it. He has been able to do that his whole life. There were times Jay would be open on the break, and he'd get it to Gregory. He'd say, "I saw you, big guy! I'll get it to you next time! It looked like the defense was moving toward you."

But I thought Jay did a tremendous job with the talent he had. And he's probably surprised I'd say that. He was always one of those enigma players to me. How much better would Jay have been if he'd worked harder? Maybe not one bit better. He could play his position just by getting in shape.

One thing Jay would always do once he got established in the NBA was keep his weight down. He would condition his body, but wouldn't practice basketball. And he was still very good at the things he did.

At 6-7 and from 230 to 245 pounds in college, Jay should have been a power forward. But he always had to play center for us. I think he always resented that. He thought it inhibited his development, when it probably enhanced it.

We put out a brochure pumping Jay for All-America honors. But with 12-15 and 13-14 records his last two years, he didn't get enough attention.

Jay blames me to this day because he wasn't drafted in the first round. What he still doesn't know is how close he came to being out of basketball.

I'd convinced Washington to take Jay with the 11th pick in the first round. Gene Shue and Bob Ferry came in. I showed them some film and told them all the things Jay could do.

I said, "What you see is not really what you get. You say, 'The guy can't run!' Actually, he runs pretty well. You say, 'The guy can't jump!' But he's a pretty good position rebounder. He can pass. He can shoot. And he can do a lot of things you need done in the pros."

Finally, the draft came, and Frank Johnson became available unexpectedly. So long, Washington!

The only other club that was interested in Jay was Phoenix. They had the 20th pick. And it seemed he'd slip from 11th to 20th. Suddenly, Larry Nance was available. Forget Phoenix!

Jay went to Dallas as the first pick of the second round—the 24th pick overall. They'd never called. They'd never seen him. They'd never had any film on him, because they figured he'd never be available.

He signed a two-year contract. But the guarantee was only half a year. When he went to training camp, he was too heavy. He was 245. After about three days there, he was 247. And they were practicing twice a day.

So I called Dick Motta, their coach, and asked how Jay was doing.

"Jud, I'm going to cut him," Dick said.

I said, "What?"

And he said, "The guy is in terrible shape. He weighs two pounds more than he did when he got here."

I said, "Wait a minute, Dick! You've got some money invested in him. Before you cut him, watch him play more closely. Watch him position rebound. Watch him pass. Watch him shoot close to the basket. Watch him shoot away from the basket. Watch all the little things he can do. Most guys you get are one-dimensional. Now, you've got a multi-dimensional player who can come off the bench and do a lot of things."

Right away, I called Jay and said, "Hey, you're going to get cut!"

He said, "No, I'm not!"

"How are you playing?" I said.

He said, "Well, they're not giving me much of a chance."

"That's because they say you're in terrible shape and you're putting on weight!" I said. "What are you eating?"

Jay said, "Well, I get so hungry at night, I have a couple of cheeseburgers before I go to bed."

To make a long story an eternity, they kept him. The next spring, I saw Motta at the NCAA Tournament in New Orleans.

He said, "Damn, am I glad you made that phone call! If you hadn't called, I'd have cut him. But I did what you said and watched him closer."

The best story was Washington had five guys responsible for making the picks. And Shue and Ferry had convinced the other three to take Jay instead of Albert King. They figured King just wasn't strong enough.

But when they took Frank Johnson and Jay dropped clear to the second round, Ferry called me and said, "Hey, Jud, the owners are on my ass! They figure I don't know what's going on."

The first time Dallas played Washington was in mid-December. Mark Aguirre, their No. 1 pick, was out with an ankle injury. And Jay had moved into the starting lineup. So Ferry was hoping the Bullets won and Jay had a good game.

Jay got 31 that night. And Dallas beat Washington.

Ferry said, "I walked out with the owner, and he said, 'I see what you mean now about that Vincent kid. He's pretty good!'"

He always was. Jay played nine years in the NBA and, even with the declining years, averaged 13.8 points per game. He had a fabulous career, including a long stay in Europe, that has gone totally unnoticed.

Unless you knew, you'd never think Jay and Sam were brothers. Jay was very quiet. He hardly ever gave an opinion. And he wasn't very emotional. Sam was kind of effervescent. He was never afraid to give an opinion. And they had different builds and played two different positions.

If there was any similarity with the Vincents, it was that neither worked very hard in the off-season. Both felt their talent would prevail.

We used to joke the Vincent workout was to jog a mile and shoot 300 jump shots. But that was still more than a lot of guys did in the off-season. And that was good enough for Jay. It wasn't good enough for Sam.

Sam was four years younger than Jay, so they never played together. But I always thought Sam could be a point guard. He always had great ball skills. But he didn't make good guard decisions.

After Sam had good freshman and sophomore years, the guys were back playing in Jenison. Earvin was there, and I said, "E, do you think Sam can make it in the pros?"

He said, "Oh, no! No way! All he can do is shoot. He can't really handle the ball. And he can't do any of the other things."

"Tell him!" I said.

Earvin said, "I can't tell him that, Coach, I'm close to the family."

I said, "E, I've been telling him he has to improve on his passing and his guard skills or he'll never make it. He thinks he could make it tomorrow! Do me a favor. In your own way, figure out a way to tell him."

Knowing Earvin, he probably told him, "Sam, you've got to work on this and that. You've got to become a total player."

Earvin said he couldn't make it, because he was too one-dimensional. But even then, that dimension was pretty good. Sam could really catch fire. He had had 36 in a win at Purdue—30 in the second half and the overtime. He was one of those players who could always get a shot. He was quicker into his shot off the dribble than anyone I had.

He led the league in scoring in '85 with a 23.9-point average and was a two-time All-Big Ten pick and an All-American in '85.

I think what hurt Sam was the fact the teams he played on never did what they might have done. They were 12-16, 17-13, 16-12 and 19-10. And Sam was kind of a victim of that. His senior year, he got 32 against UAB in the Tournament. But we were out in the first round.

Sam was a 6-1 shooting guard. But everyone wanted to turn him into a point guard. No one except Vinnie Johnson had been a 6-1 shooting guard in years. Today, they're looking at smaller shooting guards. But they weren't 10 years ago.

I was always disappointed he didn't become an even better player. He always had the potential to be a really good pro. But he never learned to be a point guard. And no one realized you could just play two guards instead of a point guard and a shooting guard.

If you look at Sam's history, the Celtics were elated when they were able to get him with the 22nd pick. They didn't think he'd be available. And he started for them at point guard. Then, he was on the bench.

He was traded to Seattle. And he started for them at point guard. Then, he was traded to Chicago.

If he could've stayed with Michael Jordan, he might still be playing. They didn't need a point guard. They just needed a good athlete. When you look at B.J. Armstrong and see how much Steve Kerr has played, they're not nearly as good as Sam was. But B.J. has played on three championship teams.

Then, Sam went to Orlando. And he started for them at point guard. He was with Milwaukee when he ruptured his Achilles. And he was starting for them at point guard.

I say Sam was given every opportunity to be successful as a point guard. But if teams had looked at him as a shooting guard, he might still be playing. The same would be true if he'd worked at developing his game.

I used to beg Sam to come up and work with our guys and analyze situations. But it was beneath him to come up and play with our guys if there weren't pros around. In Sam's mind, that wasn't beneficial. He didn't want to come back as a pro and just play with college kids.

When Sam finally came by before he went to Orlando, I said, "Hey, our guys are playing all month. You ought to come by and play with them!"

He said, "Coach, I don't leave for two weeks. I'm going to be there every day and play with them."

"Great!" I said, and we had a nice visit.

Then, he said, "By the way, Coach, if I don't see you again, good luck this year!"

In the back of his mind, he knew he wasn't coming. And we never saw him once. He was always convinced he needed time off to rejuvenate.

Who did more to rejuvenate our program? That's hard to say. Jay was our first big recruit. And Sam came in when we were down, as the state's first Mr. Basketball, and jumpstarted us.

When we were trying to revive a program Jay helped build, one we hadn't been very successful sustaining, I think Sam was a very important recruit.

I'd say they were of equal importance—very important parts of the Spartan program for nearly a decade and great kids who represented our program off the court in exemplary fashion.

THE MOST TALENTED
TEAM OF ALL

When I tell people the '83-84 team was the best I ever had, they always say, "It couldn't have been better than the national championship team!"

The sad thing is, it should've been.

That's the club I say was injured away.

We never played as well at any time in the regular season as we did in the preseason. Who are you playing against in the preseason? You're playing against yourselves. But you can still analyze what you have. And that team had a lot.

If you looked at the lineup, you saw Kevin Willis at center, Sam Vincent and Scott Skiles at the guards, Ken Johnson and Ben Tower at the forwards and Darryl Johnson and Larry Polec coming off the bench. That's an awfully good team. Not many clubs have four NBA players.

When *Sports Illustrated* came in before the season, Ivan Maisel said, "This is the best team I've seen so far—by far." But they rated us No. 8, behind North Carolina, Kentucky, Houston, Memphis State, Georgetown, Louisville and LSU.

And as strange as it seemed for a club that was 17-13 the season before, with a loss to Fresno State in the second round of the NIT, eighth in the nation seemed about right.

Kevin had just come back from the World University Games. He had been with us two years, after transferring from Jackson Community College, and was just starting to become the kind of 7-foot athlete we knew he could be—a first-round draft pick who has spent the last 11 years in the NBA.

Sam and Scott were both starting to mature. Sam was a junior. Scott was a sophomore. And they knew each other a little bit better than they did the year before.

Ken Johnson was chomping at the bit after transferring from USC. He was so big and strong we thought he had a chance to get every rebound.

And our other players were good enough to play a lot in the league, even though Darryl was just a freshman from Flint Central. In our minds, if no one else's, he was the best player coming out of Michigan.

But one by one, things began to disintegrate.

First, they declared Ken Johnson ineligible until January. The transfer rule for the NCAA said he had to sit out an academic year. The transfer rule for the Big Ten said a calendar year. So instead of being eligible December 9 under NCAA rules, he couldn't play until January 4, when winter quarter started. While Ken was sitting out, he put on 20 pounds. After that, he wasn't nearly as quick or as effective as he was in the preseason.

Then, Kevin went down in the first game of the Spartan Cutlass Classic against Central Michigan with pulled ligaments in his ankle and was supposed to be out from three to six weeks. He was back in 10 days. He was such a good athlete, we thought the ankle would heal as he played.

The ankle never did heal. He played the entire year on a foot-and-a-half. He made no power moves. Everything was a fallaway. Everything was tentative. Everything was on one leg.

And when I told people, "Willis is injured," they didn't believe it. They thought it was just a copout. See, straight ahead, he still ran like a deer. It didn't look like anything was wrong with him. What he couldn't do was go side-to-side or push off on the leg. He had no offensive moves and averaged 11.0 points a game.

We lost to St. Peter's at the Meadowlands, at Missouri and to Alabama in the Cotton States Classic in Atlanta to finish 6-3 in preconference play. A frustrating start, but hardly the worst of it.

The night Ken became eligible, we hosted Iowa and won on a last-chance shot by Darryl—not a bad Big Ten debut. People thought, "Hey, we won a big game!" But that was also when Sam injured his ankle.

Sam missed seven games. And we lost seven straight—to Northwestern, Wisconsin, Minnesota, Indiana, Ohio State, Illinois and Purdue. We'd get the Wisconsin game back on a forfeit later. But by then, it was really too late.

While Sam was out of the lineup, Scott was trying to do too much. When Sam came back, the ankle was still tender. Then, both of them were trying to do too much.

Kevin still had no agility. And Ken was still overweight. Those two guys never got in sync. All they did was get in each other's way.

Ben was strictly a support player. He couldn't carry us. And we desperately needed a lift.

Finally, we beat Michigan, then edged Oregon State. We beat Purdue and finished with a five-game win streak, starting at Indiana with one of our six wins at Assembly Hall.

We were a decent team, but not a great one. Michigan lost its last regular-season game in overtime at Northwestern and didn't get into the NCAA. Instead, they picked Michigan and Ohio State for the NIT. So we didn't even get there. We could've won the NIT. Instead, Michigan did. And instead of seeing the best club we'd ever had, all we saw was what we could've been.

How would a healthy '84 team have fared against the '79 club? We'll never know. And that seems like such a ridiculous question. The thing people don't understand is you couldn't prepare for Earvin Johnson. You couldn't really prepare for our matchup zone.

The '84 club, you could've prepared for. And when everyone was healthy, maybe that wouldn't have mattered. They could have won a championship. That's how good they were early, even though they finished 16-12.

But to win a championship, even then, you had to be lucky. You had to be healthy at tournament time. And you had to be healthy enough long enough to get there.

Why weren't we good enough? Besides all the health concerns, we never had the right chemistry.

I always thought Ben Tower would be a very good player by the time he was a junior and senior. Ben became a good defensive player. But he never had much of an offensive game.

In Saranac, they had to share one linoleum gym with the girls and the JVs. So his idea of a practice was about an hour and 15 minutes max. We didn't kill our kids in practice. A practice ran two hours from the time we started stretching to the time we were done. But I always thought practices were long for Ben.

He got better every year, but usually on defense. Ben had the kind of personality if he got 10 points, he was happy. If he got four points, he was happy. Ben never had a burning desire to be much more than he was.

Then, we had Sam and Scott on different wavelengths. They didn't get along well early. I think there was some friction—more on Sam's part than Scott's. Yet, they seemed to get along on the court. They seemed to get along off the court. So where was the friction? I don't know. But I still think there was some.

I don't think it was jealousy. But they both thought they should've had the ball more of the time. And we only had one ball. I think Sam thought he should've had the ball. And I think Scott thought he should've had the ball. And that never changed.

It wasn't, "Give me the damn ball!" or "Why the hell don't you throw it to me?" There was never any hostility. And there was never any confrontation. It was, "You're my teammate. I respect you. You respect me." But there was never any camaraderie, either. Unlike Shawn Respert and Eric Snow a decade later, Scott and Sam always went their separate ways.

And though Darryl developed into a very good Big Ten guard by his junior year, we were short a player who could've helped us, especially when Sam was out.

Randy Morrison would've been a senior that year. He'd been a high school star from Olivet. And for someone who has been the big fish in a small pond, sometimes it's hard.

The following year, when Sam came in, Randy's dad convinced him he was so much better than Sam, there was no comparison. If he'd picked someone else, maybe. But Sam was playing and Randy wasn't, and he couldn't accept that.

I still say if Randy had stayed, he would have been a pretty good player for us. I loved Randy Morrison. I thought he'd have developed into a very good guard. But he didn't have the patience to do that.

After Kevin and Ben left, we still had a decent club. We had Ken Johnson up front and got an extra year of eligibility for Richard Mudd. And for some reason, we played better. We finished 19-10; 10-8 in the Big Ten.

It was the first time we'd been back to the NCAA Tournament since '79. But we lost to UAB by two in the first round in Houston. We tipped the ball in for a basket, but had it waved away. And we stood around and watched Jerome Mincy, a 6-7 guy, outrebound us.

The only health problem that season came months before the first game. That was the summer I had my heart attack.

I'd had a shouting match, if you can believe that, with Gene Kenney, our assistant A.D. for facilities the day before. I don't even remember what it was about. But it was a good one. I was about as mad as I could get without hitting a guy.

That day, I rushed home from the office, mowed my lawn, dashed off to Walnut Hills Country Club to take a sauna, drove over to Flint to see a game and drove back. When I got home, I felt as if I was coming down with a cold.

I got up the next morning, did about 20 pushups and had that same funny feeling again. I drove to the office, called over and told Clint Thompson I was sitting down with Doug Weaver at 10, but was coming over to get some pills after that.

When Doug came in and started talking to me, I really started sweating. He has always said he had to get on me that day for comments I'd made about the Big Ten TV schedule and the fall-out he got from Wayne Duke's office.

But I said, "God, I just don't feel very good! I think I'm coming down with a cold."

And Doug said, "Maybe you're having a heart attack."

Do you know what my answer was? "I think maybe I am."

So Doug took me down to the lounge to lie down. And our doctor, Dave Hough, came over, gave me a nitroglycerine tablet and asked me what I had for dinner the night before and for breakfast that morning. He thought I had indigestion. But I still had the pain—like an elephant was standing on my chest.

I didn't want an ambulance wheeling up there. So Clint decided he'd drive me to the hospital. He drove me to St. Lawrence in Clint's little Volkswagen—bump, bump, bump, bump, bump!

"God, Clint, can you miss at least a few of the bumps?" I said. "Geez, this is a long ride!"

As soon as I walked in there and they heard I'd had chest pains, they put me in a wheelchair. They wheeled me in and took my pulse. It was 36. If I'd gotten there a few minutes later, I'd have probably been dead.

I was in intensive care for five days before they moved me. I had this cardiology team and got a horrendous bill—several thousand dollars for everything. And I got a bill from Dave Hough for $960. I didn't want to make an issue of that. I never said anything. I just paid it out of my pocket.

But lying in the hospital, my first reaction wasn't, "Am I going to die?" It was, "Am I going to coach again?" I've never been afraid of death. The one thing I've been deathly afraid of is a stroke.

They said, "In time, you're going to be fine." The original diagnosis was 20 percent damage. The final analysis was less than 10 percent. They said I was probably as healthy as 99 percent of the people age 57.

The doctors gave me all this stuff to read. I told Bev to read it. I didn't have time. I was working on basketball plays.

TRIALS,
TRIBULATIONS
AND TRIBUTES

As a head coach, you get letters from alumni and calls from boosters about lots of can't-miss prospects. We got a letter in '82 saying there was a little guard in the little town of Plymouth, Indiana, population 8,000.

Supposedly, the kid was a great player. But no one had heard of him. So we checked it out.

We asked for a film. And we got one—8 mm. We hadn't had an 8 mm film in so long you couldn't believe it. So I asked, "Does anyone know who has an 8 mm camera?"

Football did. When we took the film over, we couldn't see anything. It was like watching The Keystone Cops. It made your eyes ache to watch it. You couldn't even see the numbers.

I said, "I think he made a few baskets."

They said, "Coach, he got 54 that game!"

"He did?" I said. "Run it again!"

We didn't see any more than we saw the first time. So I sent Bill Norton down to see him. Bill was in his first year on the staff after coaching at Birmingham Brother Rice. And I still kid him about only liking the prototype Catholic point guard—the guy who's 5-7, dives all over and can't play.

Bill came back and said, "He's not a great athlete. But he's your kind of guard. He takes charge out there. I really think you ought to see him. I couldn't recommend him until I see what you think."

Plymouth was in the semi-state at Fort Wayne, where it played twice in one day. When I went to watch the players warm up, I didn't have a program. The guys were about all the same size, from 6-1 to 6-3. But I was looking for a great shooter.

Pretty soon, I saw this guy put the ball behind his head, which I hate, and shoot and shoot and shoot. He never missed. So I said, "God, I hate the way that Skiles kid shoots! . . . But he is effective."

When they introduced the starting lineups, the guy I'd been watching was playing center. Then, they said, "And at guard, No. 22, Scott Skiles!"

I swear, he was standing there with his stomach way out. And he looked like an albino. That's how white he was.

I said, "What the hell am I doing here?" But I stayed and watched the game. The kid took charge but, for a prospect, played awful. Somehow, they still managed to eke out a win.

I was supposed to drive to Ypsilanti, meet Bill and see a 6-8 player, Keith Armstrong from Ypsilanti. So help me, I put one foot on the shuttle bus, then stepped off. For some reason, I said, "I'm going to see that kid play again!"

I went across the street and found a motel. They said they'd been sold out for months. But someone said they'd just had a cancellation.

"I'll take it!" I said, and called Bill right away. "Hey, Skiles played awful. . . . But I think I'm going to watch him play again."

Scott didn't play super the second game, either. But he played very, very well—much better than his morning performance. So I said we were going to go after him. At that time, he wasn't being highly recruited—Fresno State and us were probably the main ones.

Then, at Market Square Arena, he got 30 of his team's 62 points against Indianapolis Cathedral in the afternoon semifinal and 39 points in a double-overtime upset of Gary Roosevelt for the championship that night. His 25-footer at the buzzer took the game into the first overtime.

With 900 students, it was the greatest Cinderella story in Indiana since Milan in '54, the team that inspired the film "Hoosiers."

So when he flew to Fresno State, who should happen to be on the same flight but Digger Phelps!

Scott wouldn't give Notre Dame the time of day. He said, "Here I am, 20 miles from campus. You've never recruited me. And now you have an interest? Get lost!"

He'd already written Purdue. And they wrote him back, saying they had no interest at all. An assistant wrote that note on his own, which just infuriated Gene Keady. After that, they couldn't get in.

Indiana still didn't have an interest. So with limited competition, we got him. He was the Hertz Award winner as the No. 1 prep athlete in Indiana. And a lot of people outside Indiana had no idea who he was.

Four years later, everyone knew.

Scott finished his Spartan career with 2,145 points and played his last three years without the 3-point shot. When he left, he was also No. 1 in Michigan State history with .850 career free throw accuracy. And he's still tops with 645 assists and 175 steals. Best of all, he and Earvin were the two players I had who could will a team to win.

A lot of people have asked me, "When did you know what you had?" The easy answer would be, "His freshman year, when he scored 35 in a triple-overtime win against Ohio State."

But Scott may not have been as good in any other system. He didn't start until the fourth game his freshman season. If you know Scott, you can probably guess his response to that: "I don't know why it took Coach so long to wake up!"

Scott always had something special. You could call it confidence. You could call it cockiness. Arrogance was probably a better word. There was always an arrogance about the way he played.

You may not believe it, and it may not have seemed that way, but Scott always listened to me. And he always listened to my assistant, Mike Deane. Scott understood that Coach knew a lot of basketball. He liked the fact we always made a lot of adjustments.

At 6-1, he was too small and too slow in most people's minds. But never in Scott's. He continued to get better and had a really good junior year.

At that point, I called him in and said, "Whatever you do, Scott, don't bag your books. If you're interested in coaching, you have to get that degree. You know you're not going to play pro ball."

"What do you mean, I'm not going to play pro ball?" he said, bristling at the very idea.

"You're not going to play pro ball because you can't do this, this, this and this," I told him, and listed about 10 things. "You can't shoot off the dribble. And you can't accelerate well enough."

But every year, guys have different levels of improvement. Scott didn't just improve. He raised his game another level.

I remember seeing Earvin the year before and saying, "What do you think about Scott's chances?"

"Nah," he said. "He's not big enough or strong enough. He can't do enough things. He can't play." The next summer, Earvin ran by me while they were playing and said, "Hey, Coach! Scott can play now!" We both knew what he meant.

When Sam left after his senior year, it was Scott's team. But he'd also elevated his game to the point he could do a lot more things.

He had an unbelievable senior year. But then, his last two years were incredible in a lot of ways, with all the attention focused on him. Scott was picked up by police in Indiana between his sophomore and junior years. It was August 29, 1984. He hadn't had any trouble before that.

He'd been out parking with a girl, when an officer approached and said, "Give me your driver's license." Scott had his wallet in his workout bag in the bag seat. As he reached back, the officer hollered, "What are you reaching for?"

"Hell, I'm reaching for my bag! Here, you take it!" Scott said, and threw it at him. "My wallet's in there."

I'm sure the officer didn't like his attitude. But Scott was pissed off, thinking, "What the hell are you stopping me for?"

In the bag, there was a vial. The officer took that, looked around, saw a couple of marijuana cigarette butts on the passenger side and thought he had a big drug bust. The vial was empty. But it had a white residue in it. When they ran a test on it, they said it was cocaine.

Scott said, "Hey, how that got in there is beyond me! I played at the intramural building on campus before I drove down. Somebody had to throw that into my bag. I don't know where it came from. But it's not mine."

The story broke in the media as possession of cocaine. There was no possession of cocaine, only a trace in a vial. It's not like the vial was full of anything.

His attorney, Charles Scruggs, said, "That's the most ridiculous thing in the world! It's like somebody finding a can with coffee grounds in it and saying you stole the coffee. It proves nothing."

Charlie took the case for nothing. He was a well-known attorney from Kokomo. And he got a continuance, so the case would be heard after the season.

But September 22, after Scott was back at school, he got stopped for running a stop sign near campus and was picked up for drunk driving. He tested .15. And you're considered impaired at .10.

I called him in and said, "Hey! What the hell's going on?"

"Coach, I was at a party with a couple of guys," he said. "I was at the wrong place at the wrong time, drank too much and got picked up."

"Christ, Scott!" I said. "You've got to be . . . "

"I know!" he said.

They made a big deal out of it in Indiana. And that had a big bearing on the case. He was portrayed in the press as a drunken drug addict.

Then, Charlie made a deal. They dropped the cocaine charge. And Scott was supposed to plead no contest to the marijuana. He'd get a fine and probation. I was down there as a character witness, when Charlie came storming out of the judge's chambers.

"That sonofabitch!" he said. "We're going to trial! That . . . "

I've heard a lot of curse words in my life and used most of them. But they were nothing compared to what Charlie called that judge.

"What happened?" we said.

"The judge insists Scott has to plead possession of marijuana," Charlie said.

It was 8 a.m., and we were supposed to start the proceedings at 9.

Scott said, "What do you mean, go to trial?"

"If you plead possession, you've got that on your record," Charlie said. "But we can beat it if we go to trial. The arresting officer has a very shaky record. He's lucky to have his job. He has been picked up before. Plus, there was no reason you were stopped and no reason the car could be searched. You offered no resistance."

Scott said, "How long would the trial take?"

"It'll probably take a week," Charlie said. "And we'll want some of your teammates and coaches to come down here"

"I can't do that!" Scott said. "I can't ask guys to come down here. I can't even miss another week of school. What if I plead possession?"

Charlie said, "You'll get a $100 to $200 fine and three months probation."

"Let's just do that," Scott said.

That was the second bargain—and the second mistake.

But the judge was a young guy who'd never practiced law. He was trying to make a name for himself in politics. He felt with all the media attention, it would make him look bad if he did what he originally agreed to. So he threw a curve at Scott.

When they finally entered the courtroom, instead of following what the first plea bargain was or what the second plea bargain was, he gave Scott a $100 fine, either 120 hours of community work or eight days in jail, a year's suspended sentence and a year's probation. In the plea-bargain negotiations, there was never any mention of the 120 hours or the year's probation.

Scott said, "I'd better take the eight days in jail. I don't have time for 120 hours." We talked him into the community service. He mowed lawns on weekends.

Charlie was so pissed off you couldn't believe it. He came in and said, "That lying so-and-so! He can't do that!"

Scott said, "I don't want any more publicity. I've had all I can take."

Charlie wanted to rip the judge for going back on the bargain. I guess a judge can always say, "I never made a bargain." But he did.

If it had gone to court, Scott would've gotten off, in my opinion. If you talk to Charlie Scruggs, they had absolutely no case. And if they'd gone ahead with the plea bargain as made, Scott wouldn't have been in violation of his probation when he was picked up later that year. The probation time would've already elapsed.

This was in April '85, before Scott's senior year.

He'd already been through the '85 season when they put up the "Cocaine" signs and hounded him from start to finish, largely because of how the media handled it.

And one of the provisions of his probation was he couldn't be in a place that served alcoholic beverages. We had to ignore that on road trips. We stayed in hotels and ate in hotel restaurants that served alcohol. So we were in violation of that every single time.

But the circumstances when he was picked up for DWI the following fall were what I consider about as unlucky as a guy can get.

His teammate, Ralph Walker, called him up just after midnight November 7 and said, "Hey, let's go have a beer!"

"I can't," Scott said. "I'm studying."

"Oh, c'mon!" Ralph said and talked him into going to B'zar, in downtown East Lansing.

They stayed there and drank a couple of pitchers of beer from 12:30 a.m. to 2 a.m. Scott must've had four or five beers.

He came out and saw a taxi but figured if he took it, his car would be towed for parking overnight. He knew he only had to go a few blocks. So he got in his car and drove around the corner —that's all!

The police followed him and stopped him. For what reason? None, except they were looking for guys who'd been drinking at 2 o'clock. He didn't exceed the speed limit or do anything else that would normally get you stopped.

They were really trying to crack down on drinking and driving. And they were looking for anyone. They weren't out to get Scott and weren't waiting specifically for him. He just happened to be there.

There was a witness who said he saw the whole thing. He said Scott was polite. He was courteous. He never challenged the guy. And he got nowhere. Scott passed every verbal test the guy gave him. He walked a straight line. But the officer said he wanted to give him a breathalyzer.

Scott said, "Hey, I probably won't do well on that. I drank quite a few beers in a short time. . . . Look, I'm Scott Skiles. I'm on the Michigan State basketball team. And I'm staying with guys right across the street. Why don't you give me a break?"

The guy said, "No, you're going to take the breathalyzer."

I still don't know who that officer was. But in my mind, he was horseshit.

So they gave him a breathalyzer. And he tested .10, just over the legal limit for driving while intoxicated.

They took him down to the station, booked him for DWI and tested him three more times. If you drink a lot in a short period of time, your alcohol level can jump up. They wanted a higher reading than .10. They got it to .11.

Scott got sucked in by the system. Then, he didn't get the break he should have had under the circumstances. Everyone wanted me to suspend a guy who went down to a tavern and had a few beers with a teammate before the season started. We had no rule against that. Our rule was moderation.

I always told our guys, "If you do everything in moderation, you'll be fine." Hey, if you think guys don't have a beer from time to time, you're crazy. I'm not naive enough to fall for that.

In my mind, Scott used poor judgment. Aside from that, he'd done nothing wrong that time. So the next morning, when he got out of jail, he came in to see me. His mother came in, too.

Scott was always harder on himself than anyone else. And he said, "Coach, I've embarrassed you and the program again. If you want to suspend me for the year, I'll accept that."

"What happened?" I said.

He told me, then said, "I don't know why I went down there. I haven't been drinking. I haven't been anywhere for so long. . . ."

That was when I got Doug Weaver, our A.D., involved. He suggested we suspend Scott for the year. He'd still have another season to play,

I said, "Doug, that's not fair! I know the situation. You know the situation. I've been a college student. You've been a college student. This doesn't make sense. If the guy is an alcoholic, that's one thing. All Scott did was go out and have a few beers with the guys."

Doug said, "Under the circumstances, we'd better suspend him, then make a decision."

And I said, "Doug, there's nothing to suspend him for except his past record."

Doug was adamant that Scott be suspended. But he also

indicated that if I wanted to reinstate him, he'd support that decision.

We suspended him for four days, including one of our exhibition games, then reinstated him. And I got all kinds of grief. People were saying we had a drunken drug addict on our team.

Plus, Scott faced the legal ramifications. If he'd gone to trial and gotten off, there would still have been the stigma, "Hey, he got off on a technicality!" But at least he would've gotten off. Instead, when he was picked up the second time in East Lansing, the media made him an ax murderer.

I said all the things that occurred from a legal standpoint were acceptable until February '86, when the judge in Plymouth said he'd violated his probation and had to serve 15 days in jail. To this day, I believe that to be the biggest miscarriage of justice in history. It was actually a 30-day sentence. But he served 15 days that May.

Excuse the redundancy, but I said that was a crime. He had to go in after the season and wound up serving the time in the middle of spring term.

People always said I stuck by him. Maybe to you, he'd done something terribly wrong. But to me, it was nothing like that. I don't think I saved Scott Skiles. And I don't like to say I'm the only guy in the world who would've given Scott another chance.

But when Bobby Knight came out and said, "A guy like Scott Skiles couldn't play in our program," he didn't know the particulars. All he did was read the Indiana papers, where the guy was portrayed as an alcoholic drug addict.

Hey, an alcoholic drug addict wouldn't have played on my team, either! But the fact Scott was stopped, picked up and picked up again was mostly a matter of being in the wrong place at the wrong time.

If he'd tested 2.0 and been down there all night, that was one thing. But Ralph called him at midnight. They didn't get down there until 12:30 a.m. And they were there no more than an hour-and-a-half. Why didn't the officer give him a break? It wasn't like he was falling down drunk.

But I wasn't comfortable going downtown and asking those questions. In my position, if I went down there and raised hell, I was trying to adjust the law for an ax murderer. It was an absolute no-win situation if I tried to interfere.

To this day, I've never followed up on it. But if that had happened down in Ann Arbor, at least in those days, I guarantee it would've been handled differently. Now, they seem to have a different approach. But before, they covered up everything.

We couldn't have covered anything up if we'd wanted to. And the way the media covered everything, it made Scott's performance in a sensational senior season all the more remarkable.

To play as well as he did, with the team we had and with the things that were being written and said, made it the greatest single-season performance of any player in my coaching career.

ROLES AND REFUSING
TO ROLL OVER

Sam was gone. Ken Johnson was gone. And people had written us off before the '85-86 season even began.

Bad mistake.

One thing we always took great pride in was the way our kids improved every year, from the time they arrived on campus to the day they left.

And when you had a player like Scott Skiles, no matter what the score was, you were never out of a game.

If not for a bad break in Kansas City, we might have been playing in the Final Four. And I wouldn't have put anything past that club. We might've pulled two more surprises.

Heading into the season, I always thought we'd have a pretty good team. It was just that the league was so tough again, as tough as it'd been in several years.

The question wasn't, "Are you going to be good?" It was, "Are you going to be good enough to beat the Indianas, the Michigans, the Purdues and the Iowas?"

We were good enough to go 12-6 in the league. And all that could get us was third, despite beating the champions, our friends from Michigan, twice.

By the end of the season, we were about as good a running team and as good a shooting team as you'd ever find in college basketball. Scott was great on the break. And we had a lot of perimeter shooters—guys who would've been even more dangerous today.

We led the nation in field goal shooting at .556—largely without an inside game, as amazing as that seems—and also led in free-throw shooting at .799.

Those were tremendous numbers. But we got a lot of layups off the break. And for the most part, we had the right guys shooting the shots.

Everyone knew Scott was an excellent shooter. Larry Polec was very good. And Darryl Johnson finished his career as the school's fifth-leading shooter from the field at .536. That's really good for a guard, considering the kind of shots he got.

Darryl and Vernon Carr, a 6-6 junior-college kid from Detroit, were very good college basketball players. Darryl was kind of a multi-dimensional guard. He could handle the ball. He could shoot. He could take it to the basket and do a lot of things. And Vernon could play inside or outside and really get out on the break.

But we were a small team, a three-guard team, with two 6-1 or 6-2 guards and with Barry Fordham in the middle. Barry would work and work and work, especially on defense. He was only 6-8.

And we didn't have a lot of depth. We had Carlton Valentine, Ralph Walker and Mark Brown. V was always energetic _ and always a little frustrated. And I think most people remembered Ralph for the game against Indiana when he wore his pants backwards. When we won, everyone said he should've done that more often.

Still, we only lost one pre-conference game, by one point at Iowa State. That was just a great game that went into overtime. Scott and Jeff Hornacek really played well. I remember saying, "Hornacek is a walk-on, and look how he's playing! Where do you get those walk-ons?"

But we started the Big Ten season 2-4. And nobody knew how good we were going to be.

Scott had an unbelievable game at Minnesota, where he scored 45 points—and would have had 62, I've been told, if they'd brought the 3-point line back one year earlier. To put on an exhibition like that and lose was just a shame.

What you had to do to appreciate him was see him play, not hear about him or even watch him on TV. To this day, Larry Donald of *Basketball Times* has to defend making him his National Player of the Year. But Larry was right.

I always told kids in my camp the same thing: "Scott Skiles can't run and can't jump. Yet, he had the greatest senior year in the history of Michigan State basketball. Of all the players I've ever coached, he came the closest to reaching his potential." You can talk about Earvin and all the rest. But in the 19 years I was there, Scott had the greatest year of anyone. He averaged 29.1 points per game in the league. The only guy who has done that since is Glenn Robinson. He got $80 million.

Scott shot .554 from the field and .900 at the line and averaged 6.5 assists and 1.7 steals. He talked a good game on the floor and usually played a better one.

One of his greatest tributes was being named Big Ten Player of the Year—on a third-place team.

But everything turned around for us when Michigan came to Jenison. We beat the Wolverines by 12. And Scott out-played and out-talked Antoine Joubert.

When you talk about trash talk, Steve Smith and Ken Redfield a few years later seemed to be talking to themselves. It was that much a part of their games. But Scott was kind of arrogant on the floor. If he made a big basket, it was, "Hey, you can't check me!"

And when he played against Joubert, who got so much publicity and was supposed to be the saviour in the state, Scott loved every second of it.

Before that first matchup, there'd been a lot of talk from Ann Arbor during the week. Joubert had said he was better than Scott. He and Gary Grant both said they could kill Scott one-on-one. And the media had really run with it.

When Scott got 40 points and fouled Joubert out, Joubert took off his elbow pad and threw it into the stands. That made the crowd even wilder—and it didn't need much encouragement.

Then, Joubert hollered, "We'll get you in Ann Arbor!"

That's when Scott said, loud enough for people in the stands to hear, "Not unless you lose 20 pounds, Fat Boy!"

Antoine sat there with a towel over his head in the final minutes. And when Scott scored again, he went by the Michigan bench and said, "How'd you like that one, Fat Boy?"

We beat them handily again in Ann Arbor. And we both wound up in the Midwest Region in the NCAA Tournament. They were seeded No. 2. We were No. 5. And right away, a couple of Michigan guys said, "We'd like to play Michigan State again." Our guys said to themselves, "Yeah, sure they would. We'd love to play them again! Any time!"

We figured we'd beat them 10 out of 10. They were so big, they couldn't keep up. They had a lot of size, but no quickness. Roy Tarpley was always in foul trouble. And at 6-1, Scott was tough enough to play the baseline and check Butch Wade. Remember, Wade was 6-8.

But we went to Dayton for the first two rounds of the Tournament. Meanwhile, Michigan, the No. 1 seed, went to Minneapolis and lost to Iowa State and former Wolverine coach Johnny Orr.

Our first-round game was against, of all teams, Washington. When Marv left, or was actually forced out, Andy Russo came in and said he was going to put University of Washington basketball where it belonged, He said he'd revive it and move it forward. This was after Marv had won the Pac-10 title his last two years.

After that, I rooted for Washington and Andy Russo to lose every game. I got to know Andy when we worked the Pan American Games Trials in '89. He's really a good guy. But I still never rooted for Washington.

They haven't done anything in basketball since Marv left. And when they did make the NCAA Tournament in '86, guess who beat them? Michigan State.

It was a real struggle. We almost lost it. We trailed 40-28 in the second half. But we had a 17-2 run. And Scott came through and hit two free throws with two seconds left to win it, 72-70.

Then, we got to play Georgetown, which had a vaunted press—at least, according to the press in our area. Everyone was asking us, "What about their press? How can you handle the press?"

Secretly, our guys were saying, "We hope they press!"

They pressed us twice. We went right through it for two easy baskets. And we never saw their press the rest of the game. John Thompson was smart enough to figure out the best way to play us was in a half-court game, not full-court.

That's when Scott made his famous pass—the double wraparound to Larry Polec. And as pretty a pass as that was, the key was the way Larry got out and ran, just the way he'd been doing all season.

Larry said, "You know, I should've blown that layup! Then, Scott would never have had any publicity." He'd already had enough to last a lifetime, with what he went through his last two years.

But in all my years of coaching, the best runner I ever had on the break was Larry Polec. He'd run and run and run. Every once in a while they'd throw him the ball, and he'd say, "Geez, look what I've got!"

And when it came to making guard decisions, there was Earvin, there was Scott, then there were all the rest. It went way down after that.

But we beat Georgetown 80-68, then lost to Kansas in Kemper Arena on a decision that's still hard to accept.

Danny Manning was a sophomore. But the Jayhawks had a lot of other good players, people like Ron Kellogg, Greg Dreiling and the guy who hurt us with 26 points, Calvin Thompson.

It was two years before they won the national championship back in Kansas City. But you could already see the seeds of greatness in Manning.

Our great player was a senior, though. And again, we played well enough to win. The clock stopped when it shouldn't have—more on that later. Then, they scored with nine seconds to go to tie it up. Did that mean the game should've been over and we should've won? Who knows?

Fatigue was a real factor in that game. You could really see us getting tired toward the end. We just didn't have the bodies.

And we missed a lot of free throws we'd normally make. Scott missed the front end of a one-and-one. So did Larry. And of course, Mark Brown missed the one people remember with 20 seconds left in regulation.

We lost 96-86 in overtime, despite a great effort by Barry Fordham. He was 7-for-9 from the field and outscored Dreiling, a future pro, 15-10.

The sad part was, if we'd been able to hang in there and win, we'd have had an excellent shot to get to the Final Four in Dallas. Of course, you can always beat the clubs you don't play. But in the Midwest Final, we would've played North Carolina State, with Charles Shackleford and Chris Washburn.

They were even slower than Michigan. They wouldn't even run back on defense. They trotted back. I think we'd have killed them. But they probably said, "We're so much bigger, we'd have killed Michigan State!"

If we'd won, it's hard to say how we'd have done in the Final Four that year. Louisville won the championship. And Duke was runner-up. I guess you could say we were good enough to beat anybody. We finished 23-8. But we had some definite deficiencies, too. We noticed them more the next season after Scott left.

People talk about '86 as our best coaching job. I think it's always hard to pick out the best job you've done. We might've done a better job in '90, when we won 10 straight games with a team a lot of people picked for seventh or eighth place. We might've done a better job in '94, losing four games we could have won, then making a great, late-season surge. Or did we do our best job in '95, taking what we had and making the most of it?

To be honest, we might've done a better job in the '81 and '82 seasons, when we won a total of 25 games.

Sometimes you do your best job when you have your worst record. That's when you have to hold the team together. You've got to fight off the people criticizing you and the players.

You see that in baseball, too. A guys gets fired two years after he was Manager of the Year. Why? Because he wasn't winning. He's the same guy he was two years earlier.

In '86, we didn't have nearly the players we'd had two years before. Yet, based on the record, we were a much better team.

Why were we playing three guards? Because they were our best players. We'd used three guards on occasion the year before to take advantage of Darryl. And the three-guard lineup was good at the end of the game because we could control the ball.

Maybe being able to make those changes and having them work for us was a sign we did a decent job. A key to success is always being able to adjust.

But you have to believe in something when you coach. That's what's called your coaching philosophy—the sum total of all you believe. Your basic philosophy is usually established at an early age. But it changes as you get more experience and the game changes.

One thing that'll never change was the belief the '86 players had in each other and in their coaches. That's what got us through a lot of tough times.

It was a tough year, because the staff was always pissed off. We'd go somewhere, and someone would always write something negative about Scott.

It was the same as when Muddy Waters got the job as Michigan State's head football coach. He said, "I never could figure out if '58-year-old' was my first name or my last name. Every time I picked up the paper it was either '58-year-old Muddy Waters' or 'Muddy Waters, 58 years old.'"

You couldn't pick up the paper and not read, " . . . led by Scott Skiles, a convicted drug and alcohol abuser." We saw that over and over. The media just hit it and hit it.

We said, "Why can't Scott score 45 points without the mention that he's on probation?" And time after time, we heard, "What if he was a black player?" and "What if he was a guy at the end of the bench?" They wanted answers from me to questions I always resented.

But we never lost Scott. And Scott never lost his competitive fire, despite all the criticism, especially his junior year. We didn't hear quite as much his senior year. His junior year was when they made a big deal out of the cocaine. His senior year, it was alcohol. And there aren't many college kids who can say much about a guy who has been drinking.

The Milwaukee Bucks said Scott could help them and made him the 22nd pick overall in '86. He struggled with injuries and was traded to Indiana. Then he and Sam were both picked up by Orlando.

I almost cried when they both got picked by the same team in the expansion draft. They weren't both going to start, since both were considered point guards.

Sam started at the point. But he was still better as a shooting guard, which the pro coaches failed to realize. Eventually, Scott replaced him. It wasn't that Scott was better than Sam. It was that Scott played the point position.

And in '86, he played it about as well as anyone can.

HUMOR, EVEN WHEN NOTHING IS FUNNY

Jud's Jokes was the strange idea of Tom Jamieson, a doctor in Lansing and a local athlete of some small renown.

Tom had a 900 number and obviously had no use for it. So he came up with the brilliant idea I'd tell jokes and people would call up and listen to them.

I told him, "Hey, there's absolutely no way this can make money! You've got comedy clubs, comedy hours on HBO, all the jokes you could possibly want. No one is going to call for my jokes!"

But I recorded a few stories for him once a week for three or four months. Then, I did it once every two weeks. I guess you had to do it once a month, minimum, to keep the 900 number. And that's where it ended. One time, he gave me a check for $87.

I said, "Tom, what's this?"

He said, "That's the money we got for your jokes over a three-month period."

I said, "What about your expenses? You advertised in *Basketball Weekly*. That ad had to cost you $300!"

"No, no!" he said, "I insist you take this so we can say we made some money from Jud's Jokes."

And that's what we made, $87.

But humor has been invaluable to me throughout my career. It may have even played a role in my coming to Michigan State in '76.

While I was in Chicago for the job interview, Clifton Wharton asked, "How do you rate your sense of humor?"

"Probably better than yours," I said.

They'd asked every candidate to tell his favorite joke. I told an old Montana joke, "You ate my socks!" It goes like this:

"A guy works on a sheep farm. But it's so hot during the summer, he goes barefoot in the sheep pens and develops a terrible problem with foot odor. Now, he moves to the city, gets a job with a p.r. firm, but can only go about 45 minutes without going to a bathroom and washing and powdering his feet to keep the odor down.

"He begins to date a gal who, unbeknownst to him, has a terrible breath problem. She can only last about 45 minutes before she has to go to the bathroom and brush her teeth and gargle.

"They start going together. And it works out great. Every time she'd excuse herself, he'd run to the bathroom and beat her back to the room. And when he'd excuse himself, she'd run and gargle and beat him back.

"They get engaged and finally get married—a very short ceremony, by the way.

"Now, they're preparing for their wedding night. She says, 'Dear, let me go in first.' She goes in the bathroom, and he says, 'God, I've got to get rid of these shoes!' He takes off his shoes. And they smell just awful. He takes off his socks. And they smell worse. So he puts his socks in his shoes and puts them in the closet.

"Finally, she comes out. So he goes in and scrubs his feet, scrubs his feet and scrubs his feet. He puts powder on them and everything. Suddenly, she realizes he has been in there a little too long.

"As he gets in bed, she turns toward him and says, 'Honey, I have to tell you something.'

"He says, 'Dear, you don't have to tell me anything! I know what happened. . . . You ate my socks!'"

I remember the president just cracking up when I told that joke. . . . I don't think anyone else laughed that hard.

Probably my favorite joke is about the guy celebrating his 65th wedding anniversary. His friend sees him over in the corner, sobbing and sobbing. So he goes over to see what's wrong.

He says, "Why are you crying? Are you overcome with emotion?"

The older guy says, "No, I'll tell you why I'm crying. We had a similar party on our 50th wedding anniversary. That night, I told my attorney I hated my wife and wanted to kill her.

"My attorney said, 'You can't do that! Even at your age, you'd get 15 years!'

"I was just thinking . . . tonight, I'd be a free man."

The key is knowing your audience. The reason the old cannibal joke is funny is because everyone can relate to the people you mention.

If you're at a high school and you say, "Basketball coaches' brains are $1 a pound, football coaches' brains are $2 a pound and principals' brains are $25 a pound," you have to look at the principal.

The guy says, "Why are principals' brains so expensive?"

The answer is, "Did you ever stop and think how many principals we have to butcher to get a pound of brains?"

If they don't know the principal is there and everyone in the room is looking at him, it's not that funny. The funny part isn't necessarily how you tell it. It's the people you mention.

My wife says other people could tell those jokes, and they wouldn't be funny. I told her she's a great audience, because I'll tell jokes she has heard over and over, and she always laughs. She says it's not the jokes, but the way I tell them.

Guys I play golf or handball with will say, "Remember when you said . . . "

And I never do.

The things people say I've said, I usually don't remember. Yet, people say I'm the master of the one-liner . . . like I must practice them or something.

One thing I've always had is a quick retort. Sometimes they're funny. Sometimes they're sarcastic. Sometimes they're caustic. I even do that with my wife. That's just my personality.

But I get a lot of requests to speak, inside and outside the community. I always talk at the coaches' banquet at the Final Four.

And I've talked at the Walnut Hills Country Club Stag something like 17 out of 19 years. This year, I got up and thought I told some funny jokes. I told Gus Ganakas this was the first year no one came up and said anything about it.

He said, "Yeah, they're not laughing as hard at your jokes, Jud, now that you're not the coach any more!"

There are a lot of guys who can laugh at others. I've always been able to laugh at myself. I think that gets you through some tough times.

And I've also been able to interject some humor at practice, which maybe lessens the tension of the way I coach. If I didn't do that, it would be a lot harder for the players.

They know they can come up with a joke. Kris Weshinskey the great imitator, would show everyone the way I walked. The players all know a joke on me is going to be funny to me and funny to them. And a joke on them is going to be funny to me, even if it's not funny to them.

We have what we call Sports Quiz, where we try to guess the player when something ridiculous happens. And you've got some guys who don't like being made fun of. They always think it funnier when the laugh is on someone else. But a lot of times, I think it's even funnier when the laugh is on me.

I've never taken offense to people making fun of the coach. Or if I've been the brunt of a practical joke, I've tried to see the humor in it.

A lot of times, I'll start a sentence with the phrase, "As sure as I'm fat and bald, . . ."

And I have two favorite lines about athletics and the coaching profession:

"When in danger, when in doubt, run in circles, scream and shout," and "Sooner or later, the game makes fools of us all. . . . And I'm living proof."

In '79, we were on our way back after winning the Far West Classic. And I got a little impatient at Metropolitan Airport, near Detroit. The luggage wouldn't come and wouldn't come. So I decided to go back and check on the hold-up. Naturally, the door to the loading area was locked. So I hopped on the conveyor belt and rode back with the unclaimed luggage.

Right away, a guy said, "What are you doing? You can't come back here!'

I got a quick escort back to the waiting area. . . . But pretty soon, we got our luggage.

That same year, at the Basketball Bust, the coach of the national champions got a ridiculously long round of applause.

"The last time I got a standing ovation was when I was at Montana . . . when I said I was going to Michigan State," I said. "It was in a bar. Two guys applauded. The third guy fell off his stool. And the bartender cried, because he needed the business."

But if you're going to laugh at others in this business, you'd better be able to laugh at yourself.

When I bounced the ball off my nose in frustration at Illinois, I had to make a crack about working on my dribbling—even though it hurt like hell.

When our usual group of Mid-Michigan coaches and good guys got together at the Final Four in Lexington in '85, they had some paramedics rush into the room with oxygen. I'd just had my heart attack the summer before. It was nice to know they were thinking about me.

When I heard the roof collapsed during construction at Breslin and we'd just lost in Bloomington by 37 points, I said, "We have worse structural problems than that."

And after the Parish Hickman allegations came out, we had breakfast that Sunday morning at The Gables. I said, "C'mon out and look at my new truck!" Some guy had a new pickup with "BANDIT" painted in big letters on the side. Some people might wonder how I could tell a joke like that. But as low as I was that day, and I was low, I saw the humor in it.

In my mind, Doug Weaver has a great sense of humor. He uses humor to release stress. I'm not sure I use humor for that. But I always say a good laugh takes the place of an hour of therapy.

Doug always comes up with these limericks. They're never as funny as he thinks they are. But they are clever. They're more clever than funny.

The funny thing is, Doug Weaver didn't come back to Michigan State until '80, when we started to slip for a few years. But I was never concerned about losing my job during our down periods, even when he was pressured.

Doug always said, "We've got the best basketball coach around. We'll be all right!"

I haven't always had that much respect. In '87, we went to Yugoslavia to get our guys as much experience as possible. The first game we played, we were almost sleepwalking. It was outside against a town team. And we almost got beat.

The next game, we were outside again. The wind started blowing. But we beat what we thought was the national team. We found out later it was the junior national team, with Toni Kukoc. When we did play the national team, it had both Petrovics and Vlade Divac.

I got in a tiff and, knowing they couldn't understand English, used some choice words on the officials. Then, Drazen Petrovic came over, used the same words and said, "Coach! We understand English!"

That was the same year Herb Williams and about five players got caught in an elevator for about 20 minutes. I swear, when Carlton Valentine came out, he was white. That's how panicked he was, with a claustrophobic reaction.

I'd already warned them, "Hey, quit overloading the elevator!" But they'd all pack in there because they didn't want to wait.

I never thought about coaching in Yugoslavia. But I did have a couple of other opportunities to go elsewhere, primarily back out West. How close was I to taking another job? Pretty close.

In Earvin's first year, there were rumors I was going to take the USC job. Bob Boyd announced his retirement and said he was taking another job, when he was really let go. I was contacted by an alumnus, but nothing official.

When he asked if I had an interest in the job, I said, "Right now, I'm involved in my season. When that's over, I might have an interest in the job."

Mike McGee was the USC athletic director. And he even mentioned my name. But he never contacted me. I think the fact I didn't jump on it was a factor. So I was never a viable candidate, because of the timing. They thought they had to fill the job, while we were moving on in the Tournament. So they hired Stan Morrison before the '78 season was over.

But my first year at Michigan State, I interviewed for the Fresno State job on the sly. As it turned out, I could've been Jerry Tarkanian's predecessor.

I knew Jim Sweeney, the football coach, when he worked at Washington State. He had me over to his house and said he couldn't believe the people and the support in the Fresno area.

"Jud, you'd love it here," he said. "Bev would love it here. Lucille loves it here. I'm staying here the rest of my life." I decided I wasn't going to take the job. And two months later, Jim Sweeney was with the Oakland Raiders.

I called him, laughing, and said, "Jim, you s.o.b.!"

He said, "Hey, Jud, when I talked to you, I really figured I'd be there for life. But here was a chance to get into the pros. I'd always wanted to see what I'd do at this level."

He stayed in the pros for a couple of years, then went back to Fresno State. He's two years younger than I am. And I think he has a five-year contract.

Then, Boise State tried to hire me twice. It was back in the Big Sky. And they were going do some things. They had a group that was going to raise some money on the side to sweeten the deal. And they guaranteed a radio-and-TV package.

I came to Michigan State at $25,000. When we won the NCAA Tournament, I got a tremendous $6,000 raise. I went from $33,000 to $39,000. And almost all the years I was there, I was about the lowest-paid basketball coach in the league.

I finally got a $10,000 market raise in '86, which put me in the middle salary-wise. But almost every coach who'd come into the conference would have a higher salary and a much better package, when you considered the camps and the radio and TV.

Tom Izzo will make a lot more money at Michigan State next year than I made this year. And that doesn't bother me. I've never been in it for the money. I recognize every time there's a change, the new guy gets more than the old guy. It has been that way forever.

When Marv moved to Washington, the guy before was making $22,000. Marv signed for $25,000. The new guy always gets more than the old guy. That's the way our profession works.

When you add it all up, Nick Saban is probably going to make more as head football coach at Michigan State than George Perles did. And I always say that George was the greatest money-raiser in history.

So, no, that never bothered me. I've always said if you start low and stay in one place, you stay low. If all you get are the raises the faculty gets, the three or four percent a year, you can't move up.

The funny thing is, until recently, none of the other coaches knew what you were making. They didn't discuss financial packages. But that's one thing George did, when he was chairman of the Big Ten football coaches two years in a row.

He said, "We're going to have a meeting of just the coaches. Here's what I want: what you're paying your assistants and what your TV deal is, so we can help the young guys and help ourselves through comparison."

That's one reason Barry Alvarez was able to sign that 15-year contract at Wisconsin and John Cooper was able to negotiate a better deal at Ohio State. They knew what all the others were doing.

Saban's assistants are making more than George's assistants. And I tried to tell Tom the same thing, "Whatever you do, try to start your assistants high enough."

I tried to get a market raise this year for Stan Joplin. But Merrily Dean Baker turned that down. I got Tom's salary up with the extra duties as associate head coach. Instead of making $55,000, he got a $10,000 raise.

It has gotten to the point where the top 20 guys each make a half-million dollars a year, with everything considered. I never made close to half that amount, mainly because I didn't have big camp and TV deals. And a half-million is probably more money than a college coach should make.

The only pro job I ever had a feeler on was the Denver job in '83 or '84. I was 56. And I just told them I had no interest. At my age, I couldn't see myself coaching 100 games.

Would I have liked to coach pro basketball? Yeah, I would've. But it was never a burning passion. It was never anything other than to try the pro game and match wits at the next level. It was nothing I pursued. And it was nothing I dreamed about.

In '79, after the NCAA Championship, they weren't hiring college coaches in the pros. Nobody was. So the next year, when Denny Crum won at Louisville, it was the same way for him.

The only guy with any mobility that way was Larry Brown. He went from the pros to college to the pros to college to the pros and played musical chairs.

I stayed at Michigan State and coached 13 years before we even had chairs in a new arena. . . . And maybe that was good. As mad as I got, I could never have thrown benches.

MORE GUARDS AND "THAT SKINNY KID"

A lot of people have asked if my style of coaching has ever hurt anyone's development.

I think it has with some kids. Most guys, if they've played, have learned to relax eventually. But some guys have had the idea they can't make a mistake. They've been conscious of what they can't do, rather than what they can.

I've always said, "Hey, there comes a point in time when you have confidence in me, because I have confidence in you. If I didn't have confidence in you, you wouldn't be playing!"

All my life, I've been a negative coach. I've pointed out the mistakes that were made. Consequently, when players have had the right frame of mind, we've hardly had anyone who didn't get better in our program. That was true in high school, at Washington State, at Montana and at Michigan State.

We've pointed out the limitations they've had and the things they've had to work on. We've told them what they could do and what they couldn't.

Ron Charles was a perfect example. He's still Michigan State's all-time field goal percentage leader. And he couldn't shoot a lick.

But I believe my biggest coaching failure was Patrick Ford, a two-time *Parade* All-American. Patrick was all-world as a sophomore and junior in high school and was considered a better prospect than Scott, at least by fans in the state of Michigan.

When we recruited him, his brother said, "Patrick isn't one bit better as a high school senior than he was as a freshman. So we're glad he's playing for you. We know you'll push him."

I tried to push Patrick. But he resisted any coaching or criticism. Every now and then, he'd make a Michael Jordan play and do something so quick you'd blink your eyes. Then, you'd be waiting and waiting for it to happen again.

Patrick was unhappy with his playing time and with our coaching. He transferred to Western Michigan after his sophomore year, but was never academically eligible at Western and finished his career at a Division II school in Oklahoma. I've always wondered, if I'd been a more positive coach, could I have helped Patrick realize his great talent and potential?

If you want to pick a poor coaching year, '87 might've been it. Darryl Johnson and Vernon Carr were already playing for the pro scouts, wondering why they didn't go hardship. Somebody had told them they were both going to be No. 1 draft picks.

We didn't have good chemistry. And we weren't very tough, mentally or physically. Instead of playing for us, some guys were thinking a year ahead. They wondered who was looking at them. And they were more concerned with scoring than winning.

Darryl averaged 22.1 points and Vernon 13.8. But we didn't get much better as the season went along. We lost four of our last five games, three of them at home, and finished 6-12, 11-17.

The real shame was what happened with Mark Brown. Mark thought he was the 15th man. We were trying to play Ed Wright as much as we could in practice to see if he could play the point. And Mark was hurt. He had a pulled leg muscle.

But the real reason Mark left school was because his dad and mom resented to the nth degree the idea I was ridiculing their son. They said I was bad-mouthing him at clinics. And they poisoned him against the program.

What I said at a couple of clinics was this: "Last year, we led the nation in field goal shooting at .556. We led in free throw percentage at .799. And believe it or not, if we'd made the last free throw we missed, we'd have been at .800—one of the highest percentages in history."

The guy who missed that free throw was Mark Brown in the Kansas game. But I never mentioned Mark Brown. I never even mentioned the game. And they said I was blaming Mark for the loss.

By the time he'd checked out of school, his mother hated me. His dad came to realize Mark was pencilled in as our starting point guard. But by then, it was too late.

Darryl had been our third guard for two years, with Sam and Scott ahead of him. And before he became a starter and our No. 2 scorer in '86, I said, "What you should do is always analyze who should pass where, when."

Darryl got very good at sitting with me, analyzing where the ball should go. But when he got on the floor, he couldn't do it. He was another shooting guard in a point guard's body.

He was drafted by Golden State in the third round, which was lower than we thought. But they didn't have a first-round pick. So he was actually their second selection and the only guard they took.

Darryl got 18 in one scrimmage and 20 in another. But he was so crushed when they cut him, he wouldn't come home and never came around.

Finally, I got to talk to him and said, "What did they say?"

"Coach," he said. "They said the same thing you said for four seasons—that I didn't make good guard decisions."

That can haunt so many players, because there aren't many guys who make them. Most guys aren't even thinking about guard decisions. They want to take the ball as far as they can, then either make a move for themselves or find someone else.

I know I'm very, very critical of guards. Mike Deane used to say, "I was a guard. Tom Izzo was a guard. And we can't recruit guards here! Every guard we recommend, you think is shitty."

Ed Wright was a junior college player. And Mike loved him. When I flew down to see him, he kind of went through the motions in practice. When I flew down again for a game, it was the same thing.

I asked the coach, "Does that kid EVER play hard?"

We'd watched him play in an AAU tournament a couple of years earlier and get 36 points. I think Mike was still seeing him get those 36.

Ed was another player who had a hard time adjusting to my coaching style. He was a laid-back player who would've been more comfortable as a small forward. But we played him at guard, where he struggled his first year.

He had a decent senior year, but never played quite as well as we'd hoped. It's just very difficult for most junior college players to adjust to Big Ten basketball right away.

Ken Redfield came from Chicago as a very young freshman in '86. And I'm still just sick that Ken refused to redshirt. If he had taken the extra year, I'm convinced he'd be in the pros today.

And when we recruited Kirk Manns from North Judson, Indiana, we hoped he'd be another Scott Skiles. He was another shooting forward in high school they called a shooting guard. The thing that impressed me more than anything else in recruiting Kirk Manns was he was an all-state football quarterback. You can't be an all-state quarterback without being a pretty good athlete.

So I was looking at him as a better athlete than he looked playing in high school. In basketball, he just looked like a shooter. But I thought that was the role he was supposed to play. I thought he'd be able to do more.

Wrong.

He had limited speed, limited quickness and was a great shooter. But when he came in as a freshman, we were desperate for scoring. He got 17 at TCU and 19 against BYU, the same game Darryl had 42.

Suddenly, Kirk couldn't get a shot. He figured we weren't doing what was right for him. And he was playing less and less and less. The word was out, if you crowded him, he wasn't quick enough to get around you.

He suffered through his sophomore year, playing fewer minutes and averaging just 5.0 points. He was talking about transferring. I thought that was probably good and called in his folks. At the time, they thought I had to be the worst coach in history.

His mother said, "What kind of shooter do you think Kirk is?"

I said, "Kirk is the second-best shooter I've ever coached. Mike Brkovich was the best. And he averaged 7.0 points a game for his career. Maybe the third-best shooter I ever had was a kid named George Gabriel at Washington State. And he was only third-team as a freshman. You've got to be able to do more than shoot. You've got to be able to get a shot."

"Well, how come Indiana can get all those shots for Steve Alford, and you can't get any shots for Kirk?" she said.

I said, "Because Steve Alford understands how to come off screens and get open. He's not 10 pounds overweight. And in all honesty, when he's open, they get him the ball. We don't get Kirk the ball, because he hasn't worked hard enough to get open. And if he is open, guys don't expect him to be."

"Well, Kirk is thinking of transferring," she said.

I said, "I think that'd be a good idea. We'll help him any way we can."

That really surprised them. But when he shopped himself around, programs saw a 6-foot white player. And no one offered him a scholarship.

Then, we got a call from his folks, saying, "Kirk has decided to really work on his game, dedicate himself and prove he can play at this level."

I said, "Great!"

If Kirk had gotten some decent offers, he'd have been gone. Instead, he dropped 10 pounds. He really started working on coming off screens. And he learned to get his shot off quicker.

Kirk became a very good shooting guard. As a junior, he scored 40 against Purdue, a nearby school that hadn't recruited him. And he had 29 a couple of times. As a senior, he was a very important player on a very good team.

His parents had followed Kirk all through his high school career. In their minds, if we'd done things the way we should've, he'd have averaged 20 a game. But they were very anti-Jud and anti-Michigan State his first two years and very pro-Michigan State at the end.

I still get a Christmas card from them every year, saying, "Thanks for all you did for Kirk! We really appreciate it!" And his last two years, we really appreciated him.

We always appreciated another great scorer who signed in '87. If he wasn't another Scott Skiles, he had the same initials and a lot more physical tools. He also finished his college career with 118 more points and one more Big Ten championship.

We went down to Detroit in the summer of '86 to look at a 6-11 center, Erik Wilson, who signed with Minnesota. And we saw this skinny kid out there, doing some real good things.

I said to Mike Deane, "Hey, find out that kid's name! And while you're at it, get his phone number."

His name was Steve Smith. And he became one of the greatest players in Big Ten basketball history.

When we called him, we learned he hadn't been to any camps whatsoever. Finally, he went to St. Cecilia's Summer League. We watched him there and started recruiting him very, very hard.

His high school coach, Johnny Goston, didn't want him to sign early. He wanted college coaches to see Steve and his other players, hoping they would get scholarships, too. I think he also wanted college coaches to see him coach and maybe offer him a job.

Steve was even kicked off the team briefly, when they had words over his decision. But Steve and Johnny worked out their differences. And Steve and the Pershing team had a very good year.

The common fallacy in the Steve Smith story is he was an unknown who wasn't highly recruited. The truth is he had 20 home visits—sometimes two a night. Don Monson at Oregon even had a home visit. So a lot of people knew about him by word of mouth. But not that many had really seen him play.

He made a trip to Missouri, then a visit to Michigan State, and committed to us in early October.

Right after that, I was down at the Detroit Athletic Club. And so was Bill Frieder. It was in the paper that morning that Steve had signed with us. But Bill didn't know who Steve Smith was. So he asked his former assistant, Don Sicko, the head coach at Detroit.

Bill said, "Do you know a Steve Smith?"

Sicko said, "Yeah, he was our top recruit."

"He was?" Bill said. "Geez, he must be pretty good!"

When we spoke and took some questions, they asked me, "Who are the top high school prospects in the state?"

I said, "Hey, you guys read the papers. I'm not the recruiter! Bill Frieder is the recruiter! So I'm going to let Bill answer that question."

Bill said, "Well, Michigan State just signed one of the top guard-forward prospects in the state in Steve Smith," then talked about some others.

The story was he went back to Ann Arbor and just chewed his assistants' butts up one side and down the other. They always felt if we recruited a kid in-state, they should be recruiting that kid.

I'll never forget Steve's first practice. Our first workout always came on Doug Weaver's birthday. And I always had Doug come down to say a few words to the team.

He'd always say, "It's great to be a Spartan! And I know you guys are going to kick some ass!" You know how Doug is. It'd always be the same speech with a couple of variations. And I just loved hearing it. He did a great job.

So when he came down, before he talked to the guys, he said, "How's it look?"

I said, "See that kid? He's going to be our next great guard."

"That skinny kid down there? You're kidding me!" he said.

"No, I'm not," I said.

It turned out I was right. We knew he had to get stronger. When he came in, he was really, really thin.

But after having Earvin and seeing what he could do at his size, we figured Steve could be a guard. In reality, he never was a true guard, in terms of all the things we wanted a guard to do.

Still, he was very good at the guard position because of size, ball skills and shooting range. What Steve could always do, like Sam, was get a shot for himself. With 2,263 points, Steve left as the fifth-leading scorer in conference history, a two-time All-American and a three-time team MVP.

Steve came in the same year as Jesse Hall, who'd had a lot more publicity. Jesse was all-state at Venice, Illinois —at a school with about 47 kids. He was also salutatorian of his class. In 45 years of coaching, I've probably had five truly great athletes. Eric Snow was one of them. And Jesse Hall was another. He could run and jump right out of the gym.

The difference was, when Eric struggled to be a guard, he worked and he worked and he worked. When Shawn Respert struggled to be a guard, he worked and he worked and he worked. Believe it or not, when Steve Smith struggled to be a guard, he worked and he worked and he worked.

At 6-3, Jesse Hall had to be a guard. Jesse worked on his game. But he never worked at being a guard. He'd say, "Why are you telling me I should be changing my game?"

If Jesse Hall had had Eric's work ethic, he'd be in the NBA right now or at least be a professional player. But Jesse didn't want to be coached and didn't want to work on what he couldn't do.

He always said, "Next to Steve Smith, I'm the best player out here!"

I said, "Yeah, you're the best player one-on-one. That's all—one-on-one. Not two-on-two. Not three-on-three. Not four-on-four. One-on-one. And we don't play basketball one-on-one. Nobody does. It's five-on-five."

That never changed as long as I coached. It's still five-on-five.

Jesse transferred to Southern Illinois. There, he could be a 6-3 forward. And I thought he'd go down and have a great year. Instead, he had a decent year, but nothing sensational.

We managed to keep Steve on our team for four years, though a lot of people thought he was ready for the NBA after his junior year.

If he'd left as a junior, he would've gone between 15th and 20th and made $5 million for five years. The next year, Steve went fifth and got $14.5 million for five years. He lost a million he would have gotten. But by staying, he signed for $9.5 million more. So he made an extra $8.5 million.

The thing that really hurt Steve's development as a pro was the knee injury. In order to be aggressive, you can't be fighting an injury. I know from fighting a knee injury all these years, he's probably favoring it subconsciously.

He probably came back too soon with Miami after his knee operation. But Steve has to be totally healthy before he can reach his potential. And he has to dedicate himself to that goal with Atlanta.

When I talked about Jay Vincent going unnoticed throughout his career, Steve is liable to have the same thing happen. Even though he made Dream Team II, unless Steve does a little more, that could happen.

I ran into Tucker and said, "Hey, I was disappointed in Steve in the Playoffs! He played great when he had the ball. But he did nothing the rest of the time and checked nobody!"

"Tell him that!" Tuck said.

I said, "I'm not going to tell him that! You tell him that!"

"I do!" he said. "He doesn't listen to me."

When I saw Tuck again, he said, "I told Steve what you said. . . . He doesn't want to see you. He thinks you're going to get all over him."

But I've said all along, unless Steve gets physically stronger, he'll be a good NBA player, but never a real impact player.

THE OFTEN-
FORGOTTEN FIVE

By the fall of '87, we'd started to assemble the pieces for another pretty good team. Ken Redfield and Kirk Manns were sophomores. And Steve Smith was an incoming freshman.

But the year Michigan State won the Rose Bowl, we brought in five kids from the state of Michigan. And people looked on that as a revival—the team of the future.

It just so happened some players from the state were rated high nationally that year. And when you get those players, you're listed as having a great recruiting class.

When you look at what they did for five years, great was probably too strong a word. But Matt Steigenga, Mark Montgomery, Mike Peplowski, Parish Hickman and Jon Zulauf were a very good group.

Matt started 123 of his 124 games, a Spartan career record, and scored 1,296 points between injuries, the program's 12th-best total.

Mark started 91 games and was No. 2 on the school's assist and steal lists when he left.

Pep was All-Big Ten his junior season and climbed to 16th in scoring and third in rebounding.

Parish had some moments to remember—and a few he'd like to forget.

And Jon nearly put us into the Sweet 16 with a sweet putback against Utah in the '92 Tournament.

With help from Redfield, Manns, Smith, Dwayne Stephens and Shawn Respert, they were part of a school-record 87 wins over a four-year period.

But before they scored a point, they were the focal point in a critical recruiting year—the one that signaled the start of seven straight winning seasons, with four 20-win marks.

Pep, a 6-10 center from Warren De La Salle, and Mark, a 6-2 point guard from Southgate Aquinas, committed in early October, right after a 17-11 win over Michigan in Spartan Stadium.

Pep wasn't going to go anywhere Terry Mills was. Terry Mills spit in his face when they were both in high school. So that meant Michigan was out of the running.

He was always really gung-ho. He'd been to Indiana and been to Purdue. He took a summer tour on his own. I think he was thinking about Indiana. But here was a chance to do something at Michigan State. For a year or two, Pep was leaning our way.

Mark's high school coach, Ernie Price, really helped us with him. Michigan was recruiting him. And he had been to Arizona. He was a highly recruited guy. Some guys get over-evaluated because of how they play in the summer or at a specific camp. But Mark had a lot of interest from a lot of schools.

It was funny to watch Michigan's approach with Mark and Matt. They told both players they were that year's No. 1 recruit and would be team captain their sophomore year.

Little did they know Matt and Mark were good friends and would talk on the phone from time to time. Apparently, the conversation went something like this:

"Hey, Matt, it's kind of kind of hard to turn down Michigan. I'm their No. 1 recruit. I'll be starting as a freshman and be captain there my sophomore year."

"Hey, Mark, I'm their No. 1 recruit! I'm supposed to be captain my sophomore year!"

When they compared notes on all the promises, Michigan moved down on their list of schools. But I think Mark was always leaning our way.

I think Matt was leaning our way, too. Still, there was the mystique of North Carolina. It got down to North Carolina and us. I think his step-dad, Carl Balk, thought, "Dean Smith has been in our home!" And that's impressive. You can't deny that.

But we did a good job recruiting Matt. Finally, he chose to stay closer to home. As an all-star game dunk champion, he had the biggest reputation of the five. And he was the last to sign.

By that time, we already had Parish, 6-7, and Jon, 6-6. They were both listed among the top 100 prospects in the nation.

What made it so unusual as a top recruiting class was they were all in-state kids. Matt was from Grand Rapids South Christian. Parish was from Redford Bishop Borgess. And Jon was from Port Huron.

Collectively, they were a good nucleus for any program. And they were a nice fit, in terms of position. We had a legitimate center, a power forward, a small forward, a shooting guard and a point guard, based on their college projections.

But I always thought Matt may have been better if we'd played him more at power forward, instead of always trying to play him at small forward. He was more at home around the basket. But everyone said he should be playing two-guard, because he could run and jump and shoot a little bit.

Bob Becker of the *Grand Rapids Press* thought Matt should have been the next Magic Johnson—and maybe he should've been. But one thing that always happens in-state is guys get overhyped. Here's a guy who was Mr. Basketball, but played with his back to the basket in a Class B league with no black kids. He had dominant size and athletic ability. And he was never really challenged.

For years, Tom Izzo kept saying, "Let's get Matt out of the starting lineup for a while! Maybe he'll play harder."

I said, "No, Matt will be more comfortable playing."

And if he and Pep hadn't had to overcome foot and knee problems, they could really have posted some impressive numbers.

Other programs have had injuries, too. But we've probably had more than our share over the years.

Peplowski missed his freshman year with knee reconstruction. Matt had three different stress fractures, meaning he was never the player he should have been, because he never got to practice or play in the off-season.

With Matt's personality, maybe he wouldn't have been much different. In my mind, had he been able to play more, he'd have been a much better player.

Matt was the MVP of the Oldsmobile Spartan Classic every year—Mr. Tournament, some writers called him.

One year, they had one name left to announce. And Parish was just sure they'd say, "Junior forward . . . Parish Hickman!" When they said, "Junior forward . . . " he started to get up. When they said, "Matt Steigenga!" Parish froze, then started to clap very slowly.

Everyone fell in love with Matt. He could jump out of the gym. And at 6-7, he looked like Adonis.

I still remember when Merrily Dean Baker became athletic director and had to give out some awards that May. She said, "Wow! Where did that kid come from?"

I said, "Yeah, he's kind of the women's choice."

Matt, Mark and Pep were Academic All-Big Ten selections—three straight years for Matt. Sometimes, to single out three guys as super young men and say they were great on and off the court almost puts a negative on all the other kids we've had.

It's almost the Dick Vitale syndrome: "Oh, that coach is really working the officials! Look at him!"

The guys who get up and raise hell are looked on as the ones who are coaching. The guys sitting there coaching their asses off look like they aren't doing anything.

But it's true. Matt, Mark and Pep were great kids on and off the court. They all got along. Yet, they all had deficiencies in their game.

I loved Pep. But he was one of the great talkers of all time. People were always so impressed. But he knew when to turn it on and turn it off. He told everyone he had seven knee operations—seven, my ass! What he had was one very serious, major operation, a second operation a little bit later and a series of arthroscopic flushouts and cleanouts.

That's like me saying I've had five or six operations on my knee. When people say, "Can't you do anything?" sometimes I tell them I've had five operations on my knee, because that shuts them up. But I haven't, even though they've gone into my knee five different times.

But any time you tear the anterior cruciate ligament, especially at his size, it can be a career-ending injury. Pep managed to come back. And each year, he got a little stronger.

The thing is, that really hurt Pep's development for two years. The year he came back, he only practiced half-time, because of the knee. And he hardly ever practiced hard in the off-season.

He and Matt both had a lot of things going for them. Basketball was a thing to do, not an obsession. If you're not dedicated to the game, it's hard to be great at it.

Yet, Pep and Matt were two guys that, if they hadn't been injured, would've been first-round pro picks. For the two years they were injured, they could've had the greatest desire in the world. It wouldn't have made any difference.

No one ever reaches his or her full potential. When I say the prayer before every game, I always say, "God, keep us free from injury and help us to play to our potential." Those are cliches. Yet, you're always striving to reach your potential. And we've had some guys who didn't come close, because they wouldn't put the time and effort in.

We had to make a point guard out of Mark Montgomery, who'd been an all-purpose player and more of a forward than a guard in high school. But he had two good hands. He was quick enough. He could accelerate with the ball. And he could do the things you wanted a point guard to do.

When you watched Earvin, sometimes he'd give the ball up after one dribble. You knew someone was going to be wide open. Good guard decisions mean giving the ball up at the right time, at the right place, to the right guy. Can you teach that? No. But you can talk about it until players recognize it and work on it.

Mark Montgomery recognized what he could do and what he couldn't. He had a great tournament in Maui in '91 and outplayed Lee Mayberry of Arkansas when we won the title. And for a guy we said couldn't shoot, he helped us win some games with open jumpers.

Mark led the league in assists two straight years. But he never made a lot of good guard decisions on the break. Eric Snow, to this day, never makes a lot of good guard decisions.

But what Eric and Mark did was learn to accelerate and look for guys to hit. They got better and better until you guys in the media would look at them and be fooled. And compared to the other teams in the league, they'd have given their left testicles to have a guy that good.

And Parish probably could have started for other teams in the Big Ten. He was definitely a Big Ten player. But he was a center in high school. He was kind of limited.

He was another guy who didn't work very hard at his game. He loved to play when it was playground style or St. Cecilia style. He loved a game that was 115-110, where he scored 28 points and eight of those baskets were dunks.

Suddenly, we had a center. But maybe Parish should've played more instead of Matt. You could make a case for that, I think.

Parish had some good games. He could jump and rebound. But he was a guy who was never happy. Parish always thought more of Parish than he did of the team. A lot of guys are like that.

The "me" generation of the '80s has turned into the "I" generation of the '90s. In other words, there is no difference. Kids are very selfish today. But they've always been selfish, in terms of playing time and scoring.

In my era, I was disappointed things didn't work out differently in my career. But today, kids are pissed off at the world if things don't go their way.

Parish was always going to transfer. First, he was going to go to Detroit. Then, he talked about other schools. He had a very good game against Georgia Tech in the '90 Tournament. But after the drug charge, he transferred to Liberty his senior year.

Matt was a second-round choice of the Bulls and wound up with a great financial deal in Japan. Pep was a second-round pick of Sacramento, had a fill-in shot with the Pistons and went to Spain. And Mark played in Germany.

They all played well enough to have their places in Spartan basketball history.

BRESLIN AND
OTHER BUILDING

Jenison Field House was awful—and super. It was an awful place to sell to recruits and a super place to play for a home-court advantage.

Doug Weaver always thought Jenison was the greatest thing since Pepsi-Cola. He could still relate to being a student in the early '50s and would feel the excitement. We always used to say he'd be standing on the steps, guarding the place with a gun, if anyone ever tried to tear it down.

But it was clear to almost everyone else we needed a new arena. As soon as I got here, I said, "This place is antiquated. We have to have a new building."

The kids from Indiana and the Chicago area would compare Jenison with Assembly Hall at Indiana or Assembly Hall at Illinois. That really hurt. And the kids we tried to recruit from New York just couldn't believe it.

In recruiting, we used to sell everything as a positive. We didn't badmouth anyone else. But we were always ashamed of the place we played.

We said, "This is a great school. The Big Ten is a great conference. We're on national TV a lot. And you'll get a lot of exposure. If you want to go where basketball is important, it's important at Michigan State. We sell out almost all our games. And you'll play in sold-out arenas that are exciting, whether you're home or on the road. A degree from any Big Ten school is as good as any degree there is."

Then, we'd always have to apologize for Jenison Field House.

If a kid was considering Michigan State at that point, he could say, "There's an opportunity to play. The guys are good. They like to run. And Jud has a reputation for developing players." But to a lot of kids, Jenison was a big enough minus to override all those things.

I remember when Granville Waiters came to visit. It was down to Ohio State and us. And he had to decide whether he wanted to play behind Herb Williams for two years or come in and be a starter at Michigan State. He walked into Jenison Field House and said, "You play HERE? . . . Where are the baskets?"

There weren't any baskets up. Guys were jogging around the track. And that's what it looked like—a big jogging barn.

You'd show them pictures from when it was filled and have guys tell them it was a great place to play. But it was hard for them to visualize that when they were making comparisons with top-flight programs.

We always tried to get guys to come in for big games, so they could see Jenison when it was really jumping. But it was hard to bring guys in during the season, especially out-of-state guys, because of the weather, their schedules, our schedule and everything else.

With in-state kids, it was never a problem. They could identify with it from the state tournament. And they saw nothing wrong with Jenison.

They'd tried to build a new facility and failed in '69. They let the students vote, and they voted it down. In '69, the students would have voted down anything other than free sex.

Finally, they started talking about it in the early '80s. But construction costs were escalating week by week. There was just no money. Funding for the University was being squeezed.

That's when I made the statement, "We will have a new arena! . . . It just won't happen in my lifetime."

When the trustees gave the final approval for the building in '84, naturally, I was in the hospital, recovering from my heart attack.

So when Doug came down to tell me the good news, I said, "I guess I was supposed to die, so we could get the arena. But I fooled them!" I don't know. Maybe that got us the last sympathy vote we needed.

The sad thing is Cecil Mackey, our president at the time, never got the credit he deserved. He just said the students would benefit and they would have to pay for it. If they didn't like it, he said they shouldn't come to school here.

And the students are still paying for it. Of their tuition, $2 per credit hour goes toward paying for Breslin, the new intramural building and the tennis facility. It was all a package.

Cecil was a big tennis buff. And he said, "We had to get the tennis facility! So we decided to throw Breslin in with it."

Cecil did a great job for us. I loved the guy. But by the time he learned how to be president, he'd made too many enemies on campus. He came in from Alabama with an autocratic approach and a hatchet man named Ken Thompson.

First, they got into a hassle with the alumni. If you picked up the alumni magazine, you'd read about pollution on campus and how the University was the worst culprit. And the issue about the '76 probation seemed to say we deserved it.

Cecil didn't believe the alumni magazine should take negative positions on campus issues or charge the University with violating environmental laws. And I have to agree with him.

Then, he tried to dissolve the nursing school. We had to make some cuts somewhere. But that was too drastic. With the backlash he got, we still have the nursing school. Once Cecil learned the politics of the place, it was too late.

But he was instrumental in getting the Jack Breslin Student Events Center built. I've suggested many times to many people that the tennis facility should be named after Cecil Mackey, and the indoor football facility should be named after Doug Weaver . . . . . I'm still hoping.

After we moved to Breslin, there was no reason to apologize for anything about the program. The problem was it took forever.

The new concept in those days was to go through a management firm, responsible for all phases of construction. So when we had our first planning meeting, Nick Vista, the sports information director, was there, Karen Langeland, our women's basketball coach, was there. The concert and entertainment people were there. And I was there.

A guy said, "Jud, let's start with you first. You say you'd really like a spacious locker room for the varsity."

"Yeah, I'd really like a nice, big locker room," I said.

"No problem there," he said. "Now, you could probably get by with a little less space for your junior-varsity."

"We haven't had a JV team in a number of years. We gave it up for budget reasons," I said, suspecting right then we might be in trouble.

Nick said, "We'd like computers here and here. And we'd like a big press room."

The special events people said, "We want a huge star room and several smaller star rooms."

And I said, "The big thing is, we'll need an auxiliary gym," something I don't think they'd even thought of.

At the time, they'd allocated $33 million. But there was a hidden $5 million they could get.

At about the third meeting, I said, "You know, you've never questioned one thing we've asked for. Can you build this facility with the $33 million allocated and meet all the requests we've made?" They said, "We'll have no problem with that whatsoever."

Then, they came back and said, "We can build the building everyone wants, with all the requests that have been made, for $65 million." We had to redo all the plans. And we lost a complete year.

My recommendation was to fire that management firm and start over. But it was hard to borrow money then. We'd already borrowed at least $30 million. So they didn't want to have to go through that again. Instead, they told us to cut back and see what we could do without.

And I never went to another meeting.

I said, "Hey, let someone else figure out what's going to be in there."

By not doing that, today, we have a small locker room. The visiting locker room isn't very big. The only thing we saved was the auxiliary gym.

I convinced Doug if they cut that out, we should go raise the money ourselves, because it had to be there. We couldn't come over in the middle of the winter and practice in Jenison every time there was an event in Breslin.

The cost of the auxiliary gym was $960,000. Yet, it was budgeted to cost $4 million. It wasn't in the original plan. And they were trying to cover their asses with the escalation of costs.

As it turned out, they said the building cost $43 million. They probably put $3 million more in, counting everything. So it's roughly a $46 million facility.

I'd fought since Day One to chair all the bleacher seats. Originally, the whole thing was chaired. We could've come in for another $300,000 and chaired everything. But our approach was, except for the auxiliary gym, we wouldn't use a dime of athletic department money. Originally, they tried to make the entire building an athletic department facility.

I told Doug, "Whatever you do, don't let them do that! This place has to lose money. Let some other area of the University take that loss. Don't make this an albatross around the athletic department's head."

Instead, they charged us rent. We were their biggest client— and still are.

Every year they try to escalate it, robbing Peter to pay Paul. Our vice-president, Roger Wilkinson, is in charge of both facilities. Breslin always shows a loss, and basketball shows a huge profit. Two years ago, we made $4 million in basketball. So they want to take that money through higher rent.

I told Merrily, "Don't let them do that! You can hardly make your budget now. Don't let them rob you. You've got gender equity and Olympic sports to worry about. You've got all kinds of arguments not to pay more rent."

Breslin, when it was finally built, was a great structure for basketball. But when they put in the first weight room, it was a telephone booth. It was a postage stamp.

I said to Gene Kenney, "Gene! How could you let them do that? You told us we'd have as big a weight room as we had in Jenison!"

He said, "I thought all you needed was what you said on the width."

I said, "No, that was narrow and long. This is narrow and short. Does that mean it's as big as the other one?"

Another oversight! And it took us three years of negotiation with Breslin, the facilities committee and the administration to build a new weight room for men's and women's basketball.

Everyone said the building was done on schedule. That's bullshit. It was two years late, in terms of when it was supposed to be done. For three years, I told guys, "You'll play one year in Jenison and your last three years in the new building."

It was approved in '84. And it didn't open until '89. Now, you tell me that's completion on schedule! It was completed three years after the indoor football and the tennis facility were finished.

They cut back the seats just a little bit. We were supposed to get 16,000 in there. They list 15,138 now. And we probably have 15,500 in there a lot of times.

The whole arena was supposed to have chairs like Iowa, not chairs and a few benches upstairs. Then, they cut that out to save money. I said I'd never retire until they corrected that. And every year, that was the No. 1 thing I asked for. There's a stigma attached to sitting on those benches—or anywhere near them.

When it came time to select seats, we had more people unhappy than happy. So many seats had been allocated for the trustees, for the administration, for basketball and for everything else, by the time the first people with high priority numbers walked in, 1,000 seats were already gone.

Then, a lot of people had to be moved. I argued there should be some relief for the season ticket holders of a certain period. Maybe they could only set aside 500 seats. But there should be a category for loyalty to the program that had nothing to do with contributions to anything. They wouldn't buy it. But I still believe that.

If you were in Jenison Field House for 20 years with season tickets and were moved to Breslin's upper bowl, because you hadn't given a dime to the University, I don't think that's fair. Hey, some guys can't afford to give to the University. Some people shouldn't give to the University, because this isn't their University! They live here. And they're basketball fans. That's it!

Even though I'm an Honorary Coach at Michigan State, which is a $1,200 annual donation, I give $1,000 every year to Washington State and $500 to Montana. And in my mind, I should be giving more to Washington State than to Michigan State. Washington State is my alma mater.

But through the years, the No. 1 reason coaches have been fired hasn't been wins and losses. Believe it or not, it has been attendance. Maybe those things are related. In any event, our attendance has almost always been near capacity in Jenison and Breslin. Through the years, we've had a lot of loyal fans.

With the new construction and the recruitment of Matt, Mike and Pep, there was a lot more enthusiasm about our program in '88, even more than in '86. We were talking about a new era in Spartan basketball. We were supposed to move into Breslin that year. As it was, we didn't move in until a year later.

That year, there wasn't a great, new excitement, the way there was when Earvin arrived, just an expectation we'd be better than we'd been the previous two years. And we were.

In '89, we were only 6-12 in the league. But with Steve, Kirk and Ken Redfield, we won enough games overall to get an NIT bid, which we thought was just great for that young team.

We rallied to beat Kent State by 14 in Detroit's Cobo Arena, got past Wichita State by 12 in the final game in Jenison and surprised Villanova with a seven-point win in Philadelphia.

That put us in the NIT Final Four in Madison Square Garden. But in New York, we lost to St. Louis, which had a much better team. Then, we lost in overtime to UAB in the consolation game.

Since we moved into Breslin, we've been a consistent Top 30 program. In a few of those years, we've been Top 20 and once Top 10.

But no one expected us to win the league title in '90, including us. We fooled them all, with Steve having a tremendous year and Kirk and Ken coming through as seniors.

Kirk had finally learned to catch the ball and let it go. If he caught it and held onto it a second, someone would be standing on his toe.

Ken was our second-best all-around player. He could run on the break. He could rebound. And we got him a lot of publicity as a defensive specialist —a role he detested at first, then accepted, but never embraced or relished.

Ken always saw himself as a better offensive player than he was. But every year, he got a little bit better. It wasn't as much from hard work as from better recognition. Ken went out and played a lot. He was very intelligent. He recognized what he had to do better. And he did that by playing.

We started the '89-90 season by going up to the Great Alaska Shootout. We beat Auburn, Texas A&M and Kansas State in Anchorage. And that became a springboard. We didn't expect to win that tournament. We were just hoping to win two games.

We always went into a tournament like that and said, "We're as good as those teams. Let's try to win it!"

The Great Alaska Shootout and the Maui Invitational, which we won by beating Arkansas two years later, have always drawn some pretty good teams—maybe not eight, but at least three or four. And that gave us a pretty good start.

I thought we always had a better team than the ratings did, except Street & Smith's. We knew we weren't a seventh- or eighth-place team in the conference. We'd been to the Final Four of the NIT. And we had everyone back. That should've been a sign we were decent.

We lost two games in the preseason—to Illinois-Chicago and Bowling Green. We played awful at Illinois-Chicago. But we played well at home against Bowling Green and still lost. When we beat Princeton 51-49 in the Oldsmobile Spartan Classic, I was thinking we weren't as good as I'd hoped.

But with Steve injured, we won our first three conference games at Wisconsin and against Ohio State and Iowa. We were 5-1, then, lost two in a row—a two-pointer at Michigan when Rumeal Robinson hit a running hook on the final shot and a miserable game at home against Minnesota.

After that we won 12 in a row, including two in overtime. We won 10 straight in the Big Ten and our first two in the Tournament.

The two games Steve had within 48 hours, with 36 in a win over Michigan and 39 in an unbelievable victory at Minnesota, were the two best back-to-back games in my coaching career.

His play against Michigan was flawless at both ends of the court. But then, he played even better at Minnesota. He was 28-for-49 from the field and 10-for-12 at the line.

We were one game ahead with one to go. Then, we hosted Purdue with a chance to win the outright championship. But with Kirk's stress fracture, we knew we had to play Mark Montgomery a lot.

At the end of the game, there was a wild scramble. Mark knocked the ball loose. Dwayne Stephens, a freshman, came up with it and laid it in. And all hell broke loose in Breslin.

That was the infamous no-call where Gene still says Tony Jones was fouled. I told him, "Hey, if the guy is an all-conference guard, he should be able to take care of the ball whether he was fouled or not." He always said, "You're right!"

If the '79 Ohio State game was the most memorable of my 19 seasons at Michigan State, the '90 Purdue game would have to be the best in Breslin. We still show that tape to recruits.

We went into the tournament as the top seed in the Southeast—the first and only time Michigan State has ever been a No. 1 —and had to fight for our lives.

We couldn't get anyone to believe Murray State was any good. No one had heard about Popeye Jones until he scored 37 against Pep. And we barely survived when Kirk came off the bench and made an unbelievable layup to send it into overtime. He just threw it off the board, and the ball went in. It was one of the greatest shots in Michigan State history. Otherwise, we'd have been the only No. 1 seed ever to lose to a No. 16.

We beat Cal-Santa Barbara by four. It was kind of a grinder. But we were never behind. It probably should have been a 10-point win.

Then, we traveled to New Orleans to play Georgia Tech in the Superdome. They had "Lethal Weapon III," with Kenny Anderson, Dennis Scott and Brian Oliver. We were ahead after 40 minutes had elapsed, but still lost the game. And according to the rules, that's hard to do.

We finished 15-3 and 28-6. It was the winningest season in school history and one of the best. But we could've had 30 wins —and, who knows, maybe 32 if we'd finished the job in Denver, as we had 11 years earlier in Salt Lake City.

'Stars from The Capitol City'

EARVIN "MAGIC" JOHNSON
Lansing (Mich.) Everett High School
Michigan State 1977-79
Currently with Los Angeles Lakers

JAY VINCENT
Lansing (Mich.) Eastern High School
Michigan State 1977-81
Currently with Dallas Mavericks

SPARTANS 11

Michigan State's
SAM VINCENT
Lansing (Mich.) Eastern High School
Michigan State 1982-85
All-America Candidate

Sam Vincent gets All-America publicity with a pair of prior "Stars from the Capitol City." (Michigan State University)

Jud makes a point to floor leader and future coach Scott Skiles in a surprising 1986 season. (Lansing State Journal)

Fiery Scott Skiles leads a close-but-not-quite effort against Kansas. (Michigan State University)

Jack Breslin, known as "Mr. MSU," with a hard-hatted Jud.

The long-awaited Breslin Student Events Center, a state-of-the-art facility for basketball.

The 1990 Big Ten champions: (back) trainer Tom Mackowiak, coach Jim Boylen, Ken Redfield, Parish Hickman, Matt Hofkamp, Mike Peplowski, David Mueller, Matt Steigenga, Steve Smith, Dwayne Stephens, coach Tom Crean; (front) coach Herb Williams, Jon Zulauf, Todd Wolfe, Kirk Manns, Jud, Mark Montgomery, Jeff Casler, Jesse Hall, manager Eric Spiller, coach Tom Izzo. (Michigan State University)

Jud and Michigan State hockey coach Ron Mason with their 1990 championship hardware.

Steve Smith accelerates and leaves as his school's leading scorer. (Michigan State University)

Mark Montgomery and Jud at practice during the 1990 NCAA Tournament. (Rod Sanford/Lansing State Journal)

Jud looks at the clock in disbelief after Georgia Tech's tying shot after the buzzer in Clock Game II. (Rod Sanford/Lansing State Journal)

NBA Commissioner David Stern and Steve Smith, the first-round pick of the Miami Heat in 1991. (Nathaniel Butler/NBA Photos)

Jud and Shawn Respert share a joke when Respert announces he'll stay at Michigan State as a senior. (Lansing State Journal)

Backcourt tandem Eric Snow and Shawn Respert celebrate a score in their sensational senior seasons. (Rod Sanford/ Lansing State Journal)

Shawn Respert smooches the S at center court after his last collegiate home game. (Margie Garrison/Lansing State Journal)

A.D. to coach, friend to friend. (Michigan State University)

As Jud always says, "Sooner or later, the game makes fools of us all . . . and I'm living proof." (Rod Sanford/Lansing State Journal)

Some rings you can't buy on the Home Shopping Network. (Rod Sanford/Lansing State Journal)

Don Monson and Jud can't score any baskets in 1977.

Herb Williams, Jud, and Mike Deane fight for survival in 1986.

Jud and his chosen successor, Tom Izzo, lead the Spartans to sustained success.

The brotherhood of Big Ten coaches in 1991: (back) Purdue's Gene Keady, Indiana's Bob Knight, Ohio State's Randy Ayers, Northwestern's Bill Foster, Minnesota's Clem Haskins; (front) Wisconsin's Steve Yoder, Iowa's Tom Davis, Illinois' Lou Henson, Jud, Michigan's Steve Fisher.

Purdue coach Gene Keady and Jud share a laugh before the 1995 Big Ten championship game. (Michigan State University)

Jud's Most Valuable Partner, Bev Heathcote. (Rod Sanford/ Lansing State Journal)

A good coach and a good guy says goodbye after his final game in Breslin Center. (Rod Sanford/ Lansing State Journal)

WHEN TIME
STANDS STILL

A lot of times, I think I was close to having a third national championship team.

Everyone remembers what happened in '79. But in '73, I was also the handball coach at Montana when we won an NCAA title.

Two games at Michigan State probably caused more hands to hit the top of my head —the famous Jud-thuds—than any other. And both were games we should've won in the Tournament's Sweet 16.

In '86, Kansas was the Midwest's No. 1 seed and had just beaten Temple by 22 when we faced them in Kemper Arena. They were 33-3 at the time. But we rallied from nine down in the second half to take a 62-61 lead on a Barry Fordham jumper.

When Danny Manning fouled out and Vernon Carr hit two free throws, we were up 76-72 with 2:21 to play. That's when play continued for as many as 19 seconds with no time coming off the clock. The timer, Larry Bates, said it was a clock malfunction. I said it was sheer incompetence and let my feelings be known on the sideline.

When Scott was fouled with 1:39 left, Larry Brown wanted a technical foul called on me and drew one himself for hitting the referee's whistle. Scott made the technicals, then missed a one-

and-one. And with a free possession, Barry hit another jumper to make it 80-74.

The Jayhawks scored three baskets in the last 51 seconds, the last one on a tip-in by Archie Marshall with :09 showing. If the clock had worked . . .

But we were the best shooting team in the country that year. And we missed three free throws and a chance at six points from the line in the last 99 seconds of regulation. So we can't say we didn't have our chances to win.

I still blame fatigue, more than anything else, for the missed free throws. We were just out of gas at the end. But I still thought we could hang on for the win.

The same was true four years later in New Orleans. That time, we were the No. 1 seed. And Georgia Tech was No. 4. Bobby Cremins' team had just beaten LSU, with Chris Jackson, Stanley Roberts and some guy named Shaquille.

The Yellow Jackets scored the first eight points and led for almost all the first 30 minutes. Then, we edged in front and matched our biggest lead, four points, when Dwayne Stephens hit two free throws with 13 seconds to go.

They called a timeout. And I told our players exactly what they'd do. They were going to get the ball to Kenny Anderson and have him take it the length of the court as fast as he could, just as we would've with Steve Smith. I said, "Before we let him take it all the way, we'll have to foul him, if we can't do anything else."

But Mark let Anderson go right by him for a layup that made it 75-73.

Afterward, I said, "Why didn't we foul him?"

Mark said, "Because I had four fouls," as if that makes any difference at the end of a game.

We were still two up with six seconds to go. When we threw it in, Steve held the ball for a few seconds, then was clubbed. There should have been three seconds left. But only one second came off the clock.

Steve missed the one-and-one with five seconds showing, instead of three. That was a big difference. They got the rebound. And Anderson raced down the floor for a flying 19-footer that tied the score.

I questioned Anderson's shot at the time. I ran out there, and the official said, "We'll handle it! We'll handle it! We'll decide if it's a three or a two."

I said, "No! How about the time? Wasn't the time up?"

They were so worried about whether it was a three or a two, they weren't even thinking about the time. They were supposed to have a red light behind the basket, which, of course, they didn't. And there was no calibrated clock. They were just poor facilities.

But I said again, "Didn't he shoot it after the buzzer?" They had no idea about that and finally decided it was a two. So we went into overtime. We were up one point in overtime. Then, Dennis Scott hit a 12-foot hook shot with :07 showing.

We called a timeout with four seconds left and had plenty of time to get a shot at the basket. Steve had 32 points already. We diagrammed a play. But instead, Ken Redfield wound up taking a long, poor-percentage shot.

I was so upset I could hardly talk. We had a chance to win it in regulation and a chance to win it in overtime. We didn't.

And after the game, three media guys who were sitting right on the court told me Anderson's shot was definitely after the buzzer. That's what the CBS replay had shown. The headline that Sunday in *The Detroit News* said: "'We got cheated again'— Heathcote boils after MSU's controversial loss to Tech."

The next week, I got a scathing letter from the Tournament Committee.

So I wrote a two-page letter back and said, "At no time did I say that. Under the circumstances, I think I handled that about as well as it could've been handled. Now, if you want to put the onus on somebody, please don't put it on me. Put it on the officials, who did a very poor job. After what happened with the Kansas game, if we've done something wrong, you guys have done more wrong to Michigan State."

It wasn't Larry Bates who ran the clock in New Orleans, though I thought they may have imported him from Kansas at halftime.

Actually, the Kansas game was harder to swallow than the Georgia Tech game. Two Jayhawk starters fouled out. So why couldn't we have won in overtime? Because we were absolutely exhausted. We'd played our hearts out.

The Georgia Tech game, I thought we should've been good enough to win in overtime. But we weren't.

Neither clock incident lost us the game. It might have cost us the game, but it didn't lose us the game. If anything did, it was missed free throws. Against Kansas, Skiles missed one. Polec missed one. And Mark Brown missed the last one. Against Georgia Tech, if Steve had made one at the end of regulation, we'd have won and played Minnesota again in the Southeast Final.

Instead, Georgia Tech advanced to the Final Four in Denver and lost by nine to UNLV, the national champ.

You look at the Skiles team and the Steve Smith team and wonder, "If that hadn't happened, how far would we have gone? Would we have been back in the Final Four? Did we have enough talent?"

The next season, *Basketball Times* thought we did and picked us No. 1 in the nation. I had Marv come in from Washington every year for four days. And it didn't take him long to see that wasn't going to happen.

Marv said, "Jud, this isn't nearly as good as last year's club—even in the fall, before you got better."

I said, "Marv, I know that! I keep telling the media we're not nearly as good as we were. And no one is buying it. I hope, for once, the media is right and I'm wrong. But you can't take the No. 2 and No. 3 scorers away and have no one to pick up that slack."

Kirk and Ken were gone. But everyone thought Matt would have a breakthrough season. And of course, we had Steve back. He was an All-American. Plus, we had Mark and Pep. And Parish had done a good job against Georgia Tech.

But Steve played better as a junior than he did as a senior. He played more within the framework of the team in '90. His last season, he felt he had to carry the team. He had a lower shooting percentage and took some very questionable shots.

We were decent in '91, nothing more. We tied for third in the Big Ten at 11-7 and were 19-11 overall. Seeded fifth in the West, we barely got by Wisconsin-Green Bay on a buzzer-beater from Steve. Then, we lost to Utah by a point in double-overtime in Tucson.

But those Tournaments weren't the first times we'd lost at the end. We'd been through that before—even in '79.

Arnette Hallman hit a shot for Purdue he had no business taking. Eddie Johnson beat us at the buzzer at Illinois. Keith Smith hit a foul shot at Michigan with no time left. And Wes Matthews hit a shot from his half of the court at Wisconsin to keep us from winning the title outright.

Then, there were games that were lost before the buzzer, but were every bit as disappointing.

No. 1 on the list of games I'd want back in my career was when all we had to do was beat Idaho State at home and we'd have gone to the NCAA Tournament for the first time in Montana history.

You have to remember I was an old young coach. I was older. But I'd only been coaching three years. I'd fought everybody to get the program where it was. . . . And we lost.

You always look back at games you won that did something for you and games you lost that didn't do something. Against Idaho State, they went zone, and our guards had a horrible night. That game still haunts me.

It was a home game, too. I always have great confidence at home in overtime. That's how dumb I am. The only time I haven't been confident was the Iowa game in 1993, when they made that fantastic comeback from 18 down in the second half. I knew we had nothing left.

Comebacks are great for the fans, not for the coaches. I still prefer the 45-second clock to the 35-second clock. But that's a coach's view. I'm not sure that's what's best for the game. We're involved in entertainment. And if you're going to have people pay to see you, you have to give them the best product you can.

That doesn't mean coaches have to endorse everything that turns the game into pivot-pass-and-tear-ass, because that's what a lot of casual fans want. The true basketball fans still appreciate a little chess game between the offense and the defense.

I think 35 seconds made it a better game for most fans and most players, but not for most coaches. And there's a feeling that permeates the profession that the game is for the kids, not for the coaches. But the more you limit possession time, the less control you have as a coach.

I also recognize that you're going to be behind in a lot of games. And those extra 10 seconds you don't have to play defense can give you an extra possession or two to catch up.

When you look at the Iowa game in '93 and some others when we lost big leads, it almost breaks my heart. That one probably ruined our season. And we can always say if we'd had a 45-second-clock, we'd have won.

I'm sure we've had games work the other way, too. It probably balances out. Yet, in coaching, you remember the losses a lot longer than the wins.

In '92, we finished 11-7 again, tied for third in the league with Michigan's Fab Five freshmen, but lost to Cincinnati, a team we'd already beaten in December, in the Midwest's second round in Dayton.

Matt got zero points. Pep got two. And all summer, I wondered, "Was that my fault? Was that a poor coaching job?" Maybe it was.

All you can do is prepare and adjust. That's one thing Earvin still remembers. We were always prepared. We always had a game plan.

I remember Rob Judson telling a Lou Henson story, where they were down to the last shot, and Lou said, "OK, guys. Let's go out and . . . and get a good shot!"

They did that and Illinois won. Sometimes we're guilty of overcoaching, when maybe free-lancing would yield better results.

I'll never forget when Chris Webber hit two 3's we wanted him to take in a game we fought so hard to try to win. Sometimes you do everything right and lose. It still depends on whether the ball goes in the basket.

It's funny. People ask, "What would have happened if Earvin had gone to Michigan?" But I have to wonder, "How much better would the last few years have been if Chris Webber had come to Michigan State?"

People say, "If Chris had come to Michigan State, he would've had a jump shot." I say you can't coach guys you don't have. It's hard enough coaching your own guys.

I don't think you can blame his coaches, including Steve Fisher, for anything that has happened. People talk about the illegal time out against North Carolina. In our game in Ann Arbor at the end of that season, one we lost in overtime, Chris called a timeout without knowing if they had one. They could have lost that game.

But I can empathize with Chris and Steve. In the tournament, when it's your time, it's your time. When it isn't, seconds can seem like years. And they have.

LIVING AND LEAVING
ON MY TERMS

In '92-93, we were 15-13 and lost at Oklahoma in the first round of the NIT. It was a strange year. We were better than that. But we didn't play any better than that.

And that was the first time I'd seriously considered retiring. I always said I'd coach until I was 65. That May, I turned 65. I wasn't tired of coaching. But I was disappointed in the way things had gone.

I'd always thought your last year should be a good one, if humanly possible. Yet, in reality, as the years pass, what difference does it make? When people look back at your coaching career, they look at totals and titles more than anything else.

I sensed Bev would really like to be closer to our two girls in Seattle. I'd always approached retirement with the idea there comes a time. I knew I couldn't coach forever.

When you look at some of the guys who coached a long time, Marv would still be coaching if they hadn't forced him out. Ray Meyer at DePaul quit at 70, lost his wife and, to this day, wishes he was still coaching. Ralph Miller at Oregon State stayed a year or two longer than he planned and maybe longer than he should've.

When Tom Izzo was named the next head coach at Michigan State, I was supposed to get a two-year contract extension.

But Gordon Guyer, the interim president, backed away from that and said he didn't want to obligate the new guy any longer than necessary.

Joel Ferguson was irate and thought that was something of a double-cross from the original agreement. Joel had already secured Board approval for the two-year extension. And Tom Izzo said I should take the two-year extension and forget about him. I said, "No, I'm not going to coach that long anyway. So let's not even make it an issue."

I took the one-year extension so Tom could be named the head coach when I retired. I wanted continuity in the program and felt Tom deserved the job.

It got to the point I didn't want to stay longer than I should. So in May of '93, I was about 70-30—70 percent to retire and maybe 30 percent to go one more year. I was going to make that decision in the summer. Tom was in place. And it would've been a smooth transition.

Then, the Parish Hickman allegations came up. No way was I going out because of accusations made by an attorney, planted by a newspaper guy. These weren't accusations by Parish himself.

After he was charged with conspiracy to distribute cocaine and possession with intent to deliver in April of '91, Parish was placed on University probation.

No drugs were recovered. And Parish said it was all a hoax to try to scam $28,000 out of a Drug Enforcement Administration agent—not the brightest thing any of our players had ever done.

He was acquitted late that November, while the team was in Maui, and wanted to return to the program.

He said, "Coach, I really want to stay at Michigan State!"

I said, "Parish, it's best if you get out of here—best for you."

But we never told Parish he couldn't come back and never told him he wouldn't have a scholarship. We said it was best for him to leave, under the circumstances.

Two years later, someone said, "Aren't you surprised Parish is suing the school?"

I said, "No, I knew some attorney would figure out he had a suit there. And do you think he's paying that attorney a dime? No!"

Among other things, in a story in *The Detroit News* on June 6, 1993, Parish was quoted as saying he'd received cash after games from a booster, Fred Tripp, and been given no-work jobs by Joel Ferguson, the chairman of the MSU Board of Trustees.

I was in total shock. If I had to bet my life on someone's integrity, I'd have bet on Fred Tripp a long time before I'd have bet on Parish. And if I'd taken pride in anything over the years, it was in running a clean program. So for me to go out looking like I was asked to resign because of attorney fabrications was absolutely out of the question.

On a Saturday night, June 19, or shall I say Sunday morning, June 20, my phone rang at 1:30 a.m. I jumped out of bed to answer it. And it was Parish.

"Coach, I've got to talk to you," he said. "I don't like what the attorney and that newspaper guy are telling me to say. I've got great respect for you and the program. And I don't like the way this is going. I need to talk to you and Tom."

I said, "How about Monday morning at 10?" And Parish said he'd be there.

When I got to the office Monday, I told Tom about the call. I also told him if he had anything to do that morning to do it, since Parish probably wouldn't be there. He wasn't. And I haven't seen him since.

But we got Parish a scholarship to Liberty. We called down to UTEP. They thought about taking him, then backed off. The same thing happened with New Orleans. But Liberty would give anybody a new chance.

And some other people saw a chance to build a case at my expense. The attorney said, "We want a settlement, or we're going to embarrass the school and the athletic program."

We could've settled that thing before the accusations came out. But we weren't going to let them blackmail the department. I don't even know the attorney. But anybody who'd do something like that is ridiculous. He'll hide behind the idea that those were things Parish told him. In reality, they were things he told Parish to tell him.

Fred Girard of *The Detroit News*, the guy who broke the story, is the same way. Fred Girard is an absolute sleaze, the way he writes with half-truths and innuendo.

When I talked to Fred and his sports editor, Phil Laciura, I taped the meeting. I didn't let them know it. Then, my buzzer went off.

I said, "Oh, by the way, I have to change my tape."

They were shocked. They said, "Why?"

I said, "This is liable to go to court. I don't want any second-hand hearsay like I seem to be reading in the paper."

Fred said, "All we're trying to do is be fair."

I looked at his boss and said, "You talk about being fair, and you're in a position to ruin careers with hearsay from a guy you've probably planted words with. When you guys drive home, talk to each other about what's really fair. This whole thing is totally unfair."

When the story came out in the papers in June, we'd already had a meeting with the administration.

See, I know how the NCAA operates. I've known David Berst, their head of enforcement, from being on the coaches' board of directors. But everyone runs scared. They think you have to do this and have to do that.

So I said, "We shouldn't even honor these accusations with an internal investigation. Let's invite the NCAA to come in and investigate this."

Merrily said, "Oh, no! You can't do that! Then, they'll really have it in for you."

I said, "No, the NCAA wants us to do their work. They want us to find something they can punish us for. That's how the NCAA works. And that's ridiculous!"

I was overruled. Everyone said I was overreacting, because I was involved. And I admit I had absolute tunnel vision about the investigation. My integrity was being questioned. If God had handled that, I don't think I would have been satisfied. I thought it was an insult.

You have to prove yourself innocent. The NCAA doesn't have to prove you guilty. That's not our judicial system. But that's the way they operate. And they're getting more and more litigation because of it.

But to this day, I say the NCAA should've come in and investigated. The NCAA should have come in and investigated the football allegations last fall with Roosevelt Wagner, too. We don't need to hire two outside guys and pay them. If you're going to get paid, you've really got to find something.

I told the president, Peter McPherson, I told Roger Wilkinson and I told Joel, "This isn't how the University is supposed to work. We're going to pay the investigators a half-million dollars to check on some malcontent who has no credibility."

In fact, I remember when former president Clifton Wharton just blasted the NCAA. He was at the State University of New York then. But he said Michigan State's football penalties in the '70s were more severe because the NCAA said we had a hostile attitude when all we wanted was due process.

Anyway, they appointed a three-person committee—Clarence, Mike Kasavana, the faculty rep, and Merrily. And Merrily was mainly a figurehead, with Clarence and Mike doing the investigation.

It wouldn't have mattered. There was nothing there. But Clarence started out on a mission to find something. Finally, people started telling Clarence to back off.

As the investigation progressed, it seemed to have a three-fold mission. No. 1 was to exonerate Joel Ferguson. No. 2 was to find a fall guy, who happened to be Fred Tripp. And No. 3 was to find as many minor violations as possible, so the major violations would kind of disappear.

The whole time I argued, "All we should do is investigate the jobs and the money. Nothing else is important."

They said, "Well, he made reference to the use of a phone."

I said, "So what?"

When they were finished, they had 27 violations. Then, Bob Weiss, a former county prosecutor, stepped in.

He said, "As a trustee, if you're going to say there were 27 violations, I demand you list the violations!"

If you say "27 violations," it looks like the place is running amok. But if you list 12 typed papers, five uses of the copying machine, three scammed tickets, three uses of the telephone and two scammed shoes, that's different. People read that and said "What kind of bullshit is that?"

The investigation was handled about as poorly as you could imagine. Clarence always took the approach that the more secondary violations we turned ourselves in for, the more institutional control it showed. If you had a file this big, it showed you were doing your job.

Some people couldn't believe they got it done as quickly as they did, in a span of five months. To them, that meant they didn't do a thorough job. I could believe it happened that fast, because Clarence was on a mission.

The first three guys they interviewed were players from that year—Quinton Brooks, Daimon Beathea and Anthony Miller. And Clarence tried to intimidate them. At that point, I was really upset. None of those players had played with Parish.

Finally, I said, "Mike, what are we doing? Are we just trying to find things? Why take three poor black kids from single-parent families, who are academic risks, as our first three interviews?"

Mike said, "Clarence said they were just the handiest."

I said, "We've got Shawn Respert and Eric Snow here if you want to just look at black kids. There's something wrong here. All those kids claim they were intimidated."

I was suspect of the interviews from Day One and asked Merrily to check on what was going on. She said, "We're interviewing everyone who was pre-Parish or post-Parish by two years."

I said, "Then, why hasn't Mike Peplowski, Matt Steigenga or Mark Montgomery been interviewed?" Finally, she came back and said, "Oh, I guess we're just interviewing selected people."

I said, "Why didn't you know that? And why are we doing that?" She said, "They're trying to find Mark Montgomery. And they can't seem to locate Matt or Mike."

I said, "Merrily, they're all right here! Mark worked our camp last week and could have been interviewed. Matt worked our camp both weeks. And Mike has been here the whole time."

Finally, I got a memorandum—all I ever got was memorandums. Clarence never picked up the phone and called me. But the memorandum said they wanted to interview six guys in his office at 8 a.m. Monday. I guess it was my job to find those guys.

Clarence and Mike flew out to Pocatello, Idaho, to interview Herb Williams, my former assistant who'd become the head coach at Idaho State. Herb said, "I just about ordered them out of my office. Mike was trying to get information. But Clarence, . . . he was trying to find something."

I heard Clarence told the committee he believed everything Parish had said because he was under oath at the time. Incredible!

Finally, I was one of the last guys to be interviewed. I said, "Hey, don't turn that recorder on yet. I'm so pissed off I'm going to walk out of here unless I get some satisfaction as to what direction this investigation is taking. Are we trying to prove ourselves guilty or trying to prove ourselves innocent?"

Clarence said, "We're just trying to get at the truth."

I said, "Well, then, I'm walking out of here!

"I've been here 17 years! You guys have been here the same length of time. You know me. You know my program. If we're trying to prove my program is sullied, I don't want any part of it. This is an outrage! If you knew what went on . . . Plus, you bring our kids in and intimidate them . . ."

"We don't intimidate them!" Clarence said.

I said, "Clarence, maybe you don't think they're intimidated. But why do they think they're intimidated?"

He asked if we got Parish free housing when he came up early. I'm sure Parish got free housing. But we didn't get it for him! Do you think Parish couldn't scam and move in with one of the football players or something? I'm sure a lot of athletes in different sports figured out ways to come up early and stay with someone else.

Clarence said to Tom, "Well, then, Herb must've done it!" and said to Herb, "Well, Tom must've done it!"

He just wouldn't accept the fact that we didn't arrange free housing. But that's the approach he took.

And after all the interviews and all the research, the NCAA accepted the University's corrective actions and sanctions and said the violations were secondary, Still, somewhere in the back of his mind, Clarence had it in for me. I don't know why. It was the one thing I couldn't understand.

But if I was 70-30 about leaving in '93, I was 99 percent leave and one percent stay the following winter. In fact, I told my assistants after fall recruiting, "You guys follow up and sell yourselves as the new head coach and his top assistant."

I told them I was 95 percent sure I'd retire after the season and told my wife it was 99.8 percent. That's why she went on all the trips that season, figuring, hey, it's Jud's last hurrah.

Instead, on February 27, 1994, I got a call from *The State News*, the campus newspaper, and the *State Journal* asking about a memo from Clarence to the president.

Ten days earlier, Clarence had sought the authority to ask for my retirement and, if I didn't agree, for the power to terminate my contract, with pay, effective March 31. He'd also suggested a farewell reception, where my family, friends and boosters would be invited.

When I got the calls about the memo that Sunday afternoon, I was in total shock and disbelief. But the greatest emotion was hurt.

Then, I started wondering who else was involved. Joel told me he had nothing to do with writing it. And I believe him. But he said he wasn't a bit surprised. So he may have been in on discussions with the president, because he and the president were close.

I just couldn't believe Clarence would do that on his own. I'd always considered him a good friend and a good guy.

Bev had been close to Noreece, Clarence's wife. And until the investigation, I always thought everything was fine. I'd recommended Clarence for the A.D.'s job when George Perles left and given him a 10 rating on his interview.

But when you'd talk to other coaches, they'd always say they'd gotten a ruling on something from Clarence, and it was wrong. When you'd post him up on it, he'd tell you he never said it.

After the memo came out, Gene Keady said, "How could Clarence do that to you after the way you helped him while he was at the Big Ten?"

All that time, Clarence was the liaison to basketball and struggled with that assignment because he didn't know anything about the sport. I was the chairman of the Big Ten coaches. So we worked out the agenda together. And I helped him through it.

Basically, I still think Clarence is a good person with a big heart. But he's not very smart. I know Clarence didn't write that memo all by himself. You've got to know he was told to write it, probably by the president. I think everyone was surprised by the backlash. They didn't realize Jud had friends in high places.

Immediately, Bob Weiss wanted Clarence fired. And Joel told me he wasn't surprised Clarence wrote it, because there'd been some comments made about the change.

But I say, at some point in time, you have to say, "Somebody else should do this. I can't write a memorandum like this." I think they finally realized Clarence didn't have the intelligence to be athletic director. In '92, he didn't get the job because of his close relationship with George.

The second time, he didn't get it because he isn't smart enough. And they know that. He fooled a lot of people for a while. Then, suddenly, he pulled some things . . .

So, that Sunday night, I got a phone call from the president. He said, "Don't say anything to the press until we handle this."

I said, "I want you to know I'm very upset."

"I understand that," the president said.

"I expect some support from your office," I said.

He said he'd have to analyze the situation. So we talked for about 45 minutes—most of it pauses.

The next morning, when I got to the office, I told my secretary, Lori Soderberg, "Don't worry about planning my retirement. . . . Clarence is taking care of that."

Then, Roger Wilkinson called and said, "The president has come up with a statement and wants to run it by you. It says he's very pleased with the basketball team this year. And he'll analyze the situation when the season is over."

I said, "Rog, if that's a statement of support, I'm too stupid to recognize it. You can tell the president that's unacceptable!"

A few minutes later, Terry Denbow, the president's spokesman, called and said he'd heard I wasn't happy with the statement.

"If you can't come up with anything stronger than that, it's better to say nothing at all," I told him. Ten minutes later, the president arrived at my office.

"Jud, I understand you have a little trouble with the statement we want to release," he said.

"Peter, that statement is absolute bullshit!" I said. "Unless it's something stronger than that, I'm going to go public and say I've gotten no support from the University whatsoever."

By this time, he's starting to get a lot of pressure from Bob Weiss on the Board of Trustees. And Joel is supportive, but more concerned with how it was leaked than what had been said.

If we hadn't rallied to win at Northwestern the day the memorandum was written or gone on to start a five-game winning streak, I don't know what would've happened.

But what happened was, that Monday morning, the president released a brief statement. It indicated support for the program and said any decision on fulfilling the last year of the contract would be mine.

I made it very plain to Roger I would not report to Clarence Underwood any more and told Joel the same thing. Yet, the administration never changed that chain of command.

I haven't said one word to Clarence since that day—not hello, not goodbye, not a word.

And after the team finished 10-8 and 20-12, with a win over Seton Hall and a loss to Duke in the Tournament's Southeast Region in St. Petersburg, Florida, I did what I had to do.

I said no memo is going to make me retire. I told my assistants, "Somewhat reluctantly, I'm going one more year."

FIRE & ICE AND EVERYTHING NICE

I was fortunate to have a lot of very good guards in 45 years of coaching. And I always said the two best backcourts I'd ever had were Sam Vincent and Scott Skiles from '82-85 and Earvin Johnson and whoever else was out there from '77-79.

But I finally had to stop using that line. After watching Shawn Respert and Eric Snow burn opposition guards the last few years, I had to say they were as good as any tandem—unless Earvin suddenly found a twin.

I used to go down and watch Shawn in pickup games. He was from Bishop Borgess. And we'd had Parish from there. I thought a lot of his coach, Mike Fusco. And he said, "Shawn is going to be very, very good."

I'd really liked his hand quickness and acceleration. But my assistants, Stan Joplin and Tom, didn't seem as impressed at first. He was a 6-3 high school forward. And I said, "I think he can learn to be a guard." So I made the decision to recruit Shawn over the advice and objections of my assistants.

The next year, Tom and Stan liked Eric Snow. He was the little brother of Percy, who won the Butkus Award, was Rose Bowl MVP and bruised a lot of bones as a great middle linebacker at Michigan State.

He was an Ohio kid. And we were trying to get in that state a little more. They'd watched him at the Krider All-Star Camp and could see he was a very good athlete. But he never hit a shot. And he was definitely a 6-3 high school forward at Canton McKinley. So they convinced me to offer Eric a scholarship over my initial objections.

It's kind of ironic neither player was the kind who jumped out at you. Yet, they became Fire & Ice, maybe the best guard combination in the country last season.

The reason they were both so successful wasn't their natural talent. It was because they both worked so hard on their games in the off-season. And they both had an opportunity to play early, if not immediately.

Shawn had knee surgery as a senior in high school. But he came back so fast his first year, we put him in against Detroit for about 3 minutes. When his knee swelled up, we decided to redshirt him. But the last month of practice that season, Shawn just lit it up.

People say, "Weren't you surprised the way he exploded in Maui the first games of his career?"

The answer is no. We all knew what Shawn could do by the time he became a redshirt-freshman. When he scored 25 points in his college debut, had 22 more against Arkansas and made the all-tournament team, it was no great shock to us.

Yet, any time you tear an anterior cruciate, it can be a career-ending injury. Or if you do come back, it can be at limited efficiency. If Shawn came out and favored the knee, it was subconsciously, whereas Pep favored his knee consciously.

Shawn had a lot of great shooting nights and some where he scored a lot of points and shot poorly. When he got 39 against Iowa and we lost, that didn't impress me.

But it'll be hard to forget the second half he had at Indiana, when he had 22 points in the last 8:56 with everyone in the state checking him, or the day he sprained his ankle at Michigan, got 30 points in the second half and single-handedly won the game for us.

Those may have been his best performances. But there were so many great ones. Don't forget his junior year, when he had 43 against Minnesota, the first time since Skiles in '86 anyone had scored 40 in a Big Ten game. And he also had 40 in a big win over Indiana.

When he struggled against Duke in the Tournament and

was held scoreless in the first half, he said at the press conference after the game he was definitely coming back for his senior year.

A few days later, he came in and said, "Coach, I only said that to keep the media off my back. But I've got to do what's best for me."

And I said, "Fine! Let's look into it."

We never tried to talk Shawn into staying. All we did was help gather information for him and try to figure where he'd go. We knew what kind of contract Steve Smith got in a similar situation.

So we said to Shawn, "Let's say you go 15th. The 15th pick last year was Terry Dehere. He got $8 million guaranteed over five years. The 20th pick got $5 million for four years, guaranteed."

When you looked at what Glenn Robinson and Chris Webber got, there was a tremendous difference. But if 15th money didn't seem like much, it was still more than the No. 1 pick got 10 years ago.

And when Earvin signed in 1979, he got $500,000 a year for five years. So Shawn would've gotten more than Earvin. But that was 15 years later. Salaries have escalated so far it's hard to compare.

Then, we said, "If you analyze your basketball, are you ready to be a full-time player? Probably not. You still have deficiencies. Some guys in that situation come in and sit and sit, and pretty soon they're out of the league. You'll have an opportunity to play some. But you're not going to be a star right away."

I said I was sure he'd play and play well eventually, because he'd continue to work hard enough on his game to reach the playing level. I tried to be as honest as I could with him. And when I left for Orlando and the Big Ten meetings, I figured he was 90-percent stay and 10-percent go.

Then, he said he wanted to have a meeting with his parents and the coaches. At that meeting, as we answered Diane's and Henry's questions, Shawn just stared into space. He didn't seem at all interested.

Right after that, I told my assistants, "Shawn is gone!"

The day of the press conference, he came into the office and said, "Coach, I just want you to know before I go out there, I'm staying."

Later, when I asked him about his nonchalance at that meeting with his folks, he said, "Coach, I didn't have to listen to that. That was for my parents. We'd discussed all that before."

I think it's pretty clear he did the right thing. He had a great senior year. He broke all kinds of records. He made a lot more money in the draft. And he earned his degree.

Shawn became the No. 2 scorer in Big Ten history with 2,531 points, 82 behind Calbert Cheaney of Indiana. And he wound up No. 1 in conference games with 1,545.

Averaging 25.6 as a senior, he was the Big Ten Player of the Year and the National Player of the Year of the NABC and a few publications. He was a finalist for every award handed out in Seattle except Final Four MVP.

His No. 24 was retired and will be one of four added to the rafters in Breslin, along with Scott's No. 4, Steve's No. 21 and the legendary Johnny Green's No. 24.

The only flags hung now are those of Earvin and Gregory and their crabby old coach, a great surprise after my final home game.

Was Shawn the best shooter I ever had? I say yes. I had three great shooters—Brk, Kirk and Shawn. But I've moved Shawn to the top of that list. Steve was a good shooter. And Scott was a good shooter. But they weren't great shooters. They were great scorers.

There are great shooters, good shooters, fair shooters and poor shooters. I think I'm a very good shooting coach. We can move you up a level, sometimes even two levels. We can move you from poor to fair or fair to good. The great ones don't have to be moved. They're already there.

We had a clinic before the Spartan Oldsmobile Classic last year. We wanted to do something for p.r., partly to erase the stigma from that negative article you wrote about the quality of the field.

I told the kids there, "Shooting is very important. And we happen to have one of the great shooters in college basketball, Shawn Respert. Let's bring him out!"

I hadn't told Shawn anything about it. And we had him shoot 10 shots from 3-point range, with no warmup. I figured he'd probably make six out of 10. . . . He made nine out of 10.

Afterwards, I told him, "A lot of those kids were wondering

what happened on that one you missed. They were kind of disappointed, Shawn!"

Shawn didn't move up as far as we thought he would in the Draft, even though he had an excellent year and got tremendous publicity. So many underclassmen decided to come out. The first five picks were sophomores or younger. It was just a barrage.

But going No. 8 to Portland, then being sent to Milwaukee right away, shows how much teams thought of Shawn. Every club can use another shooter. And playing with Glenn Robinson in Milwaukee won't hurt a guard's opportunities. Shawn should have a fine career in the NBA, if he stays away from injuries. And he won't be the only one who'll make it. We may have lost a couple of games because Eric missed free throws as a sophomore. But we won some games because of him, too. And not just against Iowa last season on his runner at the buzzer.

Eric had 17 games with 10 or more assists and finished with 599, just 46 behind Scott's school record. He was also named the Defensive Player of the Year by the Big Ten coaches.

Actually, Eric may have been better defensively as a sophomore than he was as a senior. He was the best player we had then at the point guard position, though he was sorely lacking at running the break.

Mark Montgomery and Eric both led the league in assists twice. That was partly because of our style of play and the personnel on those teams. We ran a lot. And you'll always get more assists from early offense than your set offense. But even then, if you can throw it to Kirk, Steve or Shawn . . .

The thing with Eric was he improved every year. And mark my words, in four years, he'll be an impact player in the NBA! He could be a bigger Avery Johnson. He'll never be a great shooter. But he'll be an adequate shooter from medium range because he works and works and works at it.

Eric Snow would be a great guy to have on your team in any league. So would Shawn Respert. They were very coachable.

Eric played well at the NBA tryout camps in Phoenix and Chicago and did very well in his workout for Seattle. Maybe that explains why the Sonics traded for him in the second round on Draft Night.

But if we hadn't had a good season last year, Eric wouldn't have gotten any attention at all. Instead, they were watching Shawn and seeing Eric. And we gave him a lot of preseason publicity, too.

Shawn and Eric weren't that close their first two years. But once they started playing together, they developed something special. They were roommates on the road. They had tremendous respect for each other—and something even deeper than that. It was the same thing Earvin and Gregory had.

What they didn't have that Earvin and Gregory had was a championship. We were close. But Shawn, Eric and I bowed out with a 14-4 conference record, one game behind surging Purdue, and a 22-6 overall mark—our fewest defeats since '79.

After we just sprinted past Louisville, we gave a game away in overtime at Nebraska and were 7-1 when we started the Big Ten season. With last-shot wins over Iowa, Oklahoma State and Minnesota, we weren't exactly dominant.

After we struggled and barely held on to beat Ohio State in Columbus, I told our players, "If we can just play as well against Purdue as we did in the second half over the weekend, we'll only get beat by 100."

We didn't know the Purdue game in Breslin would be for the championship. We never knew the Boilermakers would make the run they did. But against us, Cuonzo Martin made a couple of great plays, Shawn missed a shot he normally makes. And the game slipped away. But Purdue outplayed us and deserved to win.

We still would've tied for the title if we'd won at Iowa. From a fan's standpoint, that had to be a great game. I thought we'd won on an out-of-bounds play when Jamie Feick dunked off a feed from Eric.

And we told our guys, "Don't let them drive by you!" But Andre Woolridge hit a helluva shot with a hand up in his face.

We stole a game from Iowa here. And they stole one from us there. So that probably evened out. The team that won the title still had to win at Minnesota and beat Michigan at home in the final week. So it's hats off to Gene Keady and his players.

The NCAA Tournament and our first-round loss to Weber State was a lot harder to swallow. I say I'll never live that down. You know you're going to lose the last game you coach unless you win the national championship, take the NIT or don't make it into a tournament at all.

But to lose your last game to a Weber State was so disappointing. At halftime, I told our guys I was so glad we had a nine-point lead because we could have been nine points behind. We were only ahead because we shot about 70 percent. We were outhustled all the way.

I said, "Guys, unless we play better in the second half, our plane heads home tomorrow!"

We'd emphasized Oklahoma's loss to Manhattan and Arizona's loss to Miami of Ohio. And we'd told them how we almost beat UCLA the last time they'd won the championship when we were at Montana. But Jamie played his second-worst game of the year. And we got no play from any of the players we needed.

We fell behind, then made a run. Shawn got hacked on the arm, and they went down and traveled and scored—with no calls. That was a bitter pill to swallow. But Weber State deserved to win. They played a better game than we did. Any time you go 5-for-14 at the line . . .

But as a coach, knowing it was my last year, I thought about what a storybook ending it would be to wind up in Seattle. A Final Four experience is something you cherish and something you'd love to repeat. But we've never been able to repeat it. So few coaches ever get to relive that. Players move on.

Overall, I think we did an excellent job of ignoring all the distractions of the farewell tour. We got used to the standing ovations wherever we went.

I said, "Guys, I'll handle the media! You play basketball. Remember, it's also Eric's last year, Shawn's last year, Andy Penick's last year and the managers' last year."

The attention wasn't a nuisance. But it wasn't something I relished. It was just something I accepted. After I got the recliner at Indiana and the TV at Michigan, everyone made a presentation.

I got putters at Illinois-Chicago and Purdue and golf balls at Detroit. I got an admiralship in the Nebraska Navy. And Wisconsin came to Breslin with a cheesehead and made a $2,000 donation of cheese to the Red Cross Food Bank. At Wisconsin, in the first game of the Big Ten season, they gave me a simple standing ovation, which was probably what I deserved.

Bobby Knight gave me a custom green leather recliner. And Michigan gave me a big-screen TV. The football helmet from Illinois was a nice touch, too. When I got the antique pocket watch in Champaign, I said, "This is really meaningful because it was made in 1904, the year I was born."

And a lot of people said, "Oh, yeah!"

At Ohio State, I got golf clubs. But I think Bev was disappointed. She wanted something else she could put in our new house.

Believe it or not, they were Jack Nicklaus clubs. And even though he was playing in a tournament, they contacted him to see if he could be there.

They said, "If there's any way you can possibly make it, we'd love to have you there to present the clubs to Jud Heathcote." I guess he said, "Who's Jud Heathcote?"

At Penn State, I got a statue of the Nittany Lion. And any time you get a stool from Minnesota, you're glad when it has three legs.

Northwestern gave me a framed credo, "The Coach." And Iowa presented me with a wall clock from the Amana Colonies. What the Hawkeyes forgot was to give us the win.

Late in the season, they listed all the gifts, figured out what they were worth and asked if I was going to declare them to the IRS.

I said, "We'll declare them at face value, about like that question."

The retirement ceremony for me after the Wisconsin game was absolute overkill. I kept thinking, "This is too long!" Yet, I was appreciative of all the good wishes.

All in all, it was a special year, not just for the ol' coach, but for the players, coaches and fans—a season to remember.

BRANDY, MONS, MIKE AND TOM

Every head coach needs first-rate assistants. And as someone who has sat in more than one seat on more than one bench, I know how important a staff can be.

My first assistant at Montana was Jim Brandenburg, who'd come to Montana from Kalispell Community College in '70. He'd only been there one year. And Jack Swarthout had told him regardless of who the new head coach was, he'd still have his job.

But Jack didn't tell me that. He told me I could hire anyone I wanted. Right away, I offered the job to Don Monson. But Don was making $15,000. The job only paid $11,000. He had to turn the job down. So I told Jim I'd keep him for one year and give him a chance to prove himself.

Jim always tried so hard. He wasn't a very good assistant his first year. At first, he'd work harder and get less done than anyone I'd ever seen. And I was kind of a dominant coach. He was a little afraid to contribute anything.

But his wife was teaching. They'd bought a house. And they had three kids. So I decided to keep him on and hoped things would get better. They definitely did.

The phone bill was part of that $2,500 budget we inherited. So I told Jim to keep the calls to a minimum. But he could talk more and say less than any human being I'd ever heard. I'd ask him how long he thought he'd talked on a phone call. Then, I'd have him call the operator to verify it.

"She must have made a mistake," he said. "She said it was 17 minutes and came to $4.15!"

I said, "No mistake. I timed you at 18 minutes. So she gave you a break of one minute." Never has a guy been so focused — or, sometimes, so oblivious.

But Brandy was a great guy. He always understood the game. Once we got on the same page, we really coached well together. The last three years I was there, he was as good an assistant as anyone I've ever had. He had the confidence to do some things and really do them well. It takes a while. And it took Brandy a while to realize that I had confidence in him.

One thing I've never done—even though I think it's a good thing to do—is to sit down for an hour in the morning, talk about practice and organize it. I never did that. I ran practice. And I always told the assistants they could coach as little as they wanted or as much as they wanted.

On the Pan American Games team in 1975, Marv was the head coach. I was an assistant. And Moose Woltzen, the Lakeland College coach, was the other assistant. Moose thought, with a guy from Washington and a guy from Montana, he'd learn a lot of basketball.

One day, Moose asked what we were going to do at practice, and Marv said, "Jud, did you make out the practice schedule?"

"Hell, no!" I said. "It's your turn. I did it yesterday."

We'd alternate writing out the practice plan. And we always put it in a spiral notebook. When Marv would do the schedule, I'd come over and give it a quick look. When I'd do it, Marv would look at it for a few seconds. Either way, Moose would come over and study it.

He'd say, "I can't believe the way you guys are on the same page! Every time the whistle blows, you guys are blowing it together and telling guys exactly the same thing."

I said, "Moose, that shouldn't surprise you! We coached together for seven years."

"I know that," he said. "But that was five years ago."

I started thinking, and Moose was right. Five years had come and gone. We were still on the same page. A lot of that had to do with the way Marv coached.

He always said, "Jud and I were more co-coaches than head coach and assistant. But I used to have to remind him about every two weeks I was the head coach and he was the assistant." He gave me all the freedom I wanted. And I gave every assistant I had the opportunity to do what he wanted.

I coached my first game at West Valley against Coeur D'Alene High School in Idaho. We lost, 37-26. And the high-point man in the game was a real skinny forward for Coeur D'Alene named Don Monson.

He had 11 points. Don always claimed it was 12. Hey, I have the boxscore at home! It was 11 points.

Don went and played at the University of Idaho. But he was going with a girl who went to West Valley, so he came by the gym a lot. We had the gym open on Saturdays for anyone. And we got to know each other well in the early '50s.

Don is my best friend. He came with me to Michigan State in '76. And I kept Vern Payne from Gus Ganakas' staff. Vern played an important role in the recruitment of Earvin, then took over at Wayne State in '77.

Vern never felt he was part of the staff. Don and I were always on the same page. And I think Vern felt like an extra. But it takes some time to get adjusted when you're working for someone who doesn't outline your duties and give you a lot of specifics.

My second year at Michigan State, we hired Bill Berry, a former Spartan player. And his first season, he did next to nothing. Monson and I were just like Marv and I. People may have thought Don was the head coach.

Don was a piece of work! One night, we were at this tavern north of town. It had a pool table. And Don started playing guys for a few bucks. He took six guys in a row. The seventh guy lost at first, then started winning. Don came over and said, "Jud, lend me 20 bucks. This guy is really getting lucky!" The hustler had finally been hustled.

But in '78, Don left and took the Idaho job. Right away, I brought Bill in and said, "Hey, you simply have to do more!"

He said, "That's no problem. Coach! I could've always done more. But with you and Don, you didn't need me."

He was probably right. And he did a great job after that. After being a head coach at San Jose State, another group of Spartans, he moved to the pros. Today, he's an assistant with the Houston Rockets. He taught Hakeem Olajuwon all he knows—or so he tells me.

Before he left, Don and I were recruiting Rob Gonzalez one night. We were late. We were lost. And we finally found the gym. It said, "SOLD OUT." But I told him, "I can get us in!"

I walked up to the door, looked in and found out it was a donkey basketball game. Rob was playing in a donkey game! And Monson said, "C'mon, Jud! . . . You can get us in!"

When Don left, I hired Dave Harshman, Marv's son. He was with me for three years, was part of the national championship staff, then left for an assistant's job with the Seattle SuperSonics. He's now selling investments for the Lutheran Brotherhood.

Then, when Bill took over at San Jose State, I brought Edgar Wilson back. Edgar was working as a legislative aide in Lansing. He only played one year for me, then went out for football when his basketball eligibility was up.

I remember how my daughter, Barbie, would take a sign to the football games. We'd hold up a big No. 41 every time Edgar caught a pass. But in basketball, he wore No. 33. And he always said we retired his number, after we let Earvin wear it. Edgar was always one of my favorites. I knew he understood the program. And I had confidence he'd be a good recruiter.

After Dave, there was Bill Norton, who'd been Kevin Smith's coach at Birmingham Brother Rice. Bill was never happy in the job. He was only with us one year. There was just too much travel involved for Bill. With two young children, he wanted to be at home more.

Bill returned to Brother Rice as dean of students. I've kept in close contact with Bill over the years and always asked him, "When are you getting back in coaching?" His answer was always the same: "I don't want to leave Brother Rice. And they have an excellent coach here."

They finally made a coaching change this year. And Bill is the new—or maybe the old-new—coach at Brother Rice, back in the Catholic League. I predict he'll win a second Class A state championship before he retires.

When Bill left in '82, I hired Mike Deane from Oswego State in upstate New York. I hadn't known Mike before that. And I'd always hesitated in hiring anyone I didn't know. When Mike applied for the job, I wasn't even going to interview him until I got a call from Jerry Welch, the coach at Potsdam College.

Mike had played for Jerry at Potsdam and been a small-college All-American. Jerry must've been on the phone for 45 minutes, telling me what a great guy and a great coach Mike was. So I decided to interview Mike, was impressed and offered him the job.

Mike and Don Monson were the two best bench coaches I had as assistants. But Brandy and Tom Izzo were right behind.

The best one I ever pulled on Mike was when we went to Kalamazoo College to watch a big kid named J.P. Oosterbaan at an AAU practice. I knew the coach, Walt Hall, and Mike didn't. So driving around campus, I said, "Hey, why don't you ask those students where Walt Hall is?"

I got him to ask three different students. They all looked confused and embarrassed, admitting they didn't know where Walt Hall was. Finally, I said, "Just ask them where the Kalamazoo College gym is. Walt Hall is the coach!"

Edgar finally left to go into a family video business. It was never what he thought it would be. And eventually, he wound up back in coaching. I'm really pleased about that. Today, he's an assistant at Central Michigan. And I'm hoping he'll be a head coach soon.

In '83, I hired Tom Izzo from Northern Michigan as our part-time assistant. And when Edgar left before the '83 season, we moved Tom up temporarily. Silas Taylor, who worked in student affairs and was always close to the program, filled in for Tom for a year, because we wanted to have a black coach on the staff.

When we opened the job back up, we hired Herb Williams. Herb had been the center on the national championship teams at Evansville and was a very successful high school coach at Evanston Township High in Illinois. Herb did an excellent job in his interview. And if you rated Herb as a guy, you'd have to give him a 9 or a 10.

Tom took a step backward for two seasons, serving as our part-time assistant. For a really short guy from Iron Mountain, it was still a pretty good learning situation.

While Mike was running the team during my rehabilitation from the heart attack, Tom stepped up temporarily again and really seemed to have a knack for recruiting.

But in '86, after we'd made our Tournament run, we chased Tom out of town. He didn't want to leave Michigan State. But he'd used up all his savings. And there was no full-time job with us. So he left to work for J.D. Barnett at Tulsa, when Kevin O'Neill took a job at Arizona.

Tom had left East Lansing. And I'd already told Mike he should probably be looking for a head coaching job. He said the only place he'd have an interest in going was Siena, in Loudonville, N.Y., which probably wasn't going to open up.

I'd never heard of Siena. But that's where Mike's wife, Paula, was from. And one day, I picked up USA TODAY and saw the Siena coach had resigned. It never even registered. But I got a call from the Siena A.D. that morning, saying he wanted permission to talk to Mike Deane. When I went to tell him, it finally registered—"Siena! Oh, yeah!"

Mike said he'd look into it. But he interviewed and turned the job down.

"At this late date, I didn't think it was fair to you for me to leave," he said.

I said, "Mike, that's the wrong reason to stay! Don't turn the job down because you think you owe me anything. If you want it, you should take it."

"Maybe I'll think it over," he said.

When he called back, they'd offered the job to someone else. Instead, that guy took a job at Wagner. So Mike got the job and was written up as the second choice. He didn't dare tell anyone that job was his originally and he'd changed his mind.

Right away, I called Tom at Tulsa and offered him Mike's job. I was always going to give him a job if I could. And I could do that since Mike was gone. But when Tom told J.D. Barnett, J.D. blew up and said he was going to write a letter to our president.

When I got J.D. on the phone, I said, "Hey, I know you're mad! I understand that. But I could write the same letter to your president, saying you're unethical. Here's a guy we wanted to hire all along. And now we have."

What assistants have to do in this day and age is leave for better jobs, not just for head coaching jobs. To get ahead, it usually takes a lateral move. To go from a part-time job at Michigan State to a key full-time position was more than a lateral move. It was an important move for Tom and for us.

Sometimes it's hard to rate the part-time guys on a staff. Kelvin Sampson was here for two years, but definitely in a secondary role. But when we lost a coach and went back to four, suddenly, the part-time coach had to do more.

We had Jim Boylan, who'd started on the national championship team at Marquette, and Jim Boylen, an East Grand Rapids kid who went to Maine and played a major role in a shocking upset of us there in '87. Senior and Junior, we called them. They were great guys who enjoyed a good laugh.

Senior wasn't a real good detail guy and didn't like monitoring academics. But he was very, very good on the floor. He went to New Hampshire as head coach. And now, he's with the Cavaliers.

Junior was a very, very hard worker. And he was very good at video work. We were the first ones to put in the Lexicon system. And they actually sent Junior around the country to explain it. He used that background to land a job with the Rockets. Today, he has two NBA championship rings.

Tom Crean was here for a year in '89-90. He was always on top of recruiting. And he was already a good friend of Tom Izzo's. He was really a recruiting guru and went from here to Western Kentucky, then to Pitt with Ralph Willard.

I helped Tom Crean get the job at Western Kentucky. Just before he went in for his interview, I got Ralph on the phone and sold him on what this kid could do in recruiting. That's what he was very good at and still is. Now, he's back at Michigan State as Tom's first assistant hire.

He'll work with Stan Joplin, the guy we hired in '90 when Herb took the head coaching job at Idaho State. Herb has done an excellent job of reviving that program. And Stan did an excellent job of working with Shawn and Eric one-on-one and helping them become better players.

At our Rebounders Club luncheon, they gave away a workout T-shirt that belonged to Stan Joplin. They said he goes through two a week. But that was wrong. He goes through two a year.

I still remember when Rudy Washington of the Black Coaches Association addressed the NABC Board of Directors and said, "There are only two coaches in the country who help their black assistants get head positions. And they're both in this room—Digger Phelps and Jud Heathcote."

I think Digger had three black assistants who'd gone on. I've had Vern Payne, Bill Berry, Kelvin Sampson and Herb Williams.

I've always taken the approach you help your assistants more than anybody else. I always joke, "Hey, we'll lie for you. We'll hire someone to take your interview. We'll get you the job somehow!"

I've sold guys a bill of goods. And I always give guys the benefit of the doubt. If you've been in our program, you've learned enough basketball that you can do a good job.

I didn't think you could get a better grad assistant or part-time coach than Tom Izzo. And I didn't think you could find anyone better than Junior. But Brian Gregory, who came to us when Tom Crean left, is the best of those three at this stage of his coaching career.

Brian played with David Robinson at Navy for a year, then transferred to Oakland University and was a very good guard. Just watching him coach, you know what kind of leader he was as a player.

He has put a lot of emphasis on players' academics. And he's not afraid to get in someone's face. Junior could always play if you needed him to do that in practice. But Brian can do that, too. He's also a master with video.

He has been trying to get a full-time job. And sooner or later, he will. He's 28 years old. So he has a lot of time. Now that the court has ruled against the idea of a restricted-earnings coach, he's worth a lot of money for all the work he does.

Brian deserves a job somewhere, just as Tom deserved the job when I left. The program needed continuity. And Tom will work as hard as anyone can—if he ever gets off the phone.

Junior and Brian, who started as graduate assistants, were just snot-nosed kids when they arrived. Eventually, Junior and Brian were out there coaching, not afraid to step in. I think they realized, if something happened, Coach would always back them up.

Hey, if you played for me, you knew you were going to be coached! If you didn't want to be coached, you couldn't play at Michigan State.

Mike Deane, who's now at Marquette, was that way, too. And Tom will be the same way, to a lesser degree. If you don't want to be coached, hey, you can't play for us!

I don't think any school in our league, except maybe Indiana, spent as much time as we did in preparation—knowing what you're going to do, how you're going to check each guy and how we're going to defend each play.

But I've always said, if you look up loyalty in the dictionary, you'll see Tom's face. He's an unbelievable recruiter. And he'll do a tremendous job as the next head coach.

My wife always said the biggest mistake I ever made was getting Tom the job before I retired. I got him the job in May '93, when I thought I'd probably retire that summer.

She said, "Everyone sits around speculating about what kind of job Tom would do instead of looking at what kind of job you're doing."

Tom knew if I didn't get him the job when I did, he had zero chance to get it, maybe less than zero. The job would've been opened up. And he had no head coaching experience. Instead, he was in a situation where everyone and everything was positive. And I knew that.

So when Merrily came in, I said, "One of my top priorities is to have Tom named as my successor before I leave."

She said, "Oh, that's a good idea! I'll have to get to know Tom."

I never heard from her. So I orchestrated it through Joel, through Gordon Guyer, through Roger Wilkinson, then through Merrily, before she made the announcement.

Where Joel might take credit for it, Gordon might take credit for it, Roger might take credit for it and Merrily might take credit for it, the only way Tom got that job was from the relationship I had with Joel, Gordon and Rog. Merrily was the last and least link.

The timing was right to do that. And I have the greatest confidence Tom and his staff will do an excellent job in the years ahead.

Maybe the succession arrangement was a mistake on my part. But to me, it wasn't—not the way the black-white thing was going and the way the provost, David Scott, had talked with the black faculty and told them the next visible coaching position was to go to a black. When Merrily was hired and Clarence was bypassed, the black faculty were irate they passed over a black to hire a woman.

Equal opportunity hiring is fine. But the joke going around was that George or Jud better retire before Ron Mason. Otherwise, Michigan State would have the nation's first black hockey coach.

BOB, GENE, AND THE
BEST OF THE BIG TEN

When I was in the Big Sky, I always said it was a coach's league. You could win some games with coaching and just outsmart some guys.

In the Big Ten, right away, I recognized it was a player's league. But you could still win some games in '76 without being great. There were five teams that were terrible—and we were one of them, even though we finished fifth in the league.

I said, "We can be competitive with most of the teams in this league. But if we're going to be any good, we've got to get better players!"

In '80, after Earvin and Gregory left, we didn't have enough good players again. And you weren't going to outcoach anyone in the Big Ten.

When Johnny Orr took a beating at Michigan from the media, Johnny was a good basketball coach. Lute Olson was a good coach at Iowa. They were all over the ice cream man, Lou Henson, at Illinois. But Illinois played probably the best defense in the league. They were all over Eldon Miller, a good coach at Ohio State. And Rich Falk was a good coach at Northwestern.

Over the years, people have asked me, "What's wrong with Wisconsin?" and "What's wrong with Northwestern?"

I've always said, "Nothing! They have some very good play-ers. They just don't have as many as the other clubs do. And in the long meat-grinder of an 18-game Big Ten schedule, they're going to lose too many to even be respectable."

But over the past two decades, the league was as tough as any in the country. It produced five national championship teams and three runners-up—not bad for what used to be considered a football league.

The Big Ten has led the nation in attendance every year since '77. We've had great enthusiasm, great facilities —with a few notable exceptions—and great leadership, on and off the court.

Bobby Knight and Gene Keady will surely stand the test of time as two of the greatest coaches in the history of the game.

Bob came to Indiana from Army five years before I came to Michigan State. No wonder he's so gray! And Gene came to Purdue from Western Kentucky in '80. I hope he never leaves West Lafayette —except to come to Spokane and lose some more money on the golf course. Almost every time we play golf, I beat him. And that drives Gene crazy, because he outdrives me by almost 100 yards. I can't help it if he putts the same way. Gene can't understand it. He thinks it's my scorekeeping, when it's really my short game.

The next time you see Gene, ask him about the time Kirk Manns, a kid who grew up not too far from his campus, got 40 points against Purdue. As you can imagine, he really loves to talk about that.

He's even more incensed about Scott Skiles and one of the great recruiting gaffes of all time. His assistant wrote Scott and said, "Based on your ability, you're not one of the players we have any interest in."

But Gene Keady is a great, great basketball coach —as good as you'll find anywhere. And he's a lot of fun to be with.

When I had the heart attack, Bob and Gene talked about what they should do for me. And Gene had it all figured out.

He told Bob, "I'm going to call Jud and tell him if he needs a heart transplant, we'll send him yours. . . . I know it has never been used."

That couldn't be further from the truth. But that's the private side of Bob and an example of the way Gene always finds humor in things.

I brought Gene to our Rebounders Club luncheon my last year. And he got the biggest hand anyone ever received— including me.

After Marv Harshman and Don Monson left coaching, my best friend in the profession was Gene Keady. When you're in coaching, you hate to play your good friends. Yet, if you're in coaching very long, you're going to play your friends. And that's how you become good friends, through associations over the years.

I always challenged our players to play as hard as Purdue does. They beat us like a drum through the years, because they usually played harder than we did. We'd play hard for 30 minutes, maybe even 35. But in the last five minutes, the effort Gene would get out of his players would be the difference.

The only team that played anywhere near as hard as Purdue in our league was Indiana. Bob has been a master at instilling the team concept. Over 19 seasons, we won six times in Assembly Hall. The only coach who did better than that was Bob himself. But we also lost 12 times. And one out of three is a lot better batting average in baseball than basketball.

When Bob took his four-year sabbatical from the Big Ten meetings, I welcomed him back and said, "Nice to see you, Bobby! That was a long Montana fishing trip, wasn't it?"

One year, Bob called and said, "Jud, I've got to talk to you! . . . You're the only friend I've got in this conference."

I said, "Bob, . . . don't jump to conclusions."

But Bob has been a great coach and a great friend. He knew our philosophies were somewhat similar. He said Scott could never have played in his program. And I could've said the same thing about a lot of guys in his program. Unless you know the whole story, sometimes it's best not to say anything.

Before we're finished with Bob's and Gene's state, there's one more story about Notre Dame and Digger Phelps.

We didn't play the Irish while I was at Michigan State, except in the Tournament in '79. But in the last 30 years, we've beaten them eight out of 11 times. John Benington beat them four straight seasons. And Gus Ganakas beat them three out of six.

Suddenly, we were supposed to play them down there the day after a Saturday conference game. It wasn't even a home-and-home contract, just a game down there.

I said, "Wait a minute! We may be stupid. But we're not that dumb!"

Joe Kearney said, "I'm a good friend of Moose Krause's. Don't worry! I'll get it all worked out through the athletic director."

So when I didn't hear and didn't hear, I said, "Joe, did you get that series with Notre Dame worked out?"

He said, "Uh, Moose said Digger makes out their schedules."

But The Palace is trying to promote a game between Michigan State and Notre Dame, with games in Chicago in alternate years. I'd like to see that series. Since it's Notre Dame, I know it'd be on TV. And I could watch it wherever I am.

When you talk about places to watch a game and, more important to me, places to play, we've been everywhere from the sublime to the ridiculous.

The No. 1 place for me, as a coach, would be the Assembly Hall at Illinois. The only drawback for them is the crowd is so far back from the floor. It looks like they designed it to include a hockey rink or a track, it's so big. But the place is usually filled.

I always liked St. John Arena. Yet, as the years passed, it became more and more antiquated. I still saw it as a great basketball facility.

Third for me, believe it or not, was Crisler Arena. I always thought it was a great place for a road team to play, because the crowd was always so blah. It never became a negative factor for you or a lift for them.

Next would probably be Carver-Hawkeye Arena at Iowa. It's a good facility for basketball, with everything on one level. It has a unique look. And we won by a basket in '83 in the first game ever played there.

I think they did a nice job at Welsh-Ryan Arena at Northwestern, compared to what it was before the renovation. And I don't think the Wisconsin Fieldhouse is a bad place to play, as bad as it looks.

Assembly Hall at Indiana is kind of screwed up. It's not built like a basketball arena. It's hard to play there, because the Hoosiers play so wel,l and the crowd is always into it.

I always hated Mackey Arena at Purdue, because I still claim it's lopsided. The coaches' boxes are even on a slope. Plus, I hate arenas where you sit down below floor level.

But where Mackey Arena is bad, Williams Arena at Minnesota is an abomination. When I was going there the last time and people asked what gift I wanted, I said I wanted a bomb to go off an hour after I left. . . . They thought I was kidding.

I hate Williams Arena with a passion. The first year I went there, I said there'd be a serious injury with the dropoff and Minnesota would be responsible for it. So far, that hasn't happened. But I still think that raised floor is a joke for college basketball.

It's like at Vanderbilt. I still can't believe, in this day and age, they put the benches on the baseline behind the baskets. You know why they do that? Because they'd lose prime seating. That, to me, defies description. Arenas are important. But people still pay to see the players and the coaches.

I've always hesitated to pick an all-opponent team. And I'm not going to pick one now. But when you think of the great players we've faced, the Chris Webbers, Joe Barry Carrolls, Mychal Thompsons and Isiah Thomases, you know how tough the league has been.

Whenever that question comes up, I always start by putting Larry Bates on my all-opponent team.

Someone will say, "Larry Bates? You mean Larry Bird!"

And I say, "No. Larry Bates."

Immediately, people want to know who he played for. Then, I tell them he was the clock operator at Kemper Arena.

If I won't pick an all-opponent team, you know I'll never pick a starting five from the players I've coached. If you've read this far, you probably have a pretty good idea of who the top five are anyway.

As close as I'll come is to put Earvin on it and let you pick the other four guys. But I will talk about some of the individual skills players had.

If you say Earvin must've been the best passer, you have a wonderful sense for the obvious. But his sophomore year, he was also our best defensive player.

Our best defensive forwards ever were Ben Tower and Ken Redfield. Believe it or not, our best center defensively was Barry Fordham. Our best defensive guard was Eric Snow, especially his sophomore and junior years. And Mark Montgomery was probably our best defensive guard in the zone.

Today, no one wants to be known for that. They all want to be recognized as scorers.

The smartest player I had at Michigan State, in terms of basketball, was Earvin. The smartest guy overall was Mike Longaker, who went from the '79 team to Harvard Med School.

If I had to pick my all-fast break team, I know I'd have Larry Polec on it. He ran like a deer. And he's the only guy I ever coached who'd do that and never get mad if he didn't get the ball. He'd be wide open, not get the ball, run back, run all day and just take whatever he got.

Halfway into one game, he realized Indiana wasn't guarding him. We'd told him someone would be left open, and it'd probably be him. He was a very good shooter. And we wanted him to let it go.

Finally, in the second half, he said, "Hey, Coach! . . . They're not checking me at all!"

We said, "No kidding, Larry!"

We've talked about everyone who left the program. But Michigan State will still have some players next year. Jamie Feick and Quinton Brooks should have a lot more opportunities to score up front. Yet, they may not lead the team in scoring.

Last year, after one week of practice, not in the middle of the season, I said, "Ray Weathers will be the next great guard at Michigan State!"

And I've told him, "Now, you have to live up to that."

I saw great athletic ability and quickness in his hands. But a year off for academic reasons just kills those kids —just kills them. He had a struggling, frustrating year. But I think he'll blossom the next two seasons to be a very good basketball player.

I also think Thomas Kelley, another guard and Ray's roommate, has great potential. I used to tell my class I've only seen two or three guards in my career go left as well as they can go right. When I told Thomas that, he told me he was really left-handed.

People always ask, "Who's the next Magic?" or "Who's the next Scott?"

I tell them those two were special players. But every once in a while, you see a kid who just excites you.

The guy I love right now is Mateen Cleaves, a well-built guard at Flint Northern. Remember that name!

Of course, I've only seen Mateen on film. And I watched the final game of the Class A Tournament from Breslin on television.

I came in the next Monday and put a note on Tom's desk: "Sell the farm. Sell anything. Get Mateen Cleaves!"

The best guard prospect I've seen in the last 10 years is, guess who? Here's a hint: He's in the Big Ten now. . . . Kiwane Garris. I saw him play in high school. And he can do all the things you want in a guard. If Illinois played a different style, he could be another Kevin Johnson.

But Mateen Cleaves is as good as any guard I've seen in a long time. That's how good he is. He has great physical strength. He has great ball skills. And it looks like he makes pretty good decisions, too.

Now, he'll have one of the biggest decisions of his life. And with any kid that age, you just hope he makes the right one, for the right reasons.

He isn't Earvin. No one is. But some day, some lucky coach will talk about Mateen the way I've talked about the greatest players I've ever had.

He'd look good in any color. But he'd be on GQ's best-dressed list if he were in green and white.

GUS, THE WEAVE,
AND OTHER HEROES

Every year, I used to nominate Gus Ganakas, our assistant athletic director, for the Unsung Hero Award in Michigan. He did so many things behind the scenes that nobody ever knew.

But it was strange the way he was shoved aside in '76. They had to get rid of the football coach, Denny Stolz, because of the NCAA probation. And they were going to get rid of the athletic director, Burt Smith. Suddenly, one of the trustees said, "As long as we're making a big switch, why not get a new basketball coach, too?"

"Yeah, that's not a bad idea!" they said. And just like that, Gus was fired.

He was coming off five straight winning seasons and had been pushing for a three-year contract and a raise. Finally, he got an invitation to see the president at Cowles House.

Gus went over there thinking he'd get the three-year contract he wanted. Instead, Clifton Wharton told him he was being fired—or, as they put it, reassigned. How disappointing can it be?

As soon as I got to Michigan State, Gus said, "If you ever get invited to Cowles House, be on your guard!"

To this day, I figure the University owes Gus, more than vice versa. He shouldn't have been fired. In '75, they'd been 17-9

—the school's best record in nine seasons. And in his last three seasons, his teams finished in the top half of the Big Ten. With Earvin just around the corner, things were looking up.

The funny thing about Gus was, from Day One, he was always very friendly, very cooperative and very understanding.

I said, "Gus, how can you be as friendly to me as you are under the circumstances?"

He said, "Jud, it wasn't your fault I got fired! You had nothing to do with it."

Gus has a great sense of humor. He said, "If there's two things I enjoy, it's sex and laughs. The problem is, now I get them at the same time."

But Gus was a close friend for all the years I was at Michigan State. I was instrumental in keeping Gus involved with the basketball program as a broadcaster. He was and always has been a good basketball man. I just think he got caught in a bad situation.

That was when Darryl Rogers came in from San Jose State. A lot of times in Jenison, I'd hear a knock on the door. And it was usually the same guy knocking.

"Jud, you busy?" Darryl would say.

No matter how busy I was, I always said no.

"I need to hide for a little bit," he'd say. "Some press people are out there. And I need to get away."

Almost every week he'd do that. For about a half-hour, we'd talk about football. We'd talk about athletics. And we'd talk about our kids. I was kind of his hideaway. Guys would never think the football coach was down in the basketball coach's office.

When we came to Michigan State, there was a closeness in the overall athletic department we've never had since. In those days, we knew all the football coaches. We knew all the football coaches' wives. And the athletic department wives met periodically.

I think there was a greater appreciation of who people were and what they were trying to do. One reason was, except for hockey, we were all in Jenison, so we got to know everyone better. The other was Dory and Joe Kearney took it as a challenge to bring everyone together as close as possible.

Doug Weaver did some of that as A.D. He'd have a pig roast and a couple of other functions a year.

But Joe had a commitment to get to every single home game or match at some point, whether it was fencing, softball or football. He was really good that way, in terms of morale.

Everyone always assumed Joe and I were closer than we really were. They thought I got the job because we were lifelong friends. And they thought I influenced decisions in the department, which I didn't. Sometimes I gave Joe advice. And he didn't always take it.

I told Joe not to try to hire a guy who'd been fired at Illinois as associate athletic director. And that was almost his undoing in East Lansing. The feeling at Michigan State was if someone wasn't good enough for another Big Ten school, he wasn't good enough for us.

The president and the trustees turned down that recommendation. From that day on, I think Joe was looking to move.

Joe . . . was great. And if you see a little hesitancy there, it's because I think Joe was always a little apprehensive about his job. Joe was promised a raise after six months at Michigan State. Of course, it didn't come. I said, "Hell, you've got to remind them!"

He was a little reluctant to push the administration. A vice president at Washington had fired him. He got the ear of the president or something. And Joe was let go.

I wouldn't say Joe ran scared. He was just concerned about his future. But Joe was great to work for and was supportive of everything everyone did—sometimes to the point of trying to be too fair.

The best illustration of Joe's approach came our first year. Right away, I asked Vern Payne, my holdover assistant, what the No. 1 thing was basketball needed. He said it was to control our own practice time.

"We practice at the same time as the track team in Jenison," he said. "Guns are going off and everything."

"You're kidding!" I said.

So I mentioned that to Joe, who was a great fan of track and field. He said the facility was big enough for both teams. We just had to share it.

We tried. But the guns and the movement were just too much. So we moved upstairs for awhile and found it unsafe. We kept slipping on all the chalk dust, with gymnastics practicing at the other end.

Then, we worked out a deal where we'd practice three nights a week and track would practice two nights. Unbeknownst to me, my team had loaded up with night classes, so they wouldn't have to wake up in the morning. We had to practice in the afternoon.

Monson went in with me and said, "Joe, I've been an athletic director. Sometimes you have to have priorities. If basketball at Michigan State isn't a higher priority than indoor track, I don't know why the hell I moved here from the state of Washington!"

That hit Joe right between the eyes. So he came up with a compromise where track had to practice at night until second semester. After that, they could start at 4:30 p.m. And that's the way we worked for years and years.

Nell Jackson, the women's track coach wouldn't speak to me. Jim Bibbs, the men's coach, held it against Kearney more than me. But Jim Gibbard, the men's assistant, was mad, thinking I'd come in and emasculated the track program.

What was an obvious decision to us became an area for vacillation with Joe. He was a great guy. He just didn't want to step on anybody's toes.

I came to Michigan State for $25,000, up from $19,700 at Montana. But I said I'd taken a cut in pay every time I'd moved — from $9,200 at West Valley to $7,800 at Washington State, from $15,200 at Washington State to $13,500 at Montana and again from Montana to Michigan State.

When I mentioned that in public, Fred Stabley, our sports information director, just jumped down my throat, saying, "You did not take a cut when you came here! You were making $19,700 at Montana and came here for $25,000!"

I said, "Fred, I made $7,000 on a summer camp at Montana. That put my salary at $26,700. Here, I don't have the camp. And to enlighten you a little bit more, this is the only school in the country where the basketball coach makes less than the baseball coach—and less than the SID!"

Fred slipped quietly away.

When I came to Michigan State, Joe promised me the basketball camp and a TV show. But when I got to campus, Joe said the coach negotiated his own TV show and I was welcome to do that. I wasn't going to go out and solicit like that. So I had no TV show at first.

Then, Joe said he thought he could give me the camp. But they'd just taken camps away from Grady Peninger, the wrestling coach, and Danny Litwhiler, the baseball coach. So he couldn't really give me the camp. He said I could work the camp, but wouldn't get paid. It's probably another sign of my stupidity, but I organized the camp and worked my butt off.

I still had a 10-month contract. And all I'd ever get was the message: "Contract extended." Where coaches now have a 10-page contract, I had a one-page contract.

Then, the dumbest thing I ever did in my life was right after we won the national championship. I sat down with Joe and our president, Edgar Harden, and thought I had some leverage. I said I thought I should have the basketball camp.

Again, Joe didn't think it was a good idea, because of what it meant with everyone else. But Edgar Harden said I should take all the profits and not work the camp. That way, no one could say I was getting paid for running the camp.

My response was, "I can't do that. I wouldn't feel right not working the camp and still getting paid for it." The camp was worth from $30,000 to $40,000 at the time.

Finally, Doug came in as A.D. And in his second year, when I was thinking about taking another job, we worked out a deal where I got half the camp profits after all the administrative costs were met.

The neat thing about Doug was he came in when the program was struggling. He was very aware of the '79 championship, but wasn't a part of it. Yet, he took the approach we had the best basketball coach in the country. I don't know if he had to convince himself of that or keep telling himself that in the face of criticism.

There were two alums who came in and wanted a coaching change in basketball. Doug couldn't believe that. So he ordered both guys out of the office. He hasn't spoken to either guy since. When we started winning again, I got a congratulatory letter from one of those guys. So I wrote him back and thanked him.

"How can you do that?" Doug said.

I said, "Doug, you take everything personally. At that time, both of us were lucky there weren't more guys wanting a coaching change. It's obvious we weren't getting the job done. Now, we bounce back, and everyone's on the bandwagon again. That's part of the job! I recognize that. You should, too."

"To hell with those guys!" he said.

Once you get on Doug's shit list, it's hard to get off. But I would say Doug is, by far, the best athletic director I ever worked for.

I've always said I had a unique relationship with Doug Weaver, because I was working for a guy who was, and still is, one of my best friends. George Perles felt the same way. And I think Ron Mason felt the same way. Doug took a special interest in the revenue sports and the revenue coaches.

Doug always liked basketball. And he liked me. He liked hockey. And he liked Ron. But the sport he loved and still had a passion for was the sport he'd played and coached—football. He'd come down before every tipoff and say the same thing, "Remember, it's just another game!"

I remember when he and I went Up North to George's place in Good Hart. We played golf that day—even George—and had dinner. Then, I suggested we build a bonfire down by the lake. I built this roaring fire, and the three of us sat there asking where in the United States did the athletic director, the football coach, the basketball coach and the hockey coach get along as well as we did. The answer was nowhere.

That doesn't mean you should ignore the other programs. Tom Smith has always appreciated that, from Day One, I've lobbied every athletic director to build a new baseball field. I said Kobs Field was an embarrassment to the University. But Doug thought it was a great baseball field. You couldn't convince him of that. He loved looking out at the Red Cedar River and liked having all the facilities centrally located and contiguous.

Doug liked baseball. But I think, in the back of his mind, he thought baseball was going to be the sport the Big Ten would drop because of weather and scheduling problems. Later, I tried to convince George and Merrily about a new field, too, with no success.

Once, I sat down with Doug and said, "You've got to figure out a way to do a little more for the non-revenue sports."

He said, "Yeah. . . . But what they have to do is win some games on coaching!"

I said, "Doug, how many football games did you win on coaching when you were at Kansas State?"—a question that was like driving a wedge through his heart.

"Those coaches aren't on a level field, Doug! You've got to put some of them on a level field if you ever expect to win."

Doug always wanted to do more for the non-revenue sports, but felt the budget situation prevented him from doing it.

But he was a great boss for me. And George would tell you the same thing. We were Up North at Doug's place in Cross Village when he told me he had everything planned for his retirement.

I said, "Doug, you're too young to retire."

He said, "Here, let me show you. I've got . . . "

"Don't give me that bullshit!" I said. "I'm going in to get another beer. I don't want to hear about that."

I thought it was long-range, something in the back of his mind. But I went into Doug's office the next week and saw he had everything written on a big easel. I couldn't believe he was serious. I tried to talk him out of it. And to this day, I wish I had.

Doug wasn't a media favorite, because he'd usually put them off. He'd never give them a straight answer. He was a master of thrust-and-parry, a real hard interview. And he didn't like some of the local sportswriters and sportscasters. He thought they tried to meddle and weren't fair. Doug was a little too thin-skinned at times.

But I sure wish he'd have stayed. He was concerned about his wife, Nancy, and her health. I think he was worried about his own health, too. The stress was getting to him. And he wanted to be able to do some things while he was still young enough to do them. Since then, I think they've had some second thoughts. Maybe he retired a little earlier than he should've.

My wife has always said, "What would've happened if Doug had stayed?" We'll never know. But it always bothered Doug that the president, John DiBiaggio, took so many shots at him and disassociated himself from the department.

During the controversy over whether George should succeed Doug as athletic director, both Ron and I kind of blasted the media at a press conference over all the negative things being written. We didn't come out and specifically endorse George for the job. We came out and endorsed George as George.

The president held that against both of us. He was just starting to come around when he left two years later.

But I have a saying about loyalty, "In time of crisis, in time of fear, your best friends will all disappear." George Perles will always be a friend of mine.

When George was named A.D., the removal of the benches in Breslin was going to be done the summer of '92. Then, Merrily Dean Baker came in and moved it way down the list of priorities. That was one of the arguments I had with Merrily. What did she do for basketball? Nothing.

We were supposed to get an academic adviser for basketball. We didn't get that.

I tried to move Lori Soderberg, my secretary for 19 years, up to executive secretary. She didn't get that.

I tried to get a market raise for Stan Joplin, because new assistants were coming in above him. We couldn't get that.

And I wanted them to chair the rest of the seats. It was never even considered.

If it seems I didn't like Merrily, nothing could be further from the truth. She was a wonderful lady and was especially nice to Beverly. But she wasn't a very good athletic director. And that wasn't all her fault. She never got the chance she deserved.

She received little or no backing or cooperation from the administration. When Joel Ferguson and President McPherson maneuvered Clarence Underwood in to be in charge of football, basketball and hockey, and when Merrily accepted that without a fight, I figured her days were numbered.

Merrily was just at the wrong place at the wrong time. Tom Izzo claims if Merrily had just listened to half the advice I gave her, she'd still be athletic director. She always thought I was on "the other side," when I was just thinking of what was best for the department.

The one person who was a buffer all that time between the athletic director and the coaches was Sylvia Thompson, Duffy Daugherty's long-time secretary and the A.D.s' administrative assistant.

I could always call Sylvia and get a time to see someone I needed to see. If I wanted to see Doug, I got to see Doug. The hardest one to see was Merrily.

One of the final pieces of advice I gave Merrily was, "If you survive this job, which I don't think you're going to, remember one thing. If the football, basketball or hockey coach calls you, it isn't because it's unimportant. Make room for them immediately."

Sylvia was always great to visit with, yet would never violate confidentiality. You could try and try to pry information out of her and not get it. She never said things she shouldn't.

It's strange, but one thing I'd never, ever been able to accept in my life was the idea of having female friends. I grew up thinking if you had an interest in a female, it was more than platonic. But early on, I looked on Sylvia as a real friend with an interest more in people than in programs.

I don't think there are many employees in college athletics who've been through more changes and turmoil than Sylvia. Sylvia could probably write a best-seller, with all the things she knows behind the scenes.

But a few other people deserve some special thanks and recognition, too, including all the guys who worked so hard on the Basketball Bust and made the Rebounders Club what it is for the program.

Jake Hoffer, who was on the faculty for years and years, was one of the people at my job interview in Chicago in '76. He used to come to a lot of our practices. And when I got the community service award from the Salvation Army this year, Jake was there. I introduced him and said, "Here's a guy who was instrumental in my being hired 19 years ago. You can either give him a hand or boo him, whichever you like." I think some people may have wanted to boo. But they gave him a standing ovation, which we both appreciated.

Bob Weiss from the Board of Trustees has always been a great friend of athletics and a strong supporter of the basketball program.

And so has Joel Ferguson. Joel has a great deal of talent. He could've been anyone or anything he chose to be. Why he chose to be himself, I'll never know.

Charles Tucker was banned from involvement with the athletic department after an investigation of the football program. When they asked me about him, I said, "Tucker has always been a friend of the program and a personal friend."

I got chewed out by the administration for saying that. But it's true. I said, "Hey, let me repeat: Tucker has always been a friend of the program and a personal friend!"

See, Tuck had a way with the guys, because he played! He'd arrange games with good competition. He's almost 50 now.

But for a long time, Tuck could really play. He used to foul an awful lot. But he could still play.

And when players went to him and bitched, he said, "Hey, listen to the coach! Coach has your best interest at heart. Don't bitch about Coach to me."

He always stuck up for the coaching side. I remember in '79, when we lost at Northwestern and came back that night, Tuck was waiting in the parking lot.

He said, "Hey, Coach, it's kind of a bad time. But hang in there! Things will be OK." He has always been a program supporter, a friend of the kids and a friend of the coaches. Tuck was great to our program. And I want to thank him.

The last person on the list is Lori Soderberg, my trusty secretary. She does her job, has an interest in the program and is kind of a rock. She's always there. It's not like a wife, where you have a shoulder to lean on. But you know if you tell her to do something, it's always going to get done.

Like the student assistants we've had, I think she was kind of afraid at first, until she got to know me. At first, she worried she wasn't always doing what I wanted done. When there was a mistake, I'd tell her to do something over. Instead of being soothing, I was emphatic.

She always said she had to look up words in the dictionary, because the secretaries weren't familiar with them. Did that mean I had an extensive vocabulary or they didn't? I don't know.

Lori confided in Beth Marinez, our other secretary, "Jud has ruined half my life."

Beth said, "Why half?"

And Lori said, "Because I've still got the other half to live!"

Everyone in our office tries to be a comedian.

THE STATE
OF THE GAME

Trends occur when someone has success with an idea and gets a lot of publicity. There's nothing new in the game of basketball. If you think you've designed a great play, someone probably ran it 20 years ago.

When Indiana went undefeated in '76 with the passing game, a lot of teams started using it. But it originated 10 years earlier at a high school in Colorado. I remember when a guy was sent to scout that offense and came back with something like 86 plays.

He said, "Sorry, Coach, I couldn't get them all!" not knowing guys ran anywhere they wanted and there weren't any set plays to get.

When UCLA won its first national championship in '64, it ran a 3-1-1 press and had no one taller than 6-5. Naturally, there was an immediate proliferation of teams using the full-court press.

I was still coaching at West Valley in '57 when I first encountered what later became known as the UCLA press. We went down to play Wapato High School. I'd never seen them. But a guy told me they used a 3-1-1 press.

I called him and said, "You mean they put a guy on the ball and two guys up to fight the inbounds? They only have one guy in the middle and one guy back? . . . Geez, if you can get the ball over the first guys, you've always got three-on-two—and maybe three-on-one!"

I couldn't wait to play those guys. We were going to go over the top, break and have a lot of three-on-ones.

We did that our first three possessions and got a couple of easy buckets. Right away, they called timeout. They adjusted the press and took the second pass away. Then, where did we throw it? To make a long story short, it was the worst I've ever been beaten in my career—something like 67-35. It was a halfcourt game. And we couldn't get the ball up the floor.

But when I got to Washington State, I stumbled on a couple of things we've used ever since. In Pullman, the bleachers ran right to the bench, just like at a high school gym. The coaches would be talking, and the fans would be sitting there, poking their faces right in our huddle.

One day, I said, "Marv, doesn't that bother you?"

He said, "Yeah, but what can we do about it?"

I said, "Let's get some camp stools and move out onto the floor during timeouts."

I believe we were the first team to ever use stools during a timeout. Suddenly, a lot of teams started doing the same thing. And today, it's fairly common.

When we won the national championship in '79, we relied a lot on the matchup zone. But we'd played a lot of matchup zone through the years, not just that year.

For me, it started when Marv and I were both hard-nosed, man-to-man coaches. We were preparing to play California. They had two guards who always penetrated. So that Monday, I said, "Marv, what we should use is a zone."

"Zone?" he said. "We're not using any damn zone!"

But I said the same thing Tuesday and Wednesday. And by Thursday, Marv had heard enough. He said, "If you're so stubborn, put in your zone tonight!"

We had Jim McKean, who was a first-team *Look* All-American. And he'd held Lew Alcindor to 61 when we tried to play him man-to-man. So we had our back line cover areas and told our guards to play man-to-man in their half of the floor.

One of our guards, Ray Stein, had scored 1580 on his college boards—a perfect 800 in math and 780 in English. So Ray said, "Coach, what do I do when this guy goes here and this guy goes here?"

Marv didn't know what to do. And I had no answer. So I said, "You have to adjust!"

Then Ray said, "Coach, do I adjust to the man or the ball?"

Marv said, "Yeah, the man or the ball?"

I thought for a second, then said, "Both!"

That was it. And over the years, that's what we've preached: adjust, adjust, adjust. The guards adjust more to the ball. The inside people adjust more to the man. But all adjust to both.

We zoned about half the time I was at Montana and the same my first year at Michigan State. Then, it was Earvin's first year, and we had to do something.

He and Jay Vincent were actually pretty good one-on-one defenders. They weren't bad two-on-two. But five-on-five, they just got lost. So we started using the matchup zone as our primary defense. And teams had so much trouble, we decided to stick with it.

As the year went on, we became a much better man-to-man defensive team. But we still stuck with the zone. Al McGuire had always said, "No team can win the national championship playing a zone!"

But what we'd do was skew the zone to the personnel we faced. When Larry Bird had the ball, wherever that was, we'd charge him with an extra guy. We did the same thing with Mike Woodson of Indiana. . . . I think he only averaged about 25 points a game against us.

Since then, we've had a reputation as a matchup-zone team, when we actually played man about 80 percent of the time.

And since '79, every zone has been a matchup zone. No one uses the straight stand-around zone any more. But they were using a matchup zone a long time before we did. Some guy had even written a book on a similar amoeba defense.

In the next few years, developments on the court won't be nearly as important as what happens off it. With growing unrest, some issues have to be resolved.

I think it's a crime Pig Miller missed his freshman year under Proposition 42 and didn't get that year back later. He graduated in four years. But he only got to play three. Maybe it'll all work out for him. He's supposed to get a three-year contract from the Lakers.

I think guys will eventually get that year back. But what pisses me off, and this shows how organized the coaches are, we lost on that by seven votes the year before at the NCAA Convention. The next year, there was going to be a boycott. But at the Convention, they didn't have the extra year of eligibility on the agenda.

I called Rudy Washington, the head of the Black Coaches Association, and said, "What the hell happened?"

He said, "We had to have it sponsored by eight schools. We thought we had eight. But it turned out we didn't. One backed out at the last minute."

But I think if that gets back on the agenda, it'll pass. The presidents are adamant athletic directors and coaches are not going to run athletics as we know it. So whether they'll recapitulate or not, I don't know.

I just think once it gets on the ballot again and they have enough time for discussion and argument, it'll pass. Two years ago, the Presidents Commission endorsed it. And it still didn't pass. The Knight Commission didn't endorse it. But coaches have always fought the legislative process. It seems we're a voice in the wilderness.

One of my classmates from Washington State, Jack Peterson, has been the faculty rep at Alaska-Anchorage for eight years. And we got into a philosophical argument. He said the faculty should make all decisions for athletics. But so few of those guys have ever been in the athletic arena. I claim that's half the trouble.

I remember when Bo Schembechler came out and said, "Hey, they'll screw this up for five years. Then, the athletic directors and coaches will have to straighten it out."

I've always been conscious, cognizant and concerned about what's best for basketball. But what's best for basketball can seldom be legislated because of the ramifications for football in the past and for gender equity at present.

We could afford to give basketball players a stipend. And I've always said we should. When I was in school, we got room, board, tuition, books and a $15-a-month incidental fee. We called it laundry money, because that's how most of the guys did their laundry. With inflation, that would translate to over $100 a month.

Now, it's almost a sacrilege to some people if you suggest we need to pay the players. They say they're already getting a free education. And if you do it for basketball, you have to do it for women's basketball. Nobody wants to do that.

We've cut our scholarship numbers to the bare bone. And

that's not good for college basketball. You have coaches forcing players to transfer. And that's not good for basketball, either.

We've never done that here. And I told Tom I didn't want that done with any players I'd brought in. That isn't right. But you don't have enough guys now to carry your mistakes.

When I took the Montana job, we had 20 scholarships. Suddenly, we only had 18. So I went in, pounded on Jack Swarthout's desk and said, "Jack! How can you cut our scholarships? That's our lifeblood!"

Jack wasn't a book guy and said, "Jud, did I do that?"

"Yeah!" I said.

"I don't think I'd do that," he said. "Let's see. . . . Oh, the NCAA did that, Jud! From now on, we only get 18. It's an NCAA rule." I felt so stupid. But after they cut to 18, they cut to 16, to 15, to 14 and finally to 13. I say we've reached a point of diminishing returns.

And how do you justify women at 15 scholarships and men at 13? The rationale is they're in the developing stages, so they need more players. That's like saying we had to redshirt Vince Hanson so his feet could grow.

In spite of having serious reservations about the gender equity movement, because I don't believe women's athletics should prosper and proliferate at the expense of the men, I've always been a strong supporter of women's basketball.

In '73 at Montana, I started its first camp exclusively for girls. In '75, at the Pan Am Games, I attended a lot of the women's practices and almost all their games. And coming to Michigan State the same year as the women's coach, Karen Langeland, I've tried to be as supportive as I could, attending a lot of games when we weren't on the road.

I also believe to compare the women's game to the men's game does an injustice to some excellent players. The women may not run and jump the way men do, but their passing and shooting skills are the same.

I used to always ask Joel Ferguson to attend the Sunday Big Ten women's games. And he'd always say, "Jud, I work hard all week. On Sunday, I like to relax and slow down—just not that much."

But someone has to slow the tide of red ink in college athletics. And the first place anyone looks is at football and men's basketball.

They say 70 percent of the schools are losing money in football. Sure, you find some—a Notre Dame, a Michigan, a Penn State—that are making a fortune in football. But everyone looks at utopia instead of the usual. And what everyone wants to do for gender equity is cut football. They say the fat cats don't need 85 scholarships. Football says it needs 100.

Basketball gets caught in that cost-cutting. They think if they cut football, they ought to cut basketball. They say that's only fair. Yet, it doesn't make sense.

If we were unionized, that would change. Then, we'd have the hammer. Basketball funds the NCAA. About 83 percent of the budget comes from tournament TV revenues. We'd say we'll make our own deal or we'll boycott the Final Four for two years. Without basketball, the NCAA would be bankrupt.

I don't think you'll ever see the players unionize. If that happened, it would be some dictatorial person who got players to sign up to create chaos—someone who says, "You're being exploited. Come sign with me!"

The players would have strong representation. But it would be from someone who's running them. And that would be the height of exploitation. He'd say, "I'm going to do some things for you!" when he was really doing things for himself.

But I wouldn't be a bit surprised if the coaches are unionized in 10 years, assuming things keep going the way they're going. The idea of "To hell with the coaches! We'll tell them what we're going to do!" only works to a point.

And if they eliminate another job since the restricted-earnings restriction has been ruled illegal, don't be surprised if there's a tremendous backlash. Coaches are going to say, "Enough is enough! We're not going to take this!" And that could lead to unionization.

I say the next move by administrators will be to do away with what was the restricted-earnings position altogether. Then, instead of having five coaches, you're down to three. And that's when coaches will stand together.

You can get by with three coaches, if you're just coaching a team. But with all the things they expect you to do, you can't. They want you to handle the academics, too, and graduate every kid.

When they asked Abe Lemons of Texas how many of his kids graduated, he said, "Every single one who wanted to."

He said, "Go ask the English professor. Go ask the chemistry professor. That's their job, not mine. My job is to coach basketball."

Sure, you want the kids to graduate. But every administration expects you to be a buddy, father confessor, psychologist and psychiatrist, too.

I hesitate to say it, but more kids are mixed up now than they used to be. That's not just in basketball. That's everywhere. With the drug scene and the number of single parents, I think we understand that.

If you go by ratio, with nine football coaches for 100 kids and four basketball coaches for 13 kids, you say, "Wait a minute! The ratio is off. Let's try three coaches." Everything is viewed in terms of saving money. But I don't think the money you save justifies what it does to the product.

There's always criticism for having more people sitting on the bench in suits than people in uniform. To alleviate that, maybe the managers, doctors and trainers should all sit in the second row. But we've had to fight that image for years. Administrators say, "It just doesn't look good."

To whom? Every guy there has a responsibility and is doing something, even if it's just keeping stats. But that's why they have so many restrictions on numbers at the NCAA Tournament. Seventeen chairs are all you get.

I'd like the coaches to have a stronger voice in the future of college basketball. But I'm not sure that'll ever happen.

When I was president of the National Association of Basketball Coaches in '89, I said if I could wave a magic wand and make three things happen, I would like:

One, to see a return to old camaraderie and fellowship, instead of the greed, envy and jealousy that has permeated our profession.

Two, to see cheating eliminated in the recruiting process.

And three, to return to the days when the media were your friends and wrote positive articles instead of so many negative ones.

But if Ced Dempsey, the executive director of the NCAA, asked me for one recommendation to take to the presidents, I'd like to see scholarships increased to a minimum of 16 and make freshmen ineliegible—something that'll never happen.

I wouldn't even want to go back to playing a freshman schedule. They should just practice and adjust to college life.

In the Big Ten, you can only sign as many guys as you have scholarships. In a lot of conferences, you can sign as many as you want. Then, it's up to you to figure out which ones you renew.

My wish list included the fraternity among coaches we used to have, where there wasn't the jealousy and the constant competition for the extra dollar. It used to be when coaches got together, they talked basketball. Now, they talk about TV contracts.

The image of coaches now is they're all getting these fantastic salaries. But 80 percent or 90 percent are getting a professor's salary, maybe with a few extra bucks for a camp. The perception is that everyone's making a half-million dollars. Maybe at the top-top level, they are.

It galls my wife, that as hard as I worked, Tom Izzo in his first year will make more money by quite a ways than I ever did. There's no work-up. But that's the way it is. And that doesn't bother me one bit.

I say, compared to other coaches, the job I had should pay more! Compared to professors' salaries, it should pay less. I honestly believe our top coaches are making too much money.

I say we'd be much better off if we were paid like professors, where you didn't have these astronomical salaries and had less pressure.

I've never thought coaches should be tenured. We've got some bad coaches. But this is a performance-driven profession. This is not a hide-behind-the-books kind of job. If we have some bad coaches, they move on or move out. And that makes room for the young guys coming up. So I've never fought for tenure. But maybe that's a mistake. If you have tenure and they want to fire you, at least you have a job.

The trend now, too, is for schools to control the outside income more and more. That's probably long overdue. But they're not going to cut guys off completely. They're probably not even going to lessen what the coach makes, believe it or not.

I know Jim Harrick at UCLA said he makes less now than when the school took over that revenue. But he's probably in the top 10 of visible coaches. So I don't think he's going broke.

I was about the last coach in the country to have a shoe contract. I finally went with Pro Keds, because everyone else had one. I didn't think it was right that we got paid because someone else wore a specific shoe,

But every coach I talked to said, "Hey, how long have you been working for next-to-nothing?"

Later, I switched to Converse. But the problem is, the thing got out of line. Guys are making more from shoe companies than they are from their universities.

Presidents and athletic directors are really feeling the budget crunch. Any time they can cut a scholarship, they'll vote for that. Any time they can cut a coach, they'll vote for that. So we don't have unanimity within our own organization on what's best for our game or best for our programs, because the programs are so different.

We have high-major, mid-major and low-major. And the low-majors are always struggling. The Coppin States are playing games on the road for $25,000 guarantees just to survive. If they get beat, they get beat.

We've talked about dividing into Division I-A, I-AA and I-AAA for basketball. But no one wants to give up the Tournament money from the NCAA. It used to be you got money for just making the tournament. Now, there's a formula by conference, which still makes the rich richer.

I came up with the Heathcote proposal, where you'd get so much for getting in and so much for each game, within limits. Say you'd get $50,000 for getting in and $50,000 each time you won. If you went all the way, you'd get $350,000, plus expenses.

That's not enough to throw everything out of balance. And all the other money would be divided equally among the 302 schools.

They had a Digger Phelps proposal, too. It was similar to mine, but had Division II and Division III getting a big chunk. I had them getting five percent.

But if Michigan State gets $100,000, that's a drop in the bucket. If Montana gets $100,000, that's a big lift for their program. That means programs would be more even, rather than farther apart.

If you're going to have 302 schools competing in Division I basketball, let's try to narrow the gap a little bit with some remuneration from the Tournament. Now, they've got a formula that guarantees most of the money for the bigger schools.

Because of what some schools can do, we're always circumventing rules. For example, they come up with the idea of a part-time coach. He can only get the equivalent of an out-of-state scholarship in remuneration from the athletic department. But he can be employed anywhere else on campus.

So what does Lute Olson do? He takes Jim Roseborough, his highest-paid assistant, and makes him the part-time coach, with a campus job that pays most of his salary. And other coaches followed suit, until there was a tremendous inequity in the part-time coaches' remuneration.

The newest thing is having an administrative assistant. Football came up with that approach. Now, half the basketball programs in the Big Ten have an administrative assistant—anything to get around the resticive rules.

What you have to recognize is programs at the Big Ten level are different than Central Michigan and Valparaiso. And they've been talking about reorganization forever, saying, "Let Division I vote on Division I issues."

That's what the College Football Association kept trying to do for years. And maybe that'll happen next year. When Polytech Institute can vote you down because it doesn't understand your situation and doesn't offer scholarships, the bureaucracy of the NCAA is overpowering and baffling.

Football has been more successful than basketball in getting its points across because of numbers. You'd think the bigger the numbers, the more the influence. But it works in reverse. With 108 Division I-A football programs, they can be better organized than 302 Division I basketball programs.

What's good for the Big Ten may be bad for the Southern League. What's good for the ACC may be bad for the Big Sky. So when you come with cost-cutting measures, there's no unity and strength.

With dwindling income, higher expenses and gender equity, many schools will be fighting a losing battle with the budget. But cutting basketball will NOT solve their monetary problems.

LAST, BUT NOT LEAST . . . BEV

Wives are special people to basketball coaches.

When we were at Washington State, it was my first job in college basketball. And for almost the entire time we were there, Bev did all the basketball correspondence at home.

Why? Because we were so swamped at the office. And with the secretarial pool we had, you could turn something in and get it back in two weeks. We just couldn't operate that way. So I'd have her do it and also type all the stats for our basketball camp.

Of course, my wife could type more than 100 words a minute. So maybe she wasn't working quite as hard as it seemed. All I know is, she put in a lot of time and still managed to take care of three young children.

But I've always said my wife is my best supporter, my best friend and a shoulder to lean on, which every coach needs. You don't need someone to second-guess what you do. You need someone who's going to give you subtle advice.

She used to joke about telling me, "Don't get any technicals tonight!" That was good for the media, but not really true.

She might say, "Good luck! And take things in stride." Or she'd say, "Good luck! I'll see you after the game," letting me know she's there.

And that's all you need. I don't think many guys, in the heat of the battle, are wondering what their wives are thinking.

She has always said, "You've got to calm down a little bit. You can't let things bother you. And you can't work as hard as you do." Sometimes you listen to those things. And sometimes you don't.

My wife analyzes people very, very well. I would almost call her non-critical and non-judgmental. Yet, she's almost an expert on who's sincere and who's a phony—without ever letting them know she knows.

She's very protective. She reads more into things than I do. And if you want to take isolated incidents, you can be upset at almost every single guy.

But I think I have a special wife because of who she is. I also think I have a special coach's wife, because all the time I was gone, she was called on to do more with the family.

A coach's wife is always called on to do more with raising the kids than she would be in the normal 8-to-5 family. But what's the percentage now of single-parent families these days? It's pretty high.

If coaching takes away from your family life, it certainly doesn't eliminate you from being the father of your children and a husband to your wife. There are a lot of corporate jobs and a lot of stressful jobs that are similar to coaching.

At Washington State, one neighbor said, "Oh, I feel so sorry for you! Your husband is gone so much." She and her husband were divorced a year later. Bev and I celebrated our 37th anniversary in August of '95.

We met when I was coaching at West Valley. I lived in a big apartment house with another guy. Bev and another girl, Georgia Derks, had decided they were going to move out of Walla Walla and get different jobs in a bigger area. They thought they were treading water. She was 24 at the time.

So they drove by, saw me outside and said, "Are there any apartments available here?"

I said, "I don't know. . . . You can live with me if you want!"

They thought I was a smart ass. But I gave them directions to the manager's office. And when they drove around, they found there was another apartment available on the second floor. I was in a basement apartment, quite a ways away.

But when I drove to work, I'd see Bev walking to the bus stop. I thought she was 18 or 19, too young for me. I was 29. I finally found out she was older and called her for a date. She claims I was calling for her roommate. I really wasn't. But I didn't know which one was which.

We went together for about 18 months, then got married. I was kind of the bachelor around town, fairly well known because I was a high school coach.

I told everyone, "I had to get married. . . . But it wasn't what you think. There were about eight guys who ran around together. Four of us were in the Naval Reserve. On Wednesday nights, we'd go to the bar together. And one by one, every single one of those guys got married. I said, 'Hey, I have no choice!' "

At the time, I was working on my master's degree at the University of Washington. I spent my summers there, then came back and got married on August 25, 1958.

Carla was born on February 10, 1960, a year-and-a-half later. Then, Jerry was born December 23, 1960. I used to say we'd have been better off if she hadn't had that private room.

Actually, Jerry arrived six weeks early. They were supposed to be a year apart. But Bev had an appendix attack. He was in an incubator for a month. Then Barbie was born four years later, the last of the Heathcote kids.

All our kids had a hard time adjusting when we came to East Lansing.

I remember Don Monson had a girl who was a junior. Darryl Rogers had a girl who was a junior. Joe Kearney had a girl who was a junior. And Carla was a junior. So there were four junior girls, all trying to move into the East Lansing cliques.

My daughter would talk about school and burst into tears, saying, "Everybody knows who I am, Dad, because I'm the new basketball coach's daughter. But I don't have one friend!" The other three girls were struggling, too. So we tried to encourage them to get together. But none of them wanted to do that.

I thought it'd be different with Jerry. Right away, he was out for JV football. Then, he played JV basketball and went out for track. He had the discus record at East Lansing High. But he admitted later it was a tough adjustment for him, too.

When you're a big fish in a little pond, it's hard to adjust to being a little fish in a lake. And that's exactly what each had to do with the move from Missoula to East Lansing. Though that was somewhat traumatic at times, it was probably beneficial in the long run. All three learned to be more competitive and independent.

My oldest daugher is what I call subtly aggressive. As a senior, Carla was the editor of the yearbook, beating out some girls who'd been on the annual staff for three years.

When Carla was looking at schools, we went up to Central. We took her to Western. And we asked her if she wanted to go back to Montana.

"Maybe," she said.

Then, out of the clear, blue sky, without it ever being mentioned once, she said, "Dad, what would you think if I went to Washington State, just for a year, to see if I liked it?"

I said, "Great!"

She was there four years.

We told her, "After four years, you're on your own!"

So she made sure she graduated in four years with a degree in advertising. We paid the tuition, room and board. And she worked during the summers for her spending money.

She got a job at a little newspaper in Moscow, Idaho. But she was always selling. Then, she got a job with a printing company in Seattle. One year, she was their leading salesperson—just persistent, persistent, persistent.

But she has been married now for three years and is pregnant with our first grandchild, due in October.

If you met Carla, you'd think she's very laid-back. But my wife says she's exactly like me. She's aggressive. And she procrastinates until the last minute.

My wife always says, "Don't you have that done yet?"

And I'll say, "No. But don't worry, it'll get done."

If we leave on a trip at 7 a.m., I pack at 6. She's packed two days in advance. And it just drives her crazy that I'm not packed. She worries that I'm going to ask her where something is.

Jerry went to Miami of Ohio for two years. But he could never throw the college disc. It's bigger and heavier. So he could never earn a scholarship. We were paying out-of-state tuition. And I didn't mind a bit. Miami of Ohio is a great school. I wanted him to stay down there.

"No," he said. "It's costing you too much. I'm transferring to Michigan State."

He went out to Montana for a quarter and wanted to get into their physical therapy school. He had about a 3.1. And they only took 12 kids a year. What he didn't know was the chairman of the selection committee was our next-door neighbor and a real good friend of mine.

He came back and graduated from Michigan State with a degree in nutrition, then went to Palmer College in Iowa, the top chiropractic school in the country and finished a four-year program in three years, graduating with honors.

He has been involved in a couple of chiropractic situations that didn't work out financially. So he has put that on hold and is working at Meijer stores in their computer management program.

Barbie graduated from Central Michigan with a degree in public health. She decided if Seattle was good enough for Carla, it was good enough for her. So a tearful Bev sent her "baby" out of the nest.

Barbie worked for an insurance company, then went to work for "The Juiceman." Juicers were a hot item for a couple of years, with employees jumping from 20 to 130. But as the juicer craze subsided across the country, so did the company's fortunes.

Barbie survived severall layoffs, but could see little security for the future and decided to go back to school to get a nursing degree. She completed that a year ago and is employed in home nursing care.

She was married April 8, 1995, the weekend after the Final Four, in Seattle. We'd hoped to have a team in the Final Four and a new team as a family. We had to settle for only one.

Bev is a mother hen to both girls, especially Barbie. And she has always spent a lot of time trying to be there for all of us.

You have to understand, if you're a coach's wife, sometimes even when he's home, he's not quite with you. I don't say you take the good with the bad or the bad with the worse. You adjust to what your life is going to be and not just accept it, but build on it.

If a wife is going to complain every time her husband is gone, she can't be a coach's wife. If she's going to be unhappy when she has to do some extra things with the family, you're going to have a strained relationship.

There's enough strain and stress in the job. You don't need more at home. But most guys in college basketball have been in coaching long enough as assistants, maybe even in high school, there aren't a lot of surprises for coach's wives.

If you look at the divorce rate for coaches, I don't think it's astronomical. Certainly, there are divorces. But they're caused by the same things that cause other divorces.

I still think coaches' wives become a special breed, understanding their role and what they have to do to support their husbands, rather than being negative and creating problems, especially during the season.

Beverly has always been supportive, understanding and non-critical.

Someone said, "She must've been a saint to live with you!"

And some of that is true. But we wouldn't have the relationship we have or have stayed together this long if we didn't understand what that relationship is.

A lot of guys say, "My wife is one in a million," and don't know what they're saying. I do! And mine is!

THE FINAL-FINAL-
FINAL

I remember when we played Wisconsin on March, 11, 1989, and billed it as "the last game ever to be played in historic Jenison Field House." We invited all our former players back and combined the last game with the season-ending Basketball Bust. We had about 1,500 people attend that gala affair at the Lansing Center.

Oops!

We received an invitation to play in the NIT. And after defeating Kent State at Cobo Arena in Detroit, we hosted Wichita State in "the LAST GAME in Jenison!"

Oops again!

Earvin, Gregory and I came up with the idea to have a 10-Year Championship Reunion Game. The idea was to pit the '79 team against all the other Spartan stars. And the '79 team won 95-93 before a sold-out crowd on August 9.

Earvin was coming off a serious hamstring injury and told me to play him less than half the game. I told him, "E, you always decided how much you'd play. So nothing is going to change."

He played 38 of the 40 minutes, led everyone with 25 points, 17 rebounds and 12 assists and hit the winning free throws in the final minute. Remember what we said about Earvin and winning?

But this WAS the final game in Jenison.

I turned 68 last May and coached 45 years. It was a long career—maybe too long.

I've had opportunities to go into athletic administration, but was never really interested. I always joked, "I'm a coach! I'll coach until I'm 65, then retire," never dreaming I'd last that long. But I coached two years longer than I planned.

I'd have retired in '93 if not for the Hickman allegations. And I'd have retired last year if not for the Underwood memo. I had too much pride to retire and give my colleagues across the country the impression I was fired.

So '94-95 became my final-final-FINAL season.

Perhaps everything works out for the best. It was a special season for the Heathcote family. We had a good team that was fun to watch and fun to coach. It was disappointing to lose the Big Ten title to Purdue, with its great stretch run, and doubly disappointing to lose our first-round Tournament game to Weber State.

But the accolades, tributes and gifts made it a season my family and I will cherish forever.

Although the gifts before each road game were appreciated, the standing ovations at each arena were more important to me. I was the first coach to retire in 25 years of Big Ten basketball. And I believe the applause was for my longevity and a unique situation that doesn't occur very often these days in college basketball.

If the ceremonies before each road game were special, the tribute to Beverly and I after the last home game against Wisconsin was unbelievable. I thought an hour program was too long. But I guess the 15,138 who stayed thought it was just right.

Both Beverly and I shed some tears when they dimmed the lights and unfurled the banner proclaiming, "Jud Heathcote, Head Coach, 1976-95." And it's extra special to me to have that banner hang between the retired numbers of Earvin and Gregory. The crystal bowl for Beverly and the golf cart for me from the athletic department were frosting on the cake.

I told the crowd I'd just like to be remembered as a good coach and a good guy. Our 340 wins makes me the winningest coach in Spartan history by 108 games. But as Jack always reminds me, I'm also the losingest coach in school history, with 220 losses. So much for longevity!

The record is good, but not great. And as for being a good guy, I'll have to let others be the judge of that.

I also said I'd like to be remembered as a coach who cared about the game of basketball, about the players while they were here and after they were gone and about the welfare of my fellow coaches.

Unless you've coached, you don't know what the game stands for. The organizational chart in our basketball notebook has the program at the top, the team next, the players and coaches after that and everything on the periphery last.

We emphasize the program is bigger and more important than any team or person. In the larger scheme of things, THE GAME looms larger than anything. And if your coaching philosophy is the sum total of all you believe, the game represents all you do.

The preparation, the practice, the playing, the winning and the losing are all part of the game, but only a part. Teamwork, morale, chemistry, character, competition, desire, determination, sacrifice and on and on are all part of the game.

I have a couple of other cliches I use with coaches and fans. One is, "Coaching sucks." And the other is, "The agony of defeat is 10 times greater than the thrill of victory."

The first one, I say in jest and don't believe. I honestly think coaching is the greatest and most satisfying profession there is. I can probably count on my fingers and toes the number of times I didn't look forward to going to work. And those were usually after devastating losses.

The second one is a true statement. Losses are hard for everyone, but more for the coaches than for players or fans. And I don't think anyone in our profession took losses harder than I did.

Losing can be a cancer and can destroy teams. But good coaches put the losses behind them and move on to the next game. I think I was pretty resilient in bouncing back that way.

I served on the NABC Board for 11 years and was president in '89. When my tenure was over, Joe Vancisin, our executive secretary said, "Jud, you're one of the best Board members we've ever had. You're willing to work. And you've always cared about the game and the coaches." I took that as a supreme compliment.

I was also the chairman of the Big Ten coaches for 15 years.

The chairmanship was supposed to rotate. But I kept being re-elected. And I kept doing the extra work that assignment required.

One of my greatest sources of pride is having kept in touch with the players who've come through our program. You can name any player at Michigan State over the last 19 years and I can tell you where he is and what he's doing.

The Wisconsin tribute should have been enough for anyone. But a committee had been working all year on a retirement party for me. Lori, my secretary, contacted Beverly and asked her what I'd like.

"Probably nothing," she said. "But if you are going to have something, I want it first-class or not at all."

The committee did exactly that. It was supposed to be a secret, but who's kidding who? Finally, they contacted me to select the roasters. I chose my closest coaching friends, friends in East Lansing and three of my favorite players.

Since they're my best friends, they deserve to have their names in this book. I chose Doug Weaver as master of ceremonies and picked coaching friends Marv Harshman, Gene Keady, Bob Knight, Don Monson, Jim Brandenburg, Mike Deane and Tom Izzo. Earvin, Gregory and Scott Skiles were the players. And I wanted friends Tom Danker, Fred Tripp, Joel Ferguson and Gus Ganakas.

Earvin had a conflict back in California, but did a video I'll cherish forever. Scott also had a conflict and did a video that, for some reason, didn't come out. Bob Knight had a conflict and sent a great letter. He called and said he really wanted to roast me, but couldn't do it in a letter. So he decided to write what I'd meant to the game.

All the others took turns lambasting the ol' coach. I've joked that 800 of my closest friends paid $75 each to laugh at me for two hours. And they all seemed to enjoy it.

The committee presented Beverly and me with a new Oldsmobile Aurora at the end of the roast. Talk about a great sendoff!

But if the roast was special, how about the night before, when 15,138 filled Breslin for the All-Star Tribute Game? That was the brainchild of Earvin and Gregory, who thought the players should do something special.

Since I masquerade as a golfer, they came up with the idea of matching the first 9 ½ years against the second 9 ½ years.

Gregory and Larry Polec worked hours and hours to make that happen. The introductions were unbelievable. The game was spectacular. And the postgame reception was a chance to renew friendships and tell a few lies about the good old days, especially with players I hadn't seen for some time.

As Earvin said at the reception, "Only Michigan State could get this many players to come back in June to play a game like this."

I was almost embarrassed to receive a set of Cobra golf clubs and a trip for two to Scotland. Beverly and I have already traded that for a trip to Maui. And the committee also presented Beverly with a watch and bracelet. I've joked that if I knew we were going to receive so many gifts, I'd have retired sooner.

As Frank Sinatra sang, "Regrets, I've had a few. . . . "

I always wished I'd been able to spend more time with my children during their younger years. The demands of the job kept me on the road too much.

I also regret that I didn't finish my doctorate. After all the time and money I spent completing the coursework, it was ridiculous I didn't write the dissertation. I always kid Roy Simon on the golf course when the starter announces him as Dr. Simon. He tells me he has a Ph.D., and I have a D.E.D.—doctorate except dissertation. We just got too busy with summer camps, and I let it slip away.

After winning it all in '79, I'd always hoped to return to the Final Four. But no such luck.

And believe it or not, I've always wished I was less demonstrative on the bench and more positive with the players. But as I tell young coaches, "Don't try to be something you're not." I guess that just wasn't going to be my style.

By the time this book is published, we'll have moved to Spokane, Washington, and be living in Beverly's dream house. She designed it. And it came out even better than we expected.

Why Spokane? To be closer to our two girls in Seattle. She didn't want them on her doorstep, just close enough to spend weekends and holidays together. She has done everything for me for 37 years. So I decided it was time I did what she wanted, for a change. They say you can't go home. But Spokane is where we were married and where all our children were born.

What am I going to do there? I've been asked that question a thousand times. And so has Bev.

I used to joke that I'll finally have time to finish my book. When people said, "I didn't know you were writing a book!" I always said, "I'm not! I'm reading one."

Beverly used to tell people retirement would give us more time to spend with our grandchildren. They'd always nod and smile, not knowing we had no grandchildren or prospects for one.

Wouldn't you know, I did write a book, and our first grandchild was born in October—strange how words of jest sometimes become prophesy.

My two best friends live in Spokane—Monson and Jim Slavin, my long-time handball buddy. I'll spend time with them and with other old friends. I can't be too specific. But I know I'll keep busy. A little golf . . . a little handball . . . something.

The biggest negative on the horizon is I've been told by a number of orthopods for the past 10 years I'll have to have my left knee replaced. When people ask what I'm doing about that, I always say I'm looking for a new doctor. But I know, sooner or later, I'll have to have that done.

And although we're moving a long way from Mid-Michigan, we plan to return to East Lansing each summer to get in some golf games and visit some friends.

Of all the hundreds of congratulatory letters I received, maybe this paragraph from one of my coaching friends stands out for me:

"College coaching is becoming a very complex and cut-throat business. Integrity and character have somehow gotten lost in the shuffle, for the most part. When I think of no longer having Jud Heathcote in the profession, it makes me sad. Your career has stood for what coaching should be all about. Making kids men and turning prospects into players has been your trademark."

As I've closed most of my letters over the years, "Remember, it's great to be a Spartan!"

For me, it has truly been a Magical journey.

EPILOGUE

I wasn't sure what to think of Jud Heathcote at first, while I was a senior at Lansing Everett. He was a hot-tempered guy who reminded me of a bulldog. Today, I don't think my basketball career and my life would have been the same without his help and his influence.

As I was getting close to a decision about where I would play college ball, Jud came to see me and said, "I know you've narrowed it down to Michigan and Michigan State. It seems to me your head is saying Michigan, but your heart is saying State. Michigan is a great school, no question about that. And they have an outstanding team. But if you go there, you'll be one of several great players.

"With us, you'll run the offense. You'll be a point guard and the key to our fast break. You've seen Greg Kelser play. You know how good he is. And he would be even better if you were running the plays. You can make a tremendous difference."

Jud was right. There was a battle going on between my head and my heart. But I had been going to games at Michigan State since I was 10—not just basketball, but football, too. And that night, I dreamed about running down the court in Jenison Field House, wearing a green-and-white uniform and seeing 10,004 fans just going crazy.

The next day, I had a visit from Vernon Payne, Jud's assistant and a friend I'd hoped would get the job when Gus Ganakas was fired. Vern told me he was leaving to take the head coaching job at Wayne State, then put in one last pitch for Jud and the Spartans.

"I have nothing to gain to get you to come to MSU," Vern said. "But I think you should. I've heard that you have some reservations about Jud Heathcote."

"You heard right," I said. "I really don't know him."

"Well, I do," he said. "And if I didn't like him or I thought he was a bad coach, I would tell you. But he's good, Earvin. Really good. I think you should play for him. I know you've seen him yelling at the guys. But that's because he's intense and wants to win so badly. Behind all that yelling and screaming, Jud Heathcote is a terrific coach and an excellent teacher. I've known you for years, and I've seen how committed you are to improving your game. This is the guy who can help you do that."

Vern was right, no question. Jud was a perfectionist and expected no less from his players. If you missed a shot, that was one thing. But if you didn't do your job and made a mental error, you were in trouble. He'd point to his head and holler, "You've gotta think!" —or for those of us in the backcourt, "Be a guard, not a garbage!"

He'd talk about "Double A, Double I, Double P," which stood for: Academic and Athletic excellence, Intensity and Intelligence, Poise and Patience. And he'd always say, "KYP," which stood for Know Your Personnel. No one knew his personnel—and the opponents' personnel—better than Jud.

Jud Heathcote was a great basketball coach. But he's a better person. You couldn't find anyone more honest if you looked for another 19 years. If you wanted a drink from the pop machine, he wouldn't give you a dime. He'd built his reputation on integrity. And he would never do anything to jeopardize it.

He had a tough exterior, like a drill sergeant. Underneath, he truly cared about his players' well-being. Yet, it wasn't until after I went to Los Angeles that we became close and I appreciated what he'd done for me. I kept trying to return a few of those favors. But I never could.

In my two seasons at Michigan State, we accomplished a lot together: 51 wins, two Big Ten titles and, of course, a national championship in my first matchup with Larry Bird. When I came back to Breslin Center, I wasn't looking for that "Earvin 'Magic' Johnson—33" banner. All I wanted to see was the one that can never disappear: "NCAA Champions—1979."

Jud was such a big part of that. He was one of the last guys who could really teach you how to play. He didn't like to show you he cared. But he cared as much as anyone could. And I came back for the All-Star Tribute in June because of him, not just to show up there.

There's not another school in the country that could have gotten everyone back for a game like that. That's what makes Spartans special. They don't forget. And they keep competing. There's not a Spartan in the NBA who hasn't done well. . . . Now, these other schools, that's another story!

But I'm anxious to see what Jud does in retirement. I think he's looking forward to it. He'll miss Michigan State and the challenge of preparing a team to win. At least, he will at first. The first year is going to be difficult for him. That's how it was for me when I left the league. You don't know what to do with yourself.

I got over that. And Jud will, too. I could have come back this year. But I'm enjoying the rest of my life too much. Plus, if I came back, I'd miss the Spartans in Maui. Cookie and I are looking forward to that. And I'm looking forward to seeing a real friend, another retired competitor and someone I can always call "Coach."

Jud, I just want to say I'll miss you. You've done a lot for all of us. You've taken boys and made us men. I love you.

—Earvin "Magic" Johnson
MSU, through and through